T0129340

Living on the Edge

Memories of a Trial Lawyer

MICHAEL MAKAROFF

iUniverse

LIVING ON THE EDGE
MEMORIES OF A TRIAL LAWYER

iUniverse books may be ordered through booksellers or by contacting:

iUniverse
1663 Liberty Drive
Bloomington, IN 47403
www.iuniverse.com
1-800-Authors (1-800-288-4677)

ISBN: 978-1-5320-5230-9 (sc)
ISBN: 978-1-5320-5232-3 (hc)
ISBN: 978-1-5320-5231-6 (e)

Library of Congress Control Number: 2018912533

Print information available on the last page.

iUniverse rev. date: 10/29/2018

DEDICATION

This book is dedicated to the memory of Gray Thoron, who was the Dean of Cornell Law School when I was a student. Years after I graduated, Dean Thoron asked me to come to the law school and lecture to the students about my experiences as a trial lawyer. I did so for a period of twenty-three years. It was an honor to have participated in the unending efforts to instill in his students the requisite legal and ethical education necessary for them to succeed. In the process, I formed a longstanding friendship and working relationship with Gray Thoron as we would meet and prepare together for the talks and lectures. Gray Thoron's wisdom and deep commitment to the legal, principled and ethical education of law students was an inspiration to both the students and the fortunate few selected lawyers, like myself, who were asked to participate. Gray Thoron was tireless in his preparation and efforts to ensure that his students were exposed to all the experiences, thoughts and ideas that would help them become excellent and ethical lawyers in their communities. This was a task that he never stopped performing. We have all benefited greatly from Dean Gray Thoron's lifelong efforts, wisdom and dedication to our profession.

CONTENTS

CHAPTER 1

So, you want to be a lawyer!

I f you have ever wondered what it would be like to stand before a judge in a courtroom on behalf of a client at the beginning of a jury trial and announce that you are the counsel, then this is a book that will interest you. I have stood in courtrooms or hearing rooms before Judges, juries and administrative courts in all kinds and types of cases making arguments, pleas and, hopefully, persuasive remarks on behalf of countless numbers of clients. Whenever I would rise from my chair next to my client after the Judge had asked if the parties were ready, it was always with certain pride and pleasure that I would stand and say, "Ready your Honor." In each case, there was always the goal of succeeding on behalf of my client's needs or purpose by blending together the known and disputed facts into a mosaic that favored his or her best interests. If we were close to the end of the trial and approaching the time for the jury to receive the case, then, as the lawyer, I would strive for the final and telling points in whatever arsenal I was able to build in the case during the trial. Always, you are fighting to the very end to convince the judge or jury with the best arguments and facts you can marshal together for victory. All of this is repeated over and over with each trial or hearing as your focus and emotions are locked into the results; receiving the verdict, win or lose, and the thanks or despair of your clients.

Repeatedly, I remember similar thoughts racing through my mind as I was reaching the end of my final argument. "Have I covered everything? Is there something else I can say? Am I convincing the Judge or jury?" When there was nothing further to be said, I would sit down next to my client to wait for the final closing rebuttal statement of the opposing lawyer and the

1

Judge's closing statement of the law to be applied by the jury. Once that was completed, there was nothing left to be done but to wait for the final decision of the jury. It was now out of my hands as the process of justice was once again, moving to conclusion.

There can be no regret or second guessing after the final arguments have been made. It no longer matters. Despite many concerned thoughts, I learned by trial and error that juries would always pick up on the most crucial points from whatever evidence was finally viewed, examined and cross examined before them. The contested issues now lay fully exposed in the crucible of justice which, in the end, was the province of the jury. It was all out there to be considered and decided. There was indeed nothing left to be done. I would feel relief and, most often, a sense of calm that follows a storm. With all the necessary points having been presented, arguments made and entered, I had purged myself of the duty of presenting everything that needed to be said and done in the case. I would feel spent, but always hopeful, as I waited for the jury to return and render its' verdict. I would even begin thinking about the next case at hand waiting to be finally prepared for trial.

Juries treated me well during my career. I rarely lost a case. I must have been doing something right. They would understand what I had been attempting to convey and prove. I believe that my fellow trial attorneys all feel a similar sense of fulfillment that can only come from all the important facts and evidence having been presented and argued in anticipation of their verdict. The lawyer does not make the final decision. That is indeed the province of the jury. It is their final decision. The trial lawyer must be content with the facts presented and arguments having been made in the best light possible on behalf of the clients through the witnesses, evidence and his or her persuasive skills in the final argument. The lawyer follows a well-traveled path to the result. We bring the clients to the doorstep. It is their ultimate decision to follow their lawyer's recommendations and either settle their case and controversy or go to trial and learn the final judgment of the jury. The lawyer stands together with his clients and experiences the joy of victory or the consequences of defeat. The end of the journey is placed squarely into the laps of the jury. That is our system. It is incumbent upon the lawyer during the trial to get it right since the verdict always carries with it such significant consequences.

As client and counsel approach the end of cases, whether it be the final negotiations of an agreement, compromise, entry of a plea bargain or making the decision to go to trial, the pressure and anxiety rises. Clients become more worried and upset, calls between counsel and client increase as do the meetings and phone calls between them. Often, with the opposing counsel and, on occasion, with the judges in the cases. One enters a pressurized capsule that brings the parties and counsel together or not. All other cases and client matters are set aside or dealt with as quickly as possible as the time for final decision or trial approaches. The longer one practices; the better counsel becomes in handling this mounting pressure. However, clients are not as ready or willing to undergo the unending pressure and uncertainties that cannot be avoided. This is not a walk in the park for the participants as they become more and more burdened by the possible outcomes that vary with each passing day. Offers go back and forth between the parties and the constant pressure of the final decision grows. It is a good time for humor, if possible; and perspective as each side attempts to close the gap existing between the two sides. Most of the time, reason prevails, and things get worked out.

The usual outcome of this process is a deal that is born from the coming together of the common elements that exist in most disputes, civil or criminal. This is generally where most cases end up, with a settlement or a plea bargain. It is also good reason for lawyers to believe that most of their clients' cases and issues can and will be worked out. If not, my experience has taught me that a jury outcome will be fair and well suited to the facts and circumstances, far better than what one can expect from a trial to a Judge. This may surprise the reader. I am not saying that a judge's decision cannot be counted on. They can. However, because a Judge is one person and not the collective minds, hearts and thinking of a jury of twelve or six persons, there is always a greater risk with a Judge's final individual decision. It is simply the nature of human beings. Two minds or more are better than one. Another way of looking at this in my opinion is that there is less chance for error with more than one person making the final decisions. Think about our United States Supreme Court and the highest courts of all the states in America. What do they consist of? The answer is nine or seven justices are the choice of all the states or the United States of America for final justice. It does make you wonder about the reliability of one person to make the ultimate decision.

As client and counsel proceed through the legal journey prescribed by our Rules of Procedure for court and the system of law and order under which we operate in America, they can be comforted by the existence of a long history of good and just application in all our separate states. Most legal questions can be easily answered. If the issues raised in a case are new, then the legal process allows for the full development of good answers. My forty-eight years in law practice have led me to the conclusion which I have passed on to young lawyers who worked for me and law students in classes I have taught, that most issues and problems have been dealt with before and can be found by good research and thought. You can achieve the same result as is shown in final court decisions if you take the time to assemble the facts and think them all through to the end. As you study the issues, facts and surrounding circumstances in a case, the solutions slowly and inevitably evolve and determine what the correct outcome should be. Often, the result of your thinking will lead you to a correct decision or agreement that is supported by facts of the case and the applicable law that you find from your research. This allows you to be able to predict where a case is going once you have understood all the variety of facts, persons and circumstances that exist and thought through everything that may apply.

The wild card in all cases are the people themselves who are involved. I have no doubt that most people and certainly, law students, are surprised when I have said to them that one must think his or her way through to the final solution of cases. It is like a puzzle; the more clues you can collect, the closer you will come to the correct final solution to be argued or peacefully resolved. Having done that, there always remains the ever-present changes in the minds and hearts of the parties and witnesses. This ultimately is why we go to trial. We humans have been making the same mistakes repeatedly for centuries. All of this culminates in people testifying in court before judges and juries who, in their wisdom decide what justice requires.

I have no doubt that facts and circumstances of many of the cases I have written about in this book have happened before in Colorado or some other state, or a close approximation thereof. Of course, the separate and distinct characters of the clients and actors are new and unique as are the surrounding circumstances. The lawyer's job is to put it all together and figure out what needs to be done to make things right, fair and just. It is the same thing that we all do in our daily lives as we are confronted with the unendingly amazing things that happen. Just look around yourself and your life. All around you and with you are problems and dilemmas that need to be resolved. When harm or damages are involved, the problems rise to the level of a legal case. Still, many of issues can be resolved without the law. We lawyers turn down at least as many cases as we accept. In doing so, we often provide the additional experience and necessary thinking that the person who visited the office was unable to achieve. We regularly deal with a huge range of problems. The lawyer provides a good and necessary perspective because he or she has lived with clients through similar problems to the very end. Trial is truly the last resort. Not only is it the most expensive solution, but also must be viewed as necessarily being the final resort. Therefore, most legal problems are ultimately settled.

Inevitably, the question arises. Was it necessary to live through the anguish, fear and uncertainty of the legal process? Could things have been changed? Was there a better way? In each case, the answer is different because all of us are likely to have more thoughtful answers after the full gamut of the case has been experienced and resolved. Always, there were opportunities to resolve the disputes. Both sides have different buttons that are pushed that inevitably lead to the conclusion that is reached. Facts and law are seen differently by the opposing sides because the truth is slippery and turns into various shades and colors as it is viewed by opposing sides.

There are always a multitude of facts and factors at play in any given problem or dispute. Most of us of are not good at working through the shifting sands of decision making. The law sets up the ways and means of reaching a just decision, but most of us are unable to see outside of ourselves and the issues to make good decisions. We often become defensive and hold firmly to what appears to be best individual answer for each of us. This allows those of us who practice and participate in our justice system to achieve a sense of what can be expected as our cases proceed. I can affirm this by saying that I often found myself telling my clients, "We will work it out. Just wait and you will see." This was because, in my practice, I had been to those places before. It would lend a tone of knowledge to my words and the clients would listen, shake their heads and say. "I hope you are right." We would then make our way through the thicket and thorns of litigation to the end of the case as I predicted. Having been there before does make all the difference in the world.

I cannot even remember how many problems I was able to solve for clients during a single visit or phone call. This is a service that people only learn when they call or meet with a lawyer to see if their problem can be worked out. As a lawyer, I was always happy to be able to direct or redirect people to the right result. This is something that goes with the territory and is not so well known or understood by people who are facing important or gut-wrenching problems. We attorneys often have a key to possible solutions which study, practice and experience just makes better as the years go by. The knowledge we accumulate is often readily available for use. A lawyer in our society is well equipped to provide good and important services to the public, both large and small. In the process, both the lawyer and client gain from the services; the client having the problem resolved and the lawyer by having provided needed services and a result for the client.

My life as a lawyer on the front lines of dealing with the daily and personal tragedies, accidents, negligence, crimes and wrongdoings of my fellow human beings to one another has been a fascinating ride. It all started with my firsthand view of a great trial lawyer's mind, Clarence Darrow. In a book entitled, "Attorney for the Dammed," I read in case after case what he so brilliantly argued and said in courtrooms across America. My cases did not take me as far or as wide as Mr. Darrow, but I did experience the amazing panorama of peoples' minds and hearts, criminal acts and unusual behavior, good and bad, as they were developed and scrutinized in courtrooms and my offices. It has been an amazing ride, one that has tested my mind, heart and stamina fully.

You cannot help but grow and develop as a human being as you confront together with your clients one conundrum after another and the varied and amazing people, victims, witnesses, experts, fellow lawyers and judges that are involved. The stories never stop, and unusual facts do not have to be made up. I recommend trial work to anyone who seeks to voyage into places beyond imagination that test you physically and mentally and, as a by-product, allow you to grow and experience highs and lows of a life lived on the edge. You do not have to make it up. It simply comes to you as you live, breath and experiences the rush of standing up in front of a judge or jury to present your client's case and arguments for their consideration and the final verdict. It is a life worth living. It is my hope that this book will provide the reader with insight and an understanding of what a trial lawyer feels and experiences in court with his or her clients. Welcome aboard!

CHAPTER 2

First Steps

The first and only lawyer I worked for was very generous with the cases he gave me to work on. It turned out that he preferred to deal with the cases that had the greatest potential for making dollars, such as personal injury cases, business type cases and those of his friends and business associates. He showed little interest in going to court because he believed that he lost time and money on such matters except for the personal injury cases which did pay very well for the time spent due to the contingency fee agreements with the clients. As a result, I soon found myself representing a great many clients in all types of cases. This included criminal matters, traffic tickets, and defense of collection cases, civil disputes, and contract cases and, much to my surprise, divorce cases. It was as if I had a practice of my own.

Court appearances, motion hearings and trials immediately became a regular part of my daily life. I tried my first jury trial within a couple weeks of becoming a lawyer. It was a traffic case and I remember being upset with the Judge. He was an older fellow practitioner in an office just a few blocks away from our offices. I was upset with him because he would not grant my Motion to Dismiss at the end of the City's case. It was clear to me that the City had not proven all the elements of their case and I did not understand why the judge had failed to grant my Motion. I put on our defense and each side gave their closing arguments to the Jury. We then waited together with the opposing deputy city attorney and the Judge in his chambers well into the evening for the Jury to return its verdict. The jury decided, "Not Guilty." I was elated and partially unbelieving. I had won and, most important, believed that this would be the verdict after the trial was completed and placed into the hands of the jury. It was a great feeling. I had achieved a "Not Guilty" verdict for the first time after years of schooling, bar preparation and days and nights of day dreaming. It had happened, and I had undergone my initiation into trial work.

Soon after the verdict was received, the judge and the deputy City Attorney joined me in a celebration of my first jury victory in the Judge's chambers. The Judge smilingly said to me that, "I knew that this would be your first jury verdict and I could see as the case unfolded that you would win. If, by chance, the jury found your client guilty, I would have suggested to you to make a Motion to Set Aside the Verdict and would have granted it." I was shocked. I thanked the Judge for his thoughtfulness and willingness to take the personal time it took for us to try the case and wait for the jury verdict. I went home to my wife full of wonder about what I had been able to accomplish so soon after being sworn in as a lawyer. Ahead of me were hundreds and hundreds of victories and sometimes, deep disappointment, when the jury or the judges found against my clients. I had been baptized into my profession and was looking forward to more of the same. Ahead were more cases than I had ever dreamed of in which I began to learn my trade and pay the price that only experience, and the whims of God and law can exact.

What this Judge did was in keeping with the way lawyers treated each other when I started practicing in Colorado in the late 1960s. Older and more experienced lawyers often took it upon themselves in many courtrooms around Denver and beyond to help young lawyers like myself. The same carried over to bar association meetings and Continuing Legal Education seminars (CLEs) that we all attended where my fellow lawyers were truly interested and ready to help and give advice to fledgling lawyers. I have tried to do the same as I grew older, wiser and, hopefully, helped a few young lawyers get through some difficult thickets in which they found themselves. Sadly, much of this has disappeared during my last twenty years of practice where, instead of maintaining a professional and cordial relationship with one another, lawyers began to shoot and snipe at one another as if we were enemies. In large part, I believe this was occasioned by the introduction of more non-personal contact with one another through fax machines, email, texts and tweets. The immediacy of communication between counsel became more limited as personal contact diminished, except for court appearances. As years passed into the computer/electronic revolution, the personal contact divides it has fostered grew more and more. It seemed as if the computer age erected personal barriers between counsel despite the immediacy of the flow information and increased documentation between offices. I frankly enjoyed my last ten years of practice far less then what I experienced and enjoyed the first ten years. I do believe that the court personnel and Judges must have the same complaint.

During the next few months of the first year of practice, I experienced several more jury trials and a host of trials to the Court. The jury trials were misdemeanors such as assault, theft and DUIs. The trials to the court involved a variety of civil disputes and spilled over to domestic matters. My boss soon developed a habit of calling me in the evening or early in the morning to draft me into taking over cases that were set for hearing or trial the next day or that same morning. He would ask me to take over the cases and go to court in his place. In each case, he would tell me about the judge in the case and suggest to me to obtain a continuance, if possible. He would bring the file to my home each morning in time for me to drive to the court while giving me the facts of the cases as best he could, pat me on the back and tell me that I would do fine. I would take on the unexpected cases as is and thank him for his faith in me and for the opportunity to develop my skills.

Indeed, in some cases, the court would grant a continuance. However, in the other cases, the Judges would be upset that my boss was not there, but still ordered that the case proceed to trial, sometimes to a jury. So, having just met my client and witness or witnesses at the courthouse, I prepped as best I could and would find myself selecting a jury and trying to figure out what I would tell them in my opening statement. It is amazing how alert your mind becomes in response to the fears and danger of the imminent trial or hearing. If it was a criminal case, I had the advantage of going after the prosecution presented its case. This carried over to cross-examination of witnesses since I was able to listen to their testimony before standing up to cross-examine. I would learn the cases on the fly and found that, often, I was able to present an adequate, if not good defenses and still obtain "Not Guilty" verdicts. I must confess at this point that the prosecuting attorneys I faced were often as unprepared as I was due to their heavy caseloads. When I became a prosecutor myself, I found myself in similar circumstances, preparing for trial at the last minute when I would be speaking to the police officer and or witnesses just before entering the courtroom to try the case.

Civil cases were different from criminal. Often the clients were more upset with my boss not being present since they had paid him retainers and money was on the line in the verdicts. Whereas in the criminal courts, clients were more accepting of their reason to be there and the assistant district attorney's or city attorney's function. It made things worse if my side was the civil Plaintiff seeking damages. This meant that our case had to be presented first and I would have to start things with an opening statement to the jury or the Judge and present the client's case and witnesses having barely just met them and learned about the facts or circumstances. Getting to know the facts about my client's case and or the witnesses became even more difficult with the judge or jury waiting. It would become very intense and tested me and the clients dramatically, as their anger and tensions would spill out, in large part, because my boss was not there. In several such cases, the hearings were on motions and the client could live for another day in court regardless of the result. However, when we went to trial, it was final. Later, my boss would hear about it from the judges and his clients. Since he had thick skin and the ability to please and appease the clients and or the judges, he managed to come out of each event smiling and, often, with the client still in tow. For me, it became a growing amount of experience in all kinds of civil and criminal cases resulting from the results.

I had learned together with my clients that I can handle the stress of the situation and accusations we faced together in court. On my part, I would find myself driving back to the office or home happy with the result and exuberant that I was lucky enough to have had the opportunity to prove my worth in court under pressure. This was clearly what I wanted to do, and I loved it. Finally, I was learning the mechanics and art of courtroom advocacy and persuasion on an extemporaneous basis since I was left with such limited time for preparation. This required me to rely on my wits and, often, humor in addition to the known and unknown facts and circumstances of the trial issues. In my first few court appearances, one of my legs would be shaking as I stood at the podium speaking to the judge or jury. The shaking problem left me within the first two weeks of law practice, never to return. However, you never lose the whirling inside your brain and stomach as you attempt to put order and perspective into what you are saying, arguing or in the direct and cross examinations of the witnesses or clients in court.

By the fall of my first year in practice, having been admitted into practice in March, I had become a veteran in the courtroom in front of juries and judges. My style was one of sincerity mixed with passion. I also found myself showing anger, unexpectedly, as I reacted to what was being said by witnesses or from the direction of opposing counsel, particularly the second. I did not hide my feelings and soon learned that they could be used with some effect in courtrooms. Of course, one had to keep ones cool with the Judges. They ruled the courtroom if they chose to do so. However, many judges gave us lawyers a wide berth, and even enjoyed the skirmishes occasioned by the fighting gladiators. And so, did the juries. It did not take me long to realize that I was engaged in a show and that it paid dividends to play it both smart and even funny while representing or defending my client's interests.

The courtroom was indeed a stage and we were the actors. This required preparation whenever possible; timing which was often spontaneous and humor that would come naturally with the amazingly different circumstances and the development of each case in court. It also required the ability to characterize and sum up what the judge or jury had heard from witnesses into persuasive arguments on behalf of the client. I had entered a mammoth undertaking, one that required an ability to think fast on my feet and to be nimble in my utterances before the judges and juries. I would walk out of court happy, but sweating and tired from exertion of mind and body fully.

I began to learn about the use and misuse of objections. Good objections worked since the Judge was siding with you. I was also learning how to use objections that were ruled against me by the court. As a young lawyer, I found myself often looking at jurors as I sat at counsel's table or was standing or walking in the well of the courtroom during the testimony and questioning. I began to watch jurors during objections by myself or the opposing counsel. In the heat of battle, it became evident that jurors were not always able to hold back their reactions to the Judges' rulings or counsels' arguments. They would give off signs of their involvement in what was taking place. Sometimes, I could read their involvement with what I was saying or arguing. They were not just pieces of furniture to be ignored. In fact, I soon recognized what should have been obvious; that jurors were the principal players in the trial besides my client.

Not a single law professor in law school ever discussed in class the lawyer's unavoidable interplay with and interaction with jurors. Sometimes, it was through eye contact or facial expressions. Other times, it was body movements or reactions by jurors in the jury box and all the different ways in which they expressed themselves in eye contact, movement or spontaneous reactions. Although nothing is ever stated between counsel and jurors, it was a real interaction. I found myself making eye contact with certain jurors coming back from breaks or at times when I was returning to the podium or my chair at counsel table. As the trial progressed, I would seek out the jurors with whom I felt comfortable after having questioned them during the voire dire selection process or the ones who appeared to be friendly during the entrances and exits from the courtrooms during the trial. In the middle of trial or during difficult times or testimony, such glances would often keep up my spirits or aide in development of ease and confidence. I was learning over and over that the jurors were not only listening but feeling what was taking place in the courtroom in front of them. They were hearing my concerns and those of the litigants and witnesses. My learning curve dramatically increased in all aspects of trial by jury in the next few months as I began to try more serious cases.

The wide variety of cases set the table for my development of a better understanding of what works and does not work in trials before juries. I had already begun to have an understanding that trials to the courts before a Judge were each a unique and different experience requiring adjustment to the very different characters and personalities of the judges. The separate and varying personalities of each Judge took time to get used to as one gained exposure and experience before them, and later, confidence when appearing in front of them. It was the best learning ever. It was under fire and with no holds barred. I realized early on that you only had one shot with each witness, whether it is your witness or cross-examination of the prosecution witnesses on the other side. You must present your case the best you can and always, under the immediate fire from opposing counsel or the judge. It was all very real, live and extemporaneous. You had to fight or lose. The other side would always immediately grasp and make use of any mistakes or omissions you made, as would the judge or jury. You had to do the same or pay the consequences. One grew accustomed to doing a lot of sweating as the learning experiences in court grew and mounted. I was also learning that humor and a willingness to accept mistakes and foibles by your client or yourself can give you the food and nourishment to continue the fight for your side. It always helped if the Judge had humor in his or her makeup, since the court days were long and tiresome.

Looking back, what I experienced in the many cases I ended up trying in my first year turned out to be a compressed version of what every trial lawyer must go through to achieve an understanding and comfort zone in front of a jury. Some of us get it very fast, although it is a painful process. It is no less painful and educational to learn under less immediate circumstances and the passage of time. Either way, is not only necessary but essential in the training and growth of a trial lawyer's skills. That is why becoming a prosecutor or a public defender, or as I experienced, a deputy city attorney, can be very helpful to achieve a sense of comfort in court regardless of the problems one is facing in his or her cases. There is no other way to experience the slings and arrows of trial work but to spend a great deal of time in court while experiencing both hearings and trial, whether it is in civil or criminal cases. At some point, you find yourself ready to take on whatever the case facts and circumstances may be and know that you will be able to present your client's case as it should be presented. It is not a matter of luck. It is work done repeatedly in your chosen field of the courtroom. However, even so, there will always be surprises and unexpected developments that no one could predict.

CHAPTER 3

A Taste of Felony

The trial of my first felony case was soon upon me in the 5th month of practice. This caused me to be very concerned about my ability to handle the pressure that comes with representing a person charged with a serious crime. A loss meant jail time for my client in the Colorado penitentiary located about one hundred miles south and west of Denver in Canyon City, Colorado. This was a place I had never visited, but I began thinking about it for the first time. My client was charged with theft over five thousand dollars and a possible sentence of up to 15 years. As the trial date approached, I became more and more concerned. I felt as if a day of reckoning was approaching. I could not get the case out of my mind. In my trips to other courts with other cases and clients, my thoughts would return to this case. I started preparations for the trial much earlier than ever before.

I will call my client, John Downey. He had been the manager of a supermarket that was not at the level of a King Soopers or a Safeway. On the Friday evening in question, John closed out the store at the normal time and left for a weekend in Los Vegas. John had not been happy with his marital situation or his job. He had decided to leave Denver and have a blowout weekend drinking and gambling in Los Vegas without much thought for the future. He did exactly that and when he returned to Denver, he learned from his wife that the police were looking for him as the prime suspect in the theft of cash from his store exceeding $5000. John's immediate reaction was fright and to run. He packed up his clothes and belongings into his car and over his wife's arguments and protestations to face the police and about their children, he left Colorado for Florida.

About a year later, the police located John in Florida where he was arrested, charged and extradited back to Colorado. In the process of being returned to Colorado, he was interviewed by county Sheriff's department officers and made several incriminating statements. John agreed that he had taken with him to Los Vegas a little over five-thousand in cash that he had saved. He did not know anything about the theft of five thousand from his store and denied that he had done it. However, he admitted that he was drunk from the time he left Denver for Vegas until he returned to Denver. On top of that, during the questioning by one of the sheriff's department officers, he stated, "I must have done it." He also admitted that he ran away from Denver to Florida because he was afraid of "being convicted." These were admissions that would invariably lead to a jury instruction from the court that flight can be taken by a jury to be an indication of guilt. The case did not look good as I visited John for the first time in jail before he was bonded out with the help of his wife and family.

During the first visit, John confirmed that he had made the statements that were recorded on the police report. He also informed me that "I started drinking before I left Denver and have no recollection of taking money from the store. But I did have about five thousand in cash with me on the trip to Las Vegas which I had taken from cash I had been saving and keeping in the home. Almost all of it was spent when I returned to Denver." When he arrived in Las Vegas, John began drinking heavily, hoping to drown his sorrows regarding his marriage, job and current circumstances. The weekend was mostly a blur of gambling and drinking leading to blackouts followed by more drinking and gambling. He had never counted his money and did not know exactly the amount of money he started with. He did know that he had "just enough money left to make it back to Denver early Monday morning to open the store." He had intended to return to work as soon as he washed and changed his cloths. When he arrived home, his wife told him that the police had visited the home and wanted to speak with him. This caused John him to become immediately alarmed because the officers had informed his wife that there had been a break-in and theft at the store.

At this point, John had become panicked and put together some clothes, necessities and left home despite his wife attempting, without success, "to stop him and face the music." Obviously, he was not thinking clearly and, as he was now sitting in the County jail, he recognized that he had probably convicted himself. He told me that he was not thinking clearly when he said what he did to the investigating Sheriff's deputies who traveled to Florida and arrange for his extradition back to Colorado. He had blurted out, "I must have done it." Looking back, he recognized that in the condition he was in as he left Denver, anything was possible and he was not sure of what he had done once he started drinking. However, as he sat in jail, depressed, worn out by the experience of arrest and transportation to Denver, accusations of theft and guilt resulting from leaving his family and home, he looked the part of a man beaten down by his irresponsible behavior. I was looking at a person who was defeated. As we spoke, I could see tears in his eyes. He was sad and was having difficulty keeping himself together while we were speaking, not unlike others I had already met in jails in and around Denver. What was most troublesome was that John could not clearly remember the exact amount of money of his own that he had taken to Las Vegas other than that "it was a little over $5000." Nor was there a record of the money in a bank account. It had been accumulated over a long period of time in cash and he had kept it hidden in his home. Even his wife was not told about the money. Although, I did learn later from her that she did know about the money and ended up testifying about its existence and her knowledge about it to the jury.

John said that, "I had closed out the income and receipts of that day on Friday before I left, but I do not remember the "exact amount" other than it was a little over $5000 dollars. I left the close out receipts and cash money and checks in the desk as usual, so the assistant manager could go to the bank on Saturday morning and make the deposit." The entire weekend was blocked in his mind except for a few bursts of memory about his time in Vegas. However, I was able to confirm that he had indeed visited various Casinos where money was used to gamble during his play in various casinos, including where he had stayed in Los Vegas. The money deposits and withdrawals were subsequently confirmed in several casinos. All these facts, including his own admission, that "I must have done it" and the two separate $5,000 plus cash amounts from his home and the store did not augur well for his defense.

John told me, "I normally went to the bank in the mornings since the close-out time took place after bank hours. No note or call was necessary" since the assistant manager well understood the routine and would make the deposit in the bank the following morning with whatever money would be left in the desk drawer. Despite this being a plausible explanation, it was a hard story to swallow. My attempts to wring out of John more facts or recollections failed. His own five thousand plus cash and the five thousand plus cash receipts simply did not jive. I was also concerned about how poorly he looked. He was slumped over, looking down to the floor as he answered.

Clearly, he was facing the demons of what he had created, and they were winning. He was in no shape to face a jury and there was much work to be done. I left him in jail that day very concerned about the many unanswered questions. I did not know what could be accomplished for my client in any defense that I could raise.

As the case began to unfold with the initial court appearance, arraignment and Motions hearing, I became acquainted with the deputy DA assigned to the case and the headstrong and infamous judge in whose courtroom the case would be tried. The deputy was an experienced prosecutor and a good man. We hit it off right away. He understood the problems raised by the facts and the seriousness of the decisions that I was facing as the case proceeded. He demonstrated qualities that I have found made the best prosecuting attorneys. He was a lawyer who understood how the system affected criminal defense clients and was patient as client and counsel began to come to terms with what the client was facing in the charges and evidence as it accumulated. My instincts proved to be correct when he was later elected the District Attorney in the County which encompassed the foothills to the Rocky Mountains, creeks and rushing water filled canyons that block out the sun as you travel west towards the great fourteen-thousand-foot mountains in the continental divide.

The judge was another matter. I was soon entering one of the most bizarre experiences I have ever faced in a courtroom any place in Colorado or in other states where I have appeared on behalf of my clients. Judge Christopher Brock did everything his own way, including interpreting the law. He was demanding, domineering, paternal, friendly, outrageous and outspoken. I found myself in a buzz saw where he would tell me that he was "trying to help me" while, at the same time, he was both correcting and castigating me. In hearings, the judge would be ruling against me and pointing out what he considered to be my mistakes at the same time. He would knock me down and then try to lift me up. In truth, I was bewildered. I had heard about the judge, but now I was experiencing what I had been hearing. Judge Brock never let up on his unorthodox pursuit of my trial education during the court appearances, preliminary hearing and the trial itself. It became up to me to "adjust or be broken" in the words of courtroom chatter.

The problems began in a hearing on a Motion I had made to suppress the alleged confession of my client from being used as evidence by claiming the Sheriffs' deputies had violated the recently decided US Supreme Court case of Arizona v. Miranda that became well known as a basis of constitutional rights and law in America. My argument was that the sheriff's deputies failed to advise John of his rights that were very clearly set forth in that landmark opinion. They became known as the "Miranda advisement" required in all arrests before an interrogation by the police. When the Judge asked me to proceed with case and witnesses, I responded "Your Honor, pursuant to the Miranda case, the Supreme Court has placed the burden on the prosecution to first show to the court that the incriminating evidence had been constitutionally obtained." I went on to tell the Judge that the "DA must meet that burden before I put on any evidence." Simply as a precaution, I had subpoenaed both deputy sheriffs involved, and they were present in the courtroom. Such a hearing is exactly what I had already experienced in other courtrooms in Denver and surrounding counties. The Judge's response shocked me. He said, "In this courtroom, you either proceed with your case or I will dismiss your Motion right now." Flabbergasted, I went ahead and called the two police officers to the stand, one after the other, and examined their recollections. It should have been that I would be cross examining the officers, but due to the Judge's ruling I was forced to give them direct questions and unable to lead them as one does on cross examination. The deputy DA followed with his cross examinations of each officer, which gave him an advantage taken away by the Supreme Court when it placed the burden of going forward on the prosecution that the defendant had been properly advised of his rights. This was the practical meaning of what the Judge had ordered to take place.

Then, after the witnesses had been questioned and cross-examined, it was left for me to present my argument. Before I could finish the argument, Judge Brock interrupted me and denied my Motion to Suppress. John Downey's statement and confession remained in evidence. We were left to set the date for the trial of the case. There I was, totally bewildered by a Judge who had no intention of following the Miranda decision of the Supreme Court of the United States or, for that matter, any other US Supreme Court decisions. Leaving the courtroom, the deputy just shook his head and said, "This is how it is in his courtroom. There is no changing him." As we were leaving the courtroom, the Judge had asked that counsel come into his chambers. We complied with his order and proceeded into the judge's chambers. We then learned in more detail what the Judge had on his mind.

The first thing the Judge addressed when we were seated in his chambers was that he was aware that I had never had a case in his courtroom before. He then explained that I needed to understand that," I do not pay any attention to what they do or say in Washington. This is my courtroom and you will follow my rules. Things will be easier for you if you understand this as we proceed with your case." I could not help but to look at my fellow lawyer prosecutor sitting next to me. He had a bland look on his face not revealing his thoughts. As I turned back to the Judge, he said to me forcefully, "Do you understand?" Realizing that I had entered the land of OZ, I replied. "Yes, your honor, I understand". We then spoke a little about current events with the Judge before we both left the Judge's chambers. As we were leaving chambers, the deputy said to me when we were out of earshot of the Judge, "You have to get used to it. This is how it is and how he is. Call me if you need some help in coping with the Judge. Humor works." There it was. I had been introduced to another world I had never travelled or known had existed.

I could have appealed the Judge's ruling since this was both a procedural and a constitutional issue of some importance. It was permitted at that time to file an interlocutory appeal (An appeal made during the time that the case was unfolding in the trial court). However, the time and money involved turned out to be prohibitive to John and his family and, as I explained, if we were to lose the trial, I had already made a good record for any future appeal. We decided to go ahead with the trial which was set on the docket to go in about forty-five days. Cases went to trial much faster back then since the case dockets were not anything like they have become in the last twenty years. We were on a fast track.

As you can imagine, it was very difficult to put together my defense on behalf of John. Although, he never quite said that he stole the money, he never directly denied it. Once the police targeted him, he ran away. Being drunk as he motored to Las Vegas and all the while he was there, even with a blackout or two, did not fully account for the money he admittedly took with him and spent. He reiterated to me several times when I questioned him, that, "I had saved cash for quite a while and took it all with me. I do not know the exact total. It was about five thousand, maybe a little more". "Oh, that is great!" I replied. John was cementing the case against himself because the evidence would show that he had cashed in and out of several Las Vegas casinos a total of about the same five thousand dollars. No other person of interest had been developed by the DA' s office other than the assistant manager and he had an alibi. Moreover, John himself spoke about the honesty of his assistant manager even as the finger print evidence pointed to both John and his assistant manager and no one else. It was certainly to be expected that they would both be at the office desk counting the money and doing their jobs. John had no idea as to who else could have done it and the police were satisfied that they had the right man. As a result, they had terminated their investigation since they concluded that John was the culprit. Neither John nor his fellow employee were ever able to account for the missing five thousand plus dollars. What was I to do in his defense?

The case was made more complicated by the fact that despite John's domestic problems, both his wife and family stood behind him and paid the bail, attorney fees and expenses. The sentiment that was expressed to me by all, including the assistant manager, was that John would not do such a thing. He and his family went to church each Sunday, and he was, by all accounts, a good, decent and soft-spoken man, except for his occasional drinking. Other employees did not have information or evidence one way or the other. Yes, things at home were an issue. He had been drinking way too much and everyone was shaking their heads about him leaving town, but he could not have been the thief according to family and friends who knew him.

As I came to know John, I too found myself believing that he was innocent and a man of good character who had hit upon a rough patch in his life. In due course, as we approached the trial date, the deputy made a reasonable offer of a plea to a lower felony count with a sentence up to 5 years since John had never previously committed a crime outside of a driving and drinking misdemeanor offense a few years back. We would also have the opportunity of asking the Judge for probation. However, I had done some checking about the Judge's sentencing practices. I learned in short order and so informed John that "By all accounts, the judge was tough, and a long sentence had to be anticipated." Of course, John would have to agree to pay back the money that had been stolen as part of any plea bargain. That meant another five thousand plus dollars.

We talked about the offer several times at my office with and without his wife being present. We went back and forth between accepting the plea bargain and trying the case. The family split on the issue while John, his wife and I continued to discuss the pros and cons. Misdemeanor convictions in Colorado faced a maximum of two years in the County jail, not the penitentiary. I was unable to get the DA's office to drop the felony to a misdemeanor. This was my first taste of the tremendous risks involved for the client in the criminal justice system. I did not realize at the time that I would soon be facing similar and even more serious decisions on behalf of many of my clients. After long and careful consideration, John and I decided to turn down the offer and go to trial. I could not help thinking that maybe the blind was leading the blind.

The dye was caste. I was scared. John's life was in my hands. I did not know if I could win. I did not have enough experience yet to feel what could be accomplished in court. I also did not know what impact I could make on the jury, let alone how the jury would see John. There were a great many questions that could not be answered. This was a recurring mystery and a cloud on the horizon that I would cope with during all my early years in practice. Yet, I must say that I did in fact learn that I could win cases and that a feeling of confidence could be imparted to the juries I would be facing. This took time and experience to learn. I had never felt so strongly the need to feel confident in such an important case. Instead, I found myself struggling with that fear and, even more, with how I would go about convincing the jury that John should be acquitted. Somehow, I had to get that feeling inside me strong enough to convey it to the jury.

John's case would take longer than any trial I had previously tried. Most likely, it would take three or four days. In fact. It took one week. I had never gone beyond two days with the second day mainly for jury instructions by the judge and the final arguments to the juries before they were to commence their deliberations. The deputy had listed about fifteen witnesses, including persons from Los Vegas Casinos regarding the monies deposited and cashed in by John. I considered for the first time that it would be a guessing game as to who would really be called to testify. I attempted, unsuccessfully, to contact the Los Vegas witnesses by phone. It was a common tactic by DAs to provide the names of more witnesses than they would call. This required defense counsel to attempt to speak with all named witnesses, if possible, or risk a witness testifying with whom he had never spoken to beyond what limited information was given in the discovery that was provided under the Rules of Criminal Procedure in Colorado. This mainly consisted of the charges and the police reports.

As years went by and we become more experienced, most criminal defense lawyers learned to figure out who would be called. This was principally a question of the DA providing the court and jury with sufficient witnesses and evidence to prove the elements of the crime charged effectively, but not repetitiously. I was just beginning to understand and contemplate such questions. If I had been prone to headaches, this would have given me a doozy. But, I was not prone to headaches. Instead, I plunged into study and more study of the case long into the nights and mornings, just as in law school. The sleepless nights were added to the long time spent attempting to catch up with and speak to the witnesses that were listed. I was also beginning to learn that because of regular coaching by the deputy DA's, most prosecution witnesses would refuse to talk to me. Although, in time, I learned that sometimes they would, even the police officers. In this case, the cops would not, but a few of the civilian witnesses did. However, their recollections turned out to be peripheral at best.

The most important thing I did was to think and rethink the known facts of the case as I was learning and weighing the plusses and minuses of the evidence that the jury would see and hear. I started to run various scenarios in my head and, sometimes, making notes on paper. Early on, I did a lot of writing and note taking, but as years passed, I came to the realization that I would rarely look back or even read such notes or writing. This was because, as a case would progress, and facts became more fully known, I would be changing and re changing my thinking and ideas as to how I would present, and cross examine the case. This made previous and earlier notes irrelevant and the final notes before trial most important. Also, I came to understand that what one would visualize the facts to be presented in court often failed to come out that way in court, both in small things and large. Above all, the credibility of any witness was always the wild card. I had a somewhat credible, but highly tarnished client who had arguably confessed. But would he withstand the pressure of trial and cross examination? Once again, I did not know the answer. I simply did not have the experience to make a sound judgment about his credibility before a jury.

It became apparent that I needed to develop a game plan and strategy for the defense. First, what did the prosecution have in its arsenal? It boiled down to several things. 1. There was a theft evidenced from the store cashier register receipts for the Friday that John left the store. No deposit was ever made for the store. 2. The amount missing was a couple of hundred dollars over $5000. 3. Only John and the assistant manager had access to the locked desk drawer where the money was kept following the day's closing or, so the prosecution speculated, and no forced entry was found. 4. John took about $5000 to Los Vegas and it was all spent according to the records at the casinos that weekend. 5. John admitted that he "must have done it "and he ran away to Florida upon notification of the Sherriff's interest in seeing him. This amounted to an admission of guilt. End of story. 6. The police had not found any other evidence or prints pointing to any other person except his co-worker who had an alibi. John was the logical culprit. He had explained to me that he had indeed told the sheriff that "I must have done it" because the entire weekend was a blur for him. He had been drinking so much that he only had recollections in bits and pieces as he went from one casino to another, He was truly on a binge of drinking and gambling. I would be just shaking my head as he told me these things.

On the other hand, John's wife, who was very believable, confirmed that she was aware of John's stash of cash and that it was missing after he had left Denver that weekend. Indeed, they were having problems in the marriage and he had been drinking heavily. She had been worried about him. He was a good father to their children and an honest man who worked hard to provide for them. We were able to line up the assistant manager, church minister and a business man friend to speak on John's behalf and provide testimony as to his excellent reputation and credibility in their community. I also decided to have John's wife testify. They would all be good and reputable witnesses. My defense was one of credibility of the witnesses and that the prosecution could not conclusively show that the money John blew in Los Vegas belonged to the Super Market. Moreover, John was a man of good character Yes, he was a drinker and foolish, but not a thief. He did not have a crimnal record. I was able to have two-character witnesses who would be able to make a good impression on the jury. In the end, I concluded that my argument for the defense had to be that the DA lacked sufficient proof beyond a reasonable doubt except for the statement which was not a confession, but rather a throw away remark. John did not know how the money was taken. It was not much to hold on to, but it gave me a goal and a strategy as I entered the courtroom to fight for John.

I immediately ran into problems in the trial. They did not come so much from the prosecution witnesses, but from battling with the Judge as he ruled against my objections to the questions that were being asked by the deputy DA. He had been frequently asking leading questions, ones that embodied conclusions that should have been left for the witnesses to state or not. I had already developed a habit of including in my objections the specifics of what the prosecutor was doing wrong since this informed the jury of the evidentiary problems they were hearing. I kept losing the objections. But I continued with them until the very end of each day, often looking at the jury as I was stating the grounds upon which I was objecting, albeit losing the argument again and again. As I stood up once more near the end of second day in court to state an objection, the Judge loudly reprimanded me after ruling against me once again, "Mr. Makaroff, if you object one more time, I will hold you in contempt and call in the Sheriffs." This was serious. I had never been spoken to by a judge in such a serious way. I looked at my watch and it was about ten minutes to five when the court day would end. I figured I could make it to the end of the day. As I looked at my watch, I had also turned to the jury and smiled effectively signaling that I could make it until we recessed. Several of the men on the jury smiled back. They caught my meaning. This was a great lift for me as I was called into chambers with the deputy after the Judge had recessed for the day.

When we were seated in chambers, the judge immediately voiced his displeasure with all my objections as "unnecessary and a waste of court time." Before I could respond, the Judge added that he could see "You are losing the jury if you keep up with your behavior, mark my words." Effectively, he was advising me on how to conduct my defense of the case. I did not know what to say. Obviously, he had been on the bench a long time and knew a great deal more about trials and juries than me. What he was saying caused me a lot of concern and I was unable to process this advice on the spot. I did say to the Judge, "Without re-arguing all my objections, your honor, I honestly believe that many of them should have been upheld. In any case, Judge, the prosecution case will soon end, and I will be the one asking the questions. So, your troubles will soon end." This attempt at humor did not work and the Judge told me that he would be "watching me" as we left for the day. On the way home, I kept thinking about the jury men who smiled back at me as I was fighting the Judge. Was the case in trouble? I did not know, but a ray of hope had appeared.

Before being called out by the judge for my many objections, the DA had called the sheriff's deputy who had investigated the theft at the store to the stand to set the scene of the crime. The deputy's testimony also included traveling to Florida to bring John back to Colorado once he had waived his rights under the extradition procedures. This is when the incriminating statements were made by John that became the crux of the trial. The deputy made a good impression on the jury as a responsible and experienced law officer. I wanted the jury to know what had happened when John had not been advised of his rights to remain silent, and several of my objections related to that issue. As I began to question the deputy sheriff, once again, I was at odds with the Judge because the issue was a legal issue that had been dealt with and ruled against by the court in the Motions hearing earlier in the case. He stopped me in my tracks because the legal constitutional issue was not a question for the jury to decide. He rightly prohibited me from opening that issue before the jury. This was a score against the Defendant and not a good start for me on this cross examination. My inexperience showed and there was nothing to be done but to go forward. The cross examination failed to overcome the deputy's good impression.

As the prosecution witnesses took the stand, one by one, I was able to gain back some ground. Their testimony, which included that of the assistant manager, showed the exact amount of monies that were being used by John as he won and lost at the different casinos. It supported the prosecution claim of a little over $5000 being used, and ultimately lost by John. They also showed through the testimony of three Los Vegas casino witnesses the total amounts of money that were paid for chips at several the casinos where John gambled that weekend. It all added up to slightly more than $5000. But neither the Las Vegas witnesses nor the second Sherriff's deputy who testified were able to specifically connect the money lost to gambling with the money that had had been taken from the store proceeds. This was the point I continued to make during the cross examinations of all the witnesses connected with the casino monies and the deputy sheriff's office. I always believed that John's wife's testimony would be convincing as was the assistant Manager's when he not only admitted that John had told him about his stash of money, but also that he intended to use it when he left on Friday for the Los Vegas trip. The assistant manager also informed the jury that he was confident that the money was not taken by his boss because he was not that kind of man. This gave us some momentum going into the defense case.

Our defense went well. John's wife was very good and believable. In fact, as she was describing the family problems because of John's drinking and despair, she held the jury in her hands. They were hearing about a man in search for himself, but not a man looking to steal. When I asked her about the cash money that John accumulated, she told the jury very frankly, "It was a constant battle between us. I felt that this was money that had to be shared for the benefit of our children. He argued that he needed it to keep him going because the work was hard for him. It was sort of the light at the end of the tunnel. We never solved the problem. It was the first thing I checked when he left that weekend. I looked to see if the money was missing. It was definitely missing." I could see several jurors sit up and take notice of these compelling remarks. If they believed his wife, John could not have stolen the store money.

The reputation witnesses were two businessmen friends and John's church minister. They came across solidly and showed John to be a decent family man who regularly attended church with an excellent reputation in the business community. I recalled the assistant manager who had appeared as a prosecution witness for additional testimony. He spoke very well of

John's good character and work ethic as a manager and elaborated on what he considered to be John's depression and being out of sorts. With John's consent since he was scared to testify, just as I was very concerned that he would concede far too many of the leading questions that the DA would ask that I could not object to, I informed the court and jury that John had elected not to testify. I chose not to risk John convicting himself on the stand because of his flawed memory of the events due to his drinking binge during the Las Vegas trip. I also feared that John's sense of guilt would cause him to admit more than he should. His wife agreed with my decision and so did John. I rested the case after our last witness with John never having faced the jury.

In my closing argument, I stressed that, "The sheriff's Department had not done a good job of investigating who may have done the theft. After John had fled, they admittedly had stopped the investigation and never developed evidence that could have solved the crime." I suggested that "My client was clearly a good man under the influence of alcohol and not in his right mind. Who else would have told the police that maybe he "must have done it. This was not a confession. He did not know who took the money and neither does the DA. Also, keep in mind that his condition had not improved when he made the terrible decision to run away from all his problems. Remember, good men can make bad decisions just like the rest of us." Finally, I stressed that, "If you believe John's wife and reputation witnesses and the fact that the prosecution has not shown beyond a reasonable doubt that the money spent in Los Vegas was the store's money, then you must acquit. As we stand here today, nobody knows who stole the money from the store since the investigation never went beyond John. You must be convinced beyond a reasonable doubt and you cannot decide this case with a guess. I ask that you return a verdict of Not Guilty."

The jury was out about a half of the day on Friday. When they returned to the courtroom and their verdict was about to be delivered, I was nervous like never before as I stood next to my client. What were they to decide? The Judge asked if they had "reached a verdict?" The jury foreman stood up and replied, "Yes we have your honor." "What is your verdict?" asked the judge. The foreman replied. "We have decided that the verdict is, "Not Guilty!" Wow! It was great to hear, but also a shock which encompassed me as I turned and grabbed John in an embrace. He also appeared to be in shock. As it wore off both of us, he and his family were jubilant. I felt this overwhelming sense of relief, something that I would experience many times over as I waited for and received similar jury verdicts. A great weight is taken off your shoulders and you can feel your own strength returning once again to pursue the next case to conclusion.

After the verdict was announced and the Judge declared that the case was over, many members of the jury came around to congratulate John and speak to both of us once we left the courtroom. Several of the men asked me whether I knew from the start that I would win. I was surprised by the question since I had in fact been worried from the beginning to the end. They explained that they wondered between themselves why I was smiling as much as I did during the trial. Several also said to me that they admired how hard I had fought for my client and that they would want me to be their lawyer if they were ever placed in the same position as John. This was all great to hear. However, I did not tell them that my smiling had mostly been out of nervousness. I acknowledged to them that I had felt that they were with me during my battles with the Judge. I thanked them many times over for their verdict and left the courtroom lobby on a great high.

As I left the courthouse absorbing the verdict and remarks of the jury members, I began processing the importance of showing the jury my belief and confidence in my client's case. My smiles had been nervousness. My inexperience had stymied my confidence. However, the jury had fortunately taken my nervousness and smiles to be confidence. What I learned was that it was incumbent upon me to be confident in front of the jury for the benefit of my clients. I began to comprehend the importance of remembering always that I was being continually watched by the jurors during every part of the trial and how I comported myself with the Judge, opposing counsel, speaking to my client or reacting to testimony. The presence of the jury also meant that they were just as carefully watching the client for his or her reactions to the evidence and witnesses and the district attorney in each case. There was no escape from this. It was a given and I owed it to my clients to act accordingly from the beginning to the end of each trial and, as best as possible, to inform my clients of the scrutiny that they would be subjected to. This knowledge translated itself into how I and, hopefully, my clients behaved in the courtroom as the trial of the case proceeded. My client's chances of success were cemented to how they and I conducted ourselves. From that time forth, I was always conscious of the jury and what its members were giving off and seeing during the trial of the cases. It was vitally important, not only for myself as counsel, but for my client to know. This served me well and, as a direct result, my clients.

I carried with me from the Downey case several additional thoughts and conclusions that ended up serving me well in the future. The jury affirmed that you must fight to the end and second, how you present yourself and your case to the jury in all stages is vital. It is not just the Judge, but the jury that is watching you and your opposing counsel as the case progresses. You must remain true to yourself and who you are. It is your actions and responses to the unending wave of unexpected events and testimony during trial that matter to the jury and the court. As wise or unwise as the Judge may be, the trial lawyer will always know the case better than the Judge. And when it comes time for decisions to be made in the best interests of your client, you are the person who must make the decisions on the spot. It is you and you alone. You must also stick to your game plan as best you can that has been slowly and carefully crafted through the process of investigation, discovery and the final unrelenting study and prep for trial. Yet, despite all the preparatory work, it never fails that things turn out in court differently than expected. You are then left with only with your understanding of the case facts and your instincts about what is happening and the best response to be made. Not to be forgotten, it is you, the lawyer, who is responsible for putting together the defense which must consider various possible scenarios. Beyond that, there is no other recourse for your client. You are the person standing in front of the jury at the end of trial, speaking to them about why your client should win. It is your case, not the Judge's. Amen. These were life lessons.

I left the courtroom feeling great. I had won. It was so improbable, but the jury had not been convinced of John's guilt. My thinking, planning and final argument had been rewarded with victory. The jury had not been convinced. The battle with the Judge had been overlooked by the jury and several jurors, as it turned out, even agreed with me. They came out on my side. Final analysis of the verdict was something that would take much longer to figure out because each case is a product of all the battles of counsel with the court and the opposing counsel, each taken together with the facts, witnesses and the performance or not of the victim and your client in the witness box. There were so many variable factors. When you lay them all out, it was impossible to figure it all out in advance. That is what ends up being the province of the jury. It was a win. There were hundreds and hundreds of cases and juries ahead.

Chapter 4

Continuing Trial Education

As luck would have it, I was immediately given the opportunity to face off against one of the best deputy's DAs in Denver in a very difficult case. My client was a lawyer who had come to my boss for representation. My boss did not want the case because it involved alleged sex acts with another man in a public restroom in the City Park. He extolled my experience to the prospective client and my results in jury trials. After meeting with Leonard Dollinger in my office, he agreed to my representation of him. The case was deadly serious because Leonard was a practicing lawyer in a downtown law firm. A felony conviction would cause him to automatically lose his bar license to practice. There was another problem. Leonard was a homosexual. It was obvious when you met him or heard him speak. Moreover, he did not hide his inclinations. The prosecution case consisted of two arresting police officers and the other man in the rest room who had also been arrested at the same time after he and Leonard had exited the rest room following their alleged sex acts.

When I made my first appearance in the District Court, I was greeted by Aaron Bromberg who was appearing for the District Attorney's office. Since we were well acquainted due to him being the prosecutor in a couple of other cases I had handled in which the facts were very much against the clients. Aaron wasted no time telling me that, "Once again, I have a case that is open and shut." Good facts or bad, this was a case that had to be fought. A trial date was set within three months. There was much work and preparation to be done since my client, the lawyer, could not accept a plea bargain. It would have cost him the license to practice.

Leonard admitted that he had been at the City Park restroom at the time and place designated. He had been arrested after he had walked out of the restroom by two officers who had been watching things from next door to the restroom through a small window. Leonard told me "Mike, I never did anything like what they are accusing me of in the restroom. I never would. I had simply been in the park enjoying a beautiful day during my lunch break from the office." City Park was about a 10-15-minute ride from downtown Denver. This could be easily accomplished in the traffic situation at that time in Denver. Leonard pleaded with me that," You must believe me. I am innocent." Leonard never changed his story and maintained it throughout the case that he "did not and could not have done such a thing. Not ever!" This was a strong denial which he repeated several times. I took it seriously. This put a great deal of pressure on me since I believed him, which I was prone to do early in my career defending people. However, the evidence appeared to be insurmountable with the two eye witnesses police officers.

The police report indicated that Leonard was arrested because the two police officers were watching what was taking place near to the urinal of the public restroom in the Park through a small window from a room next door to the restroom. The room was essentially a storage shed for tools, mowing machines, rakes, shovels and other utensils necessary for use in keeping the park grounds in good shape. I visited the scene of the crime as step one in my investigation. This required coordination with the groundskeepers so that we would be given access to the all-important storage room next door to the scene of the crime. Once this was arranged after the groundskeeper checked with the DA, a time and date were worked out. I had no idea what we would see. I arranged with an investigator who had previously been a police detective, to accompany me to the location of the alleged crime.

When we arrived and viewed the restroom and were let into the storage area next door, we found a very cluttered and busy shed with wooden boxes upon which we had to stand to view the restroom. What we were able to see was from a very small screened window above the urinals. The first issue was that a ledge was set back about eight inches from the aperture that was the window itself. The ledge was located along the length of the wall dividing the rest room from the work shed. Along the ledge were collected some tools, packages and miscellaneous objects. For our purposes, it became immediately clear that anyone looking out through the window of the work shed had to cram his neck forward and up to get any kind of view of what had taken place. At my height of 6 feet one, I had to hang on tightly with my head hitting against the ceiling. As I did that, I immediately wondered how two officers could be looking out the small window at the same time. The length of the window was only about nine inches. How could two grown men be looking out at the same time with their shoulders and bodies on top of each other and somehow hanging on, particularly if they were the same size as me or even smaller? Suddenly, I had a serious question to consider as I viewed the crime scene. If the officers were taller and larger than me, they could not both view the scene below without having the same difficulties that I was experiencing?

Once I positioned myself to look through the grated window, I was surprised to learn that I could not see the urinals at all on the other side of the contiguous wall! It became apparent as time went by and I viewed men standing at the urinals that when the urinals were being used, it caused me to lose from sight the lower part of the men's bodies as they were standing at the urinals. I could see only the top of the heads and upper bodies as men stood at the urinals below. At that point, I sent my client out to the rest room next door and asked him to approach each of the two urinals directly below the window. He did, and at his height of five feet, eight inches, his torso and legs were soon lost from sight. I tried to get up as high as I could with my head, but my line of sight was held in place by the ledge, ceiling and limited window space. I was unable to make my line of sight any better. I could not see Leonard where it mattered at the urinals or close by and I could not see his torso until he was about five feet from the urinals. This was at a distance that was beyond the allegations of the complaint. The same was true for my investigator who was an inch shorter than me. We measured exactly where we lost sight of Leonard's feet and his torso. This established that we not only had a defense, but an argument that the two officers would have had a very difficult time seeing, if at all, what they had stated in their report about to have seen as thy were looking out into the rest room above the urinals. In fact, what was in the police report as having been viewed was not possible. This was a case that could not be proven beyond a reasonable doubt. I left the park with a good feeling about the chances of success for Leonard.

Soon after the investigator and I had put together our photos and exhibits of our findings, I contacted Aaron Bromberg to arrange a meeting with him in the DA's offices. I believed that I had proof of a complete defense to the allegations and felt confident that I would be able to convince him that the case should be dismissed. Aaron was polite and considerate as he heard my recollections about our personal investigation and showed him what our exhibits would be. I did not argue that my client was innocent. Instead, I attempted to convince him that the charges could not be sustained beyond a reasonable doubt. I challenged him to duplicate our investigation knowing that the result would be the same as ours was. He accepted the challenge and told me he would call back as soon as he and the officers went back to the scene. We parted on good terms and I left the meeting with a feeling of confidence that his findings would be the same as mine.

I could not have been more wrong. When Aaron called me back the following week, he told me stronger than before that nothing has changed. He told me that both officers insisted that they saw what they saw and, unless Leonard accepted the lesser felony plea that had been offered and took his chances on what jail time he would receive, we would be going to trial. I tried to convince Aaron about how devastating it would be for my client to lose his license to practice law. He replied that Leonard should have thought about this when he was engaged in the sordid activity that was alleged. "He must now face the music. The officers are both veterans, believable in court and there is no turning back. Tell your client, that his best chance is to convince the Judge at the time of sentencing that he receives probation since he has a clear record." Aaron expressed regret that this was happening to a lawyer, but said that, "This is life and we have to take as it lays'" During that conversation, I could feel how tough this case was going to be. It was all or nothing. I already knew and accepted that Leonard would not and could not accept a lesser plea. The question was how will the jury respond? I did not know, and I began to prepare and steel myself for the trial to come against the DA I knew personally to be not only very good, but a winner.

As the case approached the trial date, I kept asking Aaron whether he had been able to question the other person who had been in the rest room. We had not received in discovery any reference to the witness other than his name and address. The address was false, and it looked like the police had not been able to locate the man. My investigation led to the same conclusion. When I raised the status of the witness in passing when I would see Aaron in court, his answer was always the same. "We will find him. I will let you know whenever that is." They never did find the witness and we went to trial without him.

When the trial started, each officer testified about what they saw, as expected. As part of my cross examination of each officer, I showed each of them photos and diagrams of the rest room that we had put together in our investigation, including photos of both the urinals and the window where the police officers had viewed unsuspecting men at the urinals. These were all labeled as exhibits. The diagram contained the location of marks we had placed on the floor of the urinals designating the lines of sight from the window of a man standing at the urinal who was the same height as my client in different locations approaching and at the urinals. After considerable argument from Aaron Bromberg that the diagrams should not be admitted as unreliable, the Judge admitted them based upon my argument that both the photo exhibits, which were not contested, and diagrams accurately demonstrated the restroom as it looked and was measured by our investigator who had been a veteran police detective before retiring. These exhibits were ultimately shown to the jury, some of which over further continued objections by Aaron Bromberg. As the case progressed and my cross examinations of the officers revealed our defense, I found the jury members to be leaning forward and closely examining the defense exhibits of the scene of the alleged crime Sure enough, one of the officers was taller than me and under cross examination by me, had a hard time explaining the difficulties with the line of sight and how he crunched to see what he said he saw. He responded to the geographic impossibility of the line of sight with a statement that "I am telling you what I saw. It was plain as day." The second officer basically repeated the same story. "This is what I saw. It was plain to see, and we had to make the arrest." Both officers responded the same way when I asked how they looked together through the window as witnesses often do when they are caught in unexplainable circumstances. They gave prepared answers to fit the scenario. They each told the jury that their report "Should have said that we took turns looking through the window," effectively admitting that what was written was not accurate. Both ended up explaining that they moved back and forth while watching the show next door. As I was hearing their answers, I found myself looking at the jurors to catch their reactions. I saw mixed reactions on the part of several jurors.

I had presented all my exhibits and theory of the case to Aaron Bromberg before the trial in the hope of obtaining his agreement for a dismissal of the charges. Such agreement was not forthcoming. The officers' testimony showed that they had been well prepared to deal with my questions and the exhibits. It had become a contest for the minds of the jury. Nevertheless, I liked what I was seeing from most of the jurors. I dared to hope that there could be an acquittal.

Aaron had been very good in his presentation of the case and the officers were obviously good men who were experienced, fair and honest. They were exactly the kind of men that we wanted to have on our police forces. It was clear that the jury was having a hard time swallowing what I was showing them as the evidence unfolded. Neither one of the officers was able to contradict the line of sight shown by my photos and exhibits. They each ended up maintaining that they had seen what they were testifying about regardless of the physical difficulties shown by the geometry of the line sight that the circumstances created. The split in the case was becoming obvious. The jury would have to weigh the physical and geographic facts and data versus of the integrity of the two policemen. Aaron had obviously checked and double checked what our exhibits had shown and found that his case had to rest on the honesty and integrity of the officers. I could feel the uncertainty of the jurors as the trial unfolded. Aaron and I had had several discussions about the defense I had raised before the trial. Aaron was sticking to his guns and would not drop his insistence on a plea to a felony charge. The two of us were unable to reach an agreement since losing his law license was unacceptable to my client.

I began Leonard's defense with the testimony of our investigator. I presented through his testimony his investigation, photos and measurements all of the physical facts and photos of the tool shed, window, rest room and urinals. They included his markings of distance included everything that could be seen and measured inside the restroom and from the windows. Some of these exhibits had already been introduced and fought over during the testimony of the police officers. Much of the evidence was now admitted over the objections of the DA, who argued that, in particular, the photos taken from the window were staged and not reliable. I countered that the photos were actually taken at different and various angles to allow for the possible different lines of sight of the two officers at the time of the alleged crimes. In the end, the Judge ruled in our favor and all the photos were admitted for viewing by the jury. This was a major victory for our side. They included photos of Leonard in the rest room and at the urinal as viewed from the window above with a camera which showed that Leonard could not be viewed below his torso. When the photo exhibits were presented to the jury and passed from one juror to the next, they each took long hard looks at the photos back and forth. As I watched them, I could feel our defense working as they pondered the different photo views that were being passed between them in the jury box. The photos clearly demonstrated that any man standing at the urinals could not be seen below the waist from the vantage point of the window. The Judge, counsel and Leonard waited and watched as the members of the jury each looked closely at the photos.

My decision to have Leonard testify was not that difficult. First of all, the photos exhibits told the entire story. Having Leonard testify could only jeopardize his defense unnecessarily. I also believed that his manner of speech and presentation would have placed him in additional jeopardy. He readily agreed not to testify on his own behalf since he personally did not want to testify or be cross examined. As a fellow attorney, he understood and welcomed his right to remain silent, particularly since we had a complete defense that was being presented to the jury. We went ahead with our decision arrived at before the trial that he would not testify. We also had several character witnesses available, but used only the best two of them, a partner in his law firm and his pastor. The lines were drawn and each side made their arguments to the jury. Aaron stressed the experience and know-how of the two officers who were not likely to lie to the jury. The DA admitted that some of the defense exhibits had merit in a class room, but that "the issue before you is whether Leonard was indeed the culprit who had committed the crimes seen by the officers."

When I spoke to the jury, I reminded them that, our investigator had been on the police force for twenty-four years and had risen to the rank of a detective with far more experience than either of the two officers involved. "This is a poorly prepared case for the prosecution where the physical facts did not fit the crime scene explanations. The prosecution must prove its case beyond a reasonable doubt. Not only have they failed to do so, but they have been unable to show that their version fits what was physically possible to see. It is not up to us to prove their case. We have pointed out to you all of the unexplained and unaccounted for facts that stand in the way of proof beyond a reasonable doubt. I ask that you take all of these serious issues into consideration in determining if there exists a reasonable doubt as to the guilt of my client. I submit that once you have done so, the evidence does not support a finding of guilty. Ladies and gentlemen, in accordance with the legal instruction you have received from the court that spells out what the law considers to be a reasonable doubt, I ask that you return a verdict of Not Guilty."

The case went to the jury on a Friday morning and they failed to reach a verdict. The judge ordered the jury to return on Saturday, which was a first for me, and only happened occasionally in my years of practice. We assembled on Saturday morning and waited for the verdict. When the jury finally reached a verdict in the early afternoon after a day and one half of deliberation and were taking their seats, one of the ladies in front smiled at me. She was a school teacher recently retired. This gave me hope. We then waited through the formalities of the jury foreman giving the signed verdict form to the judge's clerk who in turn brought it to the judge seated on the bench, where the judge slowly opened the verdict and read it to himself. Leonard and I stood up in front of our seats and the Judge proceeded to read the jury verdict out loud. The verdict was "Not Guilty"! I shook hands and hugged Leonard. I also shook hands with Aaron who had approached me at our defense table. Not all prosecutors are able to show similar respect for a jury's decision. However, Aaron was such a lawyer and continued in the same manner when he was elevated to the bench where he served as a wonderful judge for the rest of his legal career during which I very much enjoyed appearing in cases.

Many of the jurors left right away since it was a Saturday, but among those who remained to speak were the two ladies and a man who had smiled earlier in the case. Clearly there had been a serious division in the jury room, but with the passage of time in the manner that only jurors use to reach decisions, they had come to agreement that there was indeed a reasonable doubt that had not been overcome. This was great to hear since that was what I had concentrated on in my closing argument to the jury. However, the last thing I heard was amazing.

The retired school teacher had been waiting to speak to me after I had spoken to other jurors and as we began to speak, she smiled and said to me, "Please tell your client to never do it again." Wow! As we talked further, the teacher told me that this had been the sentiment of the majority of the jury members including the man I had noticed. Yet, over the hours of the decision-making process, which totaled about sixteen hours, one by one, the jurors came around to the defense point of view. They kept reviewing the legal instructions given to them by the Judge that the case had to be proven beyond a reasonable doubt. In the end, they all agreed that the case had not been so proven in view of their split about the verdict. I was learning specifically the greatness of our jury system. Jurors feel bound to follow the law despite where their natural leanings would take them. What she told me was powerful. It constitutes the very basis of how well our system of justice actually works. I have found this to be true over and over again in my years of practice in front of juries.

I learned from this case what I have found to be true in so many cases that followed. Investigation and double checking the facts and the scene of the crime is a prerequisite to success. I also learned that no matter how good the opposing lawyer is, and Aaron Bromberg was one of the very best I ever faced, everyone can be beaten. Juries are persuaded by the facts and witnesses involved regardless of how good the lawyers may be. This was brought home to me in numerous verdicts when jurors told me frankly that they really liked the job I had done, but they had to vote against my client. Pure and simple, the facts, evidence, the client, witnesses and exhibits involved are the ultimate decider. What really matters is how well your case plays in court, including the client whenever possible. Learning the best way to present your case is something that with time and understanding of your own strengths and weaknesses, you can improve. In order to receive the verdict, you seek, it is your job to use all the evidence and persuasive abilities you have in the best manner possible. This is always uncertain until the case fully unfolds in front of the jury with the different personalities, strengths and weaknesses of each witness and, of course, your client. You are the director of your case and the face and voice of your client. You become the wild card in any trial. This is what we must learn to do in dealing with the ever-changing facts and evidence of each case. More importantly, each of us lawyers must learn how best to present our cases and ourselves before the jury.

I do not remember smiling very much in Leonard's case. I was too involved in making sure we had covered all the exhibits and other evidence that was necessary to rebut the testimony and evidence presented by the other side. was up against a lawyer who knew how to get the most out of even a struggling prosecution case. However, I was both earnest and a true believer in our defense. It is always helpful to show the jury that you believe in your client and the case. This was a truth that could not be hidden and I exploited it to the fullest extent possible as only a young and determined lawyer can. The jurors cannot help but to feel your commitment as the case proceeds, if it is real. Time and experience does teach the lawyer if he is getting his case across to the jury. There are numerous tell signs that occur as the trial progresses often without the jurors themselves being aware. You must expect this and watch for them as you attempt to cover all of the weaknesses and loopholes that exist on your side. It is a never-ending process. However, it does not take away the agony of uncertainty in your mind while you are waiting for the jury to reach a final decision.

As You watch the jury members returning to their seats, your mind is always racing through the most graphic and important happenings during the trial. You are asking yourself, "Did I get the points I wanted across to the jury? Did they believe your client or the chief witness or witnesses for the prosecution? What did you forget to raise in your final argument?" Then, as you are about to hear the jury foreman or the judge read the verdict, all disturbing thoughts leave your mind and you look at the jurors as they move towards their respective seats in the jury box. Some talk to one another and you can see that relationships have developed among them. The strange and curious process of a jury determination has been accomplished and you are about to learn their verdict. This is justice alive and well in our American courts.

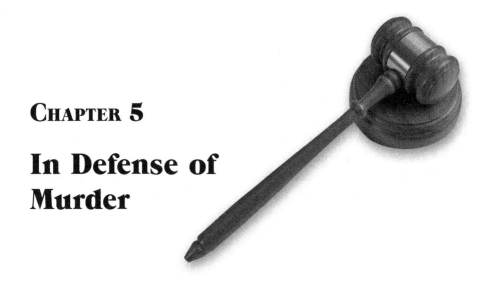

CHAPTER 5

In Defense of Murder

I n my second year of practice, my first murder case walked into the office. Once again, my boss did not want the case and I ended up with two men in my office asking for help in a grossly unpleasant situation. The two of them had picked up a woman in a bar who was just as drunk as they were. Between the three of them, they decided together to leave the bar and find a place to park and have fun. They found such a place immediately south and east of where the bar was located. The scene of the crime was alongside a county road where there was an open field. The three of them proceeded to enjoy what men and woman do. After the fun was over, the woman began to barf and collapsed onto the ground and passed out. The two guys were not in much better shape than she was, turned to each other, and decided that it was time to leave. They did leave and left the woman lying curled up on the ground. Time went by and the woman was found dead in the field. Some good police work by the Sheriff's department located the two men through their regular attendance at the bar where the woman had been picked up by my clients. My two clients were identified, found and arrested. They were charged with murder and had just been bailed out with the help of family and friends when they visited my office. At that time, bail could be obtained in certain murder cases. The charges against each of them were Murder in the Second Degree.

The men had been interrogated by the Sherriff's office and admitted to the basic facts as they had occurred. Both of them were construction workers and hard drinkers who enjoyed their beers at the local bar before heading home to their wives. They were regular guys without criminal records except for traffic offenses. They each insisted that neither one of them had struck the woman or forced her in any way. They were supported in this because the woman did not show any scars or bruises on her body. They had no adequate responses as to why they left her where they did, except that they were drunk and not thinking clearly. We were scheduled to attend the arraignment the following week.

As the case progressed through the initial court appearances, we were set for a preliminary hearing. This was the mandatory hearing which required the Judge to determine if there was probable cause to proceed with the case to trial. I had done my homework reviewing the police report and witness statements, including lengthy interviews with my clients. I went to the scene of the incident alongside the county road, went back over the statements made by my clients, visited the bar where they had met the unlucky woman and learned the recollections of the regulars who saw them meet the woman in question before the three of them left the bar. All of this always is a must if you are the defense lawyer in a case. A full investigation is a prerequisite. I cannot tell you how often a careful review of the scene of a crime or other important locations pays off. The actual lay out of the scene of the crime often brings unexpected results as the cases proceed. There can be bonuses when witnesses are found whose recollections can be the difference in the final results that are achieved in the cases.

It all starts with the fact that many prosecutors do not have the time to visit the scenes of all the crimes in cases for which they are responsible. They must rely on what they are told by the investigating officers or detectives. However, the officers are also busy and, depending on their different abilities and experience, do not always pick up all the facts and information that is available at the scene of the crime. Later on, when the cases go to trial, police officers sometimes do not double check their notes and records or revisit the scenes of the crimes before their testimony. This gives the defense counsel an edge where it can really matter during the preliminary hearing or, later, the trial. Often, when I was the defense counsel in a case and cross examining the police witnesses, I would be the one who had the last look at the scene of the crime. A recent memory always trumps the older and receding memories of the police officers or detectives who had originally viewed the crime scene. The time and caseloads of the police witnesses works against them when they appear in court weighted down by the volume of other cases to be attended to before the court appearance. It is an advantage that must be made use of in each case, if at all possible.

As a result of my homework, I could see that my clients had essentially told the truth. Their final decision to leave the woman where she lay was certainly questionable, but was it a crime? Was there any intent or was it simply two men, drunk and stupid, doing what drunk and stupid people do? The more I thought about the case, the more I believed that there was not a provable intent to commit a crime, let alone murder in the second degree. Since the preliminary hearing was fast approaching, I decided to visit the DA's office one block away from the courthouse and see if I could speak to the DA himself since he had appeared as counsel in the initial court hearing. I chose to visit the DA's office on a day in which I was appearing in another case two or three days before the preliminary hearing.

The DA was a person I had met before. He had actually offered me a job to work in his law office on civil matters which was permitted for DA's to do at that time. I liked Matt Martin from the first time I met him in the interview for the job in his office. Sadly, the morning after he had offered me a job and I had accepted and celebrated with my wife that evening, he called me at home and told me that he had second thoughts about another DA being hired for his staff and decided to rescind the offer. This was a real hard blow to a brand-new lawyer seeking his first job. However, I got over it and I had seen and met with Matt a number of times since, either in court or his offices as my caseload took me to court in his county. We developed a joking relationship about the rescinded offer as I would tell him jokingly, "You beat me to the punch. I was going to tell you that I decided not to take the job after learning about your "reputation." He would reply that, "Now that I know you, you would not have lasted more than a few days!" We would laugh and get along fine. I really liked and respected Matt and would have loved to have worked for him.

Matt was available that day and I met with him in his office. As I began to speak with him about the case and present my concerns and arguments for dismissal, he stopped me and said that he had also been giving the case a lot of thought since he personally reviewed and handled all of the murder cases in the office. He then proceeded to raise with me each and every concern that I had been thinking about. His review of the police report and statements led him to the same conclusion that I had reached. My clients were drunk and stupid and it boiled down to whether there was intent to commit a crime by leaving. His staff was divided on that issue and there had been discussion about lowering the charges to manslaughter or less, and or simply dismissing the case. We talked some more and as I was about to leave and wait to hear from him about what he had finally decided, Matt said to me, "You know,

I have made my decision. I am going to dismiss the case. If I am in doubt about intent in a Murder or Manslaughter, then there is no need to pursue this case at any lower level. I think a jury at any level will have the same trouble convicting these two jerks same as we do as we speak. When you come to court for the preliminary hearing, I will dismiss the charges." This was wonderful news and I left Matt's office and found a phone nearby to call my clients with the good news.

Matt did as he said and my clients left the courtroom a couple of days later considering themselves the luckiest guys in the world. On my part, I received a lesson that I followed ever since the meeting with Marty Martin. If the questions raised by the case are serious enough for a dismissal or a lowering of charges, and you cannot convince the deputy DA you are working with, it is very worthwhile to meet with the DA himself or the next level of deputy in the given DA's office. It has worked for me on almost every occasion that I have done so. However, as the size of the District Attorney offices grew in Denver and the surrounding counties, I found this was something I did judiciously since maintaining my reputation mattered in the continuing relationship one develops with the front-line deputy DAs that you deal with on a daily basis. As the years went by, however, I learned that many of the deputies' I faced welcomed a review of their thinking from above or at the Chief Deputy level. Substantive issues can and will be discussed by the more experienced DAs. In fact, this makes for camaraderie between DAs, deputy DAs and defense counsel that helps the justice system work.

Having personally and successfully handled a murder case was a confidence builder. The fact that the case turned around easier than many other lesser felony cases I had handled was a complete surprise. The truth was that one never knows what kind of problems a case will bring or what it will take to have it resolved. This was what made things so interesting and often, fascinating, in the practice of law. Each case creates its own agenda and timeline, often interrupted with new and surprising developments. This would strike easier cases just as often as the more difficult ones. The lawyer must react accordingly, be thankful when things are easier and accept the problems and difficulties when they arise in the other cases. No one ever promised it to be a rose garden over and over again. On the contrary, the trouble that clients find themselves in generally translates into trouble for their counsel. There is no escape from the changing scene and pitfalls in case after case.

I returned to my other cases with more zest and eagerness to see what problems they brought. Often, I would face problems in areas of law with which I was unfamiliar. I developed a routine which worked well for me that became a part of my practice ever since. Since we did not have computers at this time, all research had to be done either in a fellow lawyer's library's in the same building or beyond in other lawyers' offices, the law library of the Supreme Court or the court libraries in each of the courthouses where I practiced. What I would do was to start from scratch in each case by reviewing the law and applicable cases that outlined the specific issues and problems of the new case I had taken. This information could be found in our general reference books such as Corpus Juris, American Jurisprudence and many others. Once, I familiarized myself with the general principles and applicable statutes even when I had a memory of the issues from law school study, I would then be ready to tackle the facts of the specific case and to speak intelligently with the client, draft the Answer and Counterclaim in civil cases or begin to develop a plan on how to defend against the criminal allegations against my client. This would often be done the day or week before court appearances or prior to a civil case deadline for an Answer or other required filing.

When I was in court waiting for my cases to be called, I would meet with and watch the other lawyers and deputies involved in their cases and hear their presentations and arguments in court. I discovered something totally unexpected. Many lawyers were unprepared and this would often make a difference, if not in the outcome of the case, then in the particular ruling or decision to be made by the court. I soon recognized that by being prepared, this would make an impression on the judges involved that would stay with them from case to case as I grew and developed as a lawyer. Your reputation with judges mattered and was something to be taken seriously. Judges were more likely to accept what a prepared lawyer would say over the sloppy or ill-informed counsel. As time passed, I also learned from the judges themselves that they would talk to each other about the lawyers appearing before them. You are always on stage as you practiced your profession. Everything counted

My studying increased as I learned the benefits to be derived for my clients and their cases. On the down side, my evenings and weekends of work increased as I fully accepted the work and time requirements of the job that had to be spent to be successful. Then too, the results on behalf of clients were consistently paying off. I felt as if I was on a roll. Clients were pleased and I was beginning to get business coming to me and not just from my boss. Other lawyers began referring cases to me and so were the clients whom I had successfully represented. Winning counted. Being prepared counted.

Knowing and being known by the DAs and judges counted. The manner in which I treated clients counted, even if we ended up taking plea bargains. Reaction of my fellow lawyers counted. Just as I watched others, they were watching me and I began to receive referrals from them. This knowledge gave me confidence and good reason to keep doing what I had been doing.

It appeared as if in no time at all, I had become fully engaged in the profession I wanted to practice. I was doing well with my clients and had developed a good relationship with the Judges in different counties where I was appearing. Most important, and surprisingly, clients were asking me when I would start my own practice. Such thoughts were really not in my mind as I was experiencing all the things one had to learn about appearing in court; winning and losing in front of juries and judges and dealing with the unending differences between clients and how they dealt with the pressures and ups and downs of the cases they were living. You find yourself always having to care for and look out for your clients' needs as they were going down the winding road to an outcome that could take months or even a year. In many ways, this helped mask the anxieties I felt as I traveled the same winding road together with my clients. During the days, there was never time to sit back and think about the problems that were appearing as your cases progressed. That would only start at the end of my days heading home from court or during the sleepless nights and weekends when I would try to unwind without from the days' work. The practice of law was burning itself into my life and soul. I was captivated by it and was ready for anything that may come my way.

A month before it happened, I would not have predicted that I would leave the lawyer who had hired me and had given me the opportunity to spread my wings as a lawyer. I was having some thoughts about starting my own practice, but my thoughts had not yet coalesced into a plan. Then, a couple of weeks into December, my boss called me into his office and offered me a partnership in his law practice that included a good raise and fifteen percent of any profits. This was totally unexpected and I told him that I needed time to consider the offer. I liked him but did not trust him. I was wary of how he treated clients. His focus was primarily on his own personal businesses, of which there were many, and the more lucrative cases that came into the office. I thought it over during the weekend decided on staying for a few months so I could clean up the various cases I was responsible for and then begin looking for a place to open my own practice. When I informed my boss of my decision and suggested a time period before I left his office, he responded by telling me, "You are done in this office as of the end of the year. Good luck to you. That is how I became a sole practitioner in January 1968.

I found offices on the 12ᵗʰ floor in a twenty-three-story office building in downtown Denver. It was one of the largest buildings at that time. I was scared and did not know what to expect. It was an adventure. There was no certainty about who may follow me or where I would meet or develop new clients or business. That is a story that I ended up recounting to Cornell law students a few years later when I was invited by the Dean of our law school to speak to them about the vicissitudes of practice and how one goes about developing a law practice and clients. After the first talk I gave in the early 1970s, I was invited back to Cornell Law School for the next twenty years. My talks were increased to speak in seminars, small groups of students and a general lecture about the problems lawyers face in court with clients, judges and juries. The other topics that I began to speak about were the ever present moral and ethical issues raised during the cases and, sometimes, opposing counsel. These were issues that happened to be the chief interest of the Dean of Cornell law school and later professor emeritus who had invited me to speak at the law school. Doing this caused me to developed a third eye view of what was taking place around me as I was practicing law. While I would be working my way through the many different types of cases, I became ever mindful of what I would be telling the Cornell students the next time I appeared in Ithaca, New York to lecture at the law school. After giving talks for a few years, my interest and knowledge of the ethics of practice grew and I began representing lawyers facing grievances and ethical violations. My knowledge and experience grew further as I found myself regularly appearing on behalf of my fellow attorneys before the Grievance Committee and prosecutors appointed by our Supreme Court before three-person trial panels that included a Judge selected by the Colorado Supreme Court and, lawyers or citizens who volunteered their services. Representing lawyers facing ethical charges became an integral part of my law practice for the rest of my years in practice

Fortunately, as I was going through the steps of locating an office in Denver that I could afford, I learned that an Assistant City Attorney job was available in a neighboring city to handle the docket of criminal cases together with another attorney. I jumped at this chance and arranged to meet the City Attorney whom I had previously met and worked with on a few matters. I was hired and, beginning in January 1968, became a prosecutor. I worked part-time each week and was responsible for the City court docket every other day together with another lawyer hired to do the same part time job for the other half of court cases. He and I soon became friends as we handled and took responsibility for all of the cases on the court docket. There were times when one of our cases would carry over from one day to the next and we would both appear in court at the same time since we were each responsible for the docket of that day or the case we had handled the day before. It was up to the two of us to make sure that the City Court interests were taken care of to the best of our abilities and as we saw fit. We had both received the same instructions from the city attorney, "You handle things. Stay out of my way. I have way too much to do. Talk to the other city attorney if there is a problem, and work things out with the Judges." I never needed to go to my boss, the city attorney, during my stay as prosecutor, except one time. I had been alerted by city detectives that they were about to arrest my boss's friend for illegal gambling and thought he should know. When I informed him, his response was, "Tell the detectives to do their jobs as they deem necessary." Consequently, his friend was arrested and my co- deputy city attorney ended up with the case on his docket and worked out a plea to the charges. As a result of my boss's attitude regarding the conduct of our jobs, I developed great respect for him.

For the following year, I tremendously enjoyed being prosecutor every other day, meeting with the people charged with traffic tickets, domestic violence, theft, assaults and a whole host of other city code violations. I learned to work out pleas and plea bargains and, in those cases that could not be worked out, they would be set for trial beginning late morning or in the afternoon, before the Judge or jury. Each day, whenever we would complete the docket, a jury would be empaneled and we tried the case or cases that we had been unable to work out with a plea. We might have two jury trials in an afternoon, but that did not happen often, but when it did, I would be waiting for a second jury verdict well into the evenings. Most days, we would finish and the Judge and counsel would leave court well before 5 PM. It was a great job and increased my abilities as a trial lawyer tremendously

I tried twenty-five jury trials and scores of trials to the court before the two trial judges who split the days on the bench same as we prosecutors did. Trying cases as a prosecutor allowed me to think and plan on how to meet the burden of proof in each case. Not only was I broadening my trial experience, I was also learning in depth what worked and did not work for me as I tried to persuade the judges and the juries. I was able to achieve a comfort zone in court that only trial after trial can bring.

The best part was that I was being paid and, at the same time, was handling the cases in my own practice, whether they were civil or criminal, all around the Denver area. If either I or my fellow prosecutor had a jury trial of more than one day in our separate practices, we covered for each other and the city always had a city attorney ready to handle the docket. I was certainly busy with my growing practice and met many people in the municipal court who eventually became my clients. It was a win-win situation which I highly recommend to any young lawyer who is starting out.

Trying all of the cases gave me the opportunity to watch and work opposite many different lawyers. Many were good and experienced. Others were younger like me and just beginning to grow into the lawyers they were to become. A few were not good at all and should have stayed out of the courtroom. I wondered if their clients understood how deficient their representation was. I figured that it does take time for the poor ones to work themselves out of appearing in court and developing their practices into more office type of practices. Each of us who practices law must learn and find the area of practice which best fits his or her particular talents. Law practice is full of opportunities other than in the courtroom and facing juries. I was learning from all of the lawyers I faced as each of them presented themselves in a different way to the juries. I must admit that I enjoyed watching opposing lawyers in action, even if their plan was to attack the prosecutor. I was discovering that there were a great many different ways to defend your client even though many were off base and sure to lose. Win or lose, the better lawyers all had one thing in common. They were prepared! However, one lawyer stood out and impressed me with his overall abilities.

The best lawyer I faced was a very experienced African American lawyer who had a deep and commanding voice. I had heard good things about him from several different lawyers when the topic of really good trial lawyers was being discussed. His name often came up as one of the best we had at that time. When we started the trial and began selecting the jury in an assault case, I was mesmerized by his command of the jury from his first questions. He did not waste time asking about the issues and what they thought about the law that was to be applied. Instead, he went right to the main point of his concerns. Would his black client receive justice from what was likely to turn out to be an all-white jury of 6 persons? Would the individual jurors keep their word when they swore to apply the law of the case to without discrimination to his client? He indicated that this was his main concern and "Can I count on your word to view the facts and evidence fairly?" He was in control of himself and what he wished to accomplish. The jurors were surprised at first but all responded affirmatively to the questions and to him personally. It was clear that they meant what they said and he did not spend much time questioning further. I recollect that we were given about a half hour to forty-five minus for the jury selection process because of the time limits under which we worked.

The presentation of evidence proceeded normally and I did the best I could with what we had to support the charges. The lawyer carefully put his client through the events and it became clear that the defense was that the victim was lying and the police accepted the victim's version of what had taken place. I could see the credibility issue being slowly developed and grow. This was the battle from the start. The lawyer was both clever and credible as he pursued it in his cross examinations of the police officer and victim. I could tell from looking at the jurors that he had captured their interest and had entered their heads. Within an hour, the jury returned a verdict of "Not Guilty." I had been beaten by a master. I congratulated him after the verdict and found myself wondering if I would ever be able to command the courtroom as well as he did. I now realized that I had seen an example of what it took to do that. You not only must know your case, but you must yourself be fully involved and credible as you present, object and argue the evidence in the case. It was a complete package that I had observed. This was something that would take time, patience and a gravitas that I could only hope to attain. He was great! I fully understood why he was considered one of the best. I admitted to myself that I had enjoyed the beating I had received. It turned out to be the only jury trial I lost during my tenure as a deputy City Attorney. I now had a picture of how I wanted to be in the courtroom as I developed my knowledge and abilities as a trial lawyer. I had been given a clear image of what to strive for. It was up to me to achieve it.

CHAPTER 6

The jury selection Puzzle

A s I became accustomed to my offices in downtown Denver, I developed relationships with several lawyers who were in the same building and who had similar practices to mine. Often one or two of them would be heading for court just two blocks away in the City and County Building or walking back to my building or some other one nearby. While walking and talking to the fellow lawyers, all of whom were more experienced than I was, this allowed me to learn from their anecdotes and stories about fellow lawyers and the judges before whom I was appearing. When we all gathered in the separate courtrooms for the docket calls, I would be sitting next to other lawyers I had never met as well as lawyers I did know. Slowly, I began to learn the names and faces of many more lawyers than before. Although my work had previously taken me to Denver many times, the cases I had been handling predominately took me to the outlying county courts where I had developed similar acquaintances with lawyers, not always learning if their offices were in Denver. This was a never-ending process that took place over a period of months and years. It was both fun and very informative to be walking, talking and sitting next to practicing lawyers. There was so much to learn and people to know. As time passed, we often had cases in common with co-defendants or opposite each other in divorce or civil cases. I was learning that the trial bar in Colorado was a small world.

One of the lawyers I met in the same office building where I worked was

Ron Ramirez. Ron was a former deputy DA. He was carrying a wealth of criminal cases and was very busy. We had an occasional lunch together and he shared with me his experiences as a prosecutor and now, as a defense lawyer. Ron had tried many murder cases. I was very impressed and eagerly took in the information he was freely providing about his former fellow prosecutors and the District Court Judges on the bench at that time. I was going to school in real life and loved it. One day, Ron was complaining about not having enough time to properly prepare for his next murder case that was coming up for trial. I jumped at that and offered to help him free of charge if I could second chair him in the trial and handle one or two of the witnesses on direct or cross-examination. I explained that the year before, I had represented the two men in the murder case and the dismissal that had been achieved. I told Ron that I wanted to participate in a murder trial and learn the ropes first hand. He agreed to let me help him in his case.

I began visiting Ron's office just a few floors above my floor to work on his files in the case and catch up on the facts and circumstances. I joined him speaking to witnesses and also attended a couple of meetings with his client, Arman Ortiz. The charge in the case was 1st Degree Murder. Arman was one of the tenants in the home of a woman who was the victim of the murder. His room was on the 2nd of three floors and directly above the owner's living quarters. It was well known that he and she did not get along and there had been several shouting matches between them as evidenced by the other tenants who were witnesses for the prosecution. On the day in question, no one had been home at the time of death, including our client according to what he was telling Ron and previously, the police. The owner had been stabbed to death with a knife. The problem was that when Arman arrived in the mid-afternoon at the apartment of a friend where a group of guys were playing cards, Arman had blood on his shirt which later tested to be his own on his left hand tightly wrapped. He told the card players that he had accidently cut his hand, and in his effort to stop the blood, had caused his blood to spill on the front of his shirt while he was wrapping his hand. The guys played cards for several hours. However, it turned out that the time of death of the landlady was about thirty minutes before Arman arrived at the card game. This was a damaging coincidence or not. He had no alibi for the actual time of death. He said that he had been walking around Denver and the neighborhood before joining the card game about twenty minutes from his apartment. The cut on his hand was quite evident and wrapped after he said he had used a knife to slice some chicken for his breakfast. He left his apartment before the time of death and had seen the landlady as he passed by the living room and they had acknowledged each other. The other tenants were not home. Other prominent facts were the continuing arguments that Arman had with the landlady that were witnessed and over heard by the other tenants. Two of the other tenants testified that they had heard Arman make verbal threats to physically harm the landlady if she did not leave him alone. Apparently, he was behind in the rent and she would not let up.

The trial lasted several days. Ron let me question a couple of the prospective jurors during the voir dire jury selection process and allowed me to handle the cross examination of one of the other tenants and one of the card players. Ron was good and very professional in the trial. He had been there many times before and it showed. He gave a solid final argument that proved to be insufficient to convince the jury after it had heard Arman's testimony. We had discussed the pros and cons of putting Arman on the stand between ourselves and with him. Arman wanted to testify and Ron agreed. When I raised the issue that Arman was not going to do well on the stand, which Ron acknowledged, Ron's position was that this was his client's right to decide whether he would testify. As expected, Arman did not make a good witness. This case brought out once again the vital importance in any trial of a client testifying or not. It is always dangerous since the members of the jury get to see, hear and feel the client in the courtroom for better or worse.

The jury members were very clear in telling us after the verdict that they simply did not believe Arman's testimony. They thought he had motive and the opportunity. The decisions to have the client testify or not are crucial and there is no turning back once your client takes the stand. I was grateful for the opportunity to participate in the trial and thanked Ron. I had learned that a murder trial was essentially just like other trials but with more at stake. Jurors' paid close attention since murder always draws attention. However, it was the last time I second chaired in a criminal defense case. I learned something I had not anticipated. It was not for me to second chair. I needed to be up front and before the judges and jurors myself. I could feel it in my blood as Ron did the actual work in the courtroom and I watched and listened. This is something that we must each learn about ourselves as we enter trial work. I did end up sharing representation of some civil plaintiffs and defendants with other lawyers on two or three occasions where it worked out pretty well. However, there can only be one captain of the ship for the sake of the criminal defendant in court. The connection with the jury for the defense lawyer is personal and should not be tampered with. Of course, the OJ Simpson case is a huge example to the contrary. However, that case stands by itself as a departure from all norms and strategies in criminal defense. The defense lawyers won the case, but they sure did have trouble getting along and a circus surrounded them throughout the trial. They also failed to gain the respect or admiration from their peers as we watched the show that was displayed on TV across America instead of a trial for justice.

I took over a rape case from another lawyer who had recommended to the client to waive the jury. I found myself facing trial before a judge which worried me throughout the trial. As with most judges, I was unable to sense whether I was winning or losing since the Judge would not give off any signals like juries are prone to do. Being accustomed to court and trial, the judges rarely give off what they may or not are thinking as jurors often do. This particular judge knew very well how to mask his thinking and maintained an unreadable continence. I hated that since I was not receiving the feedback that jurors unintentionally would be giving off as the trial proceeds. I vowed never to waive a jury in any felony case and pretty much kept my vow for the rest of my career, except one time in a case a few years later. It was a case in which I became convinced that the prosecution would not be able to prove its case during several court appearances before the trial date of the case. Also, the Judge had been expressing similar concerns about the lack of evidence by the prosecution during those court appearances before the trial date. Since the court was echoing my feelings, I decided to waive the jury. In part, this was also because my client was very worried about the fees and costs and the fact that a trial to a judge would take less time and money. He was urging me to waive the jury since he had also heard the Judge's stated concerns about the evidence. The result was that I agreed to waive the jury due to the wishes of my client, but not without real fear and trembling.

Once we were in trial, this particular judge took on another visage and kept his thinking to himself and his face unreadable as the trial unfolded. I kept telling myself as we progressed through the case evidence and witnesses that I had been so stupid to have gone along with my client's wishes. As a result, both my client and I proceeded to suffer throughout the presentation of evidence as the case went forward to its's conclusion. At the end, I held my breath and was praying when the Judge announced his verdict in favor of my client "Not Guilty." My prayers were answered but I never did try a felony case to the court again. You do live and learn about what works for you in the courtroom. I discovered that I did not trust a single person, whether he was an individual or a judge to decide guilt or innocence. I had already developed a great amount of trust and confidence in juries and their results. This distrust never left me for the rest of my career. Trying a case before a judge was always a nail bitter. It was something we all did, particularly in misdemeanor cases where clients had often waived a jury before hiring counsel or the costs became a major factor in the decision to have a jury or not.

The result of a trial to the court was that once we had concluded all of the testimony, evidence and arguments in the case and the judge was left with making his decision, he or she would often take time for deliberations same as a jury. We would be instructed counsel that the court would let us know when he or she had decided on the verdict. This would leave things up in the air, sometimes for almost a week, similar to waiting days for a jury verdict. Once we were called back to the courtroom for the decision, after the days of uncertainty and concern, the judge would announce that he or she found that the prosecution had failed to prove their case beyond a reasonable doubt and acquitted my client or the opposite, that the case had been proven which would lead to sentencing. It was an especially painful and highly uncertain wait for client and counsel.

The next serious case that year I taught me still more about the trial process and remained in my memory as an unforgettable trial. My client was a juvenile sixteen-year-old Mexican-American who had accidentally shot his twin brother. When I met him and his parents in my office, I was deeply affected by them and the terrible tragedy and loss they had suffered. Young Ramon Chavez had gone upstairs to retrieve a pistol that he and his twin brother, Jose, liked to use shooting at squirrels and small game in a field near their home. When he went upstairs, his brother had said to him, "Pick up the gun so that we can go shooting when you come back down the stairs." Ramon picked up the weapon and twirled it as he came down the stairs. He then pointed the gun at his brother and pulled the trigger. He thought that the gun was not loaded and that they would collect the bullets in the basement before leaving the house. It was loaded. When Ramon thoughtlessly pulled the trigger, he ended up shooting his brother in his face. Just before it happened, he had been joking about what a bad shot he was. It all ended in a sudden and terrible tragedy. Jose was dead.

I could feel the depth of despair and suffering of the parents and their remaining son as they relayed the sad event to me in my office. As a juvenile, Ramon faced a sentence of incarceration in the juvenile system until he was 27 years old or whatever time the Judge may impose at sentencing after conviction. The boy was charged with Manslaughter. This was heavy price to pay on top of the loss of his brother. I accepted the case and believed that it could be won. He had been foolish and negligent in not knowing the gun was loaded. I did not believe that there was sufficient intent for Ramon to be found guilty.

The prosecuting attorney was a young lawyer like me, highly motivated and fully believing in his case. As our separate careers unfolded, we remained in contact and became friends. However, at the time of the case, I was exasperated in dealing with him because he was unmoved by the depth of the tragedy that had unfolded. My client was already locked up in guilt and the terrible memory of his momentary lapse of reason as he playfully pulled the trigger. I was unable to convince the young DA to take a lesser plea to a misdemeanor instead of the felony due to the personal loss suffered by him and his family. He would not agree. We went to trial.

The trial unfolded before the Chief Judge of the Juvenile court who was a warm and considerate woman who was clearly distressed over the sad facts as they unfolded, same as were the prospective jurors. During the jury selection process, I learned that one of the jurors was a sergeant in the police department who had never been assigned to the Juvenile division. She was impressive and appeared open to being persuaded by the facts. When both sides began eliminating the prospective jurors and it came time for my last decision to eliminate a juror, the police sergeant was still on the jury panel. I had to decide, knowing that she was a cop, whether to let her stay or not on the jury. I decided to keep her on the jury after being impressed with how she handled herself and trusted that she would be a fair and impartial juror. This was a serious mistake in jury selection.

Attorneys each have the power to decide who they wish to eliminate from the jury panel for cause or at will Our decisions about who stays can be crucial to the final verdict as I was about to learn. The trial went as expected and I felt that we had clearly established that there was no statutory criminal intent on the part of my client who had broken down and cried before the jury as did his mother who was still mourning the loss of Jose. Despite the deep emotion felt by all of us in court, the verdict of the jury was "Guilty" of Manslaughter. I was deeply upset with the verdict and also with what I learned from a few of the jurors after we had received the verdict. I learned from some of the more sympathetic jurors that soon after the police sergeant became foreman of the jury, she lobbied strongly for the conviction of my client. One by one, she disposed of the arguments by jurors who were sympathetic and understanding of the depth of Roman's sorrow over his act and the lack of any intent, negligent or otherwise, to cause harm to his brother. Several jurors had considered an acquittal or the lesser misdemeanor charge regarding the weapon itself. The police sergeant was the juror who made the difference.

I had failed to take into account that the Sargent would likely become the jury foreperson and have considerable influence since she had a complete understanding of the criminal justice system. Indeed, she had put to good use her knowledge and experience in the jury room with her successful lobbying for the guilty verdict. I did not listen to my own internal concern and trepidation about the lady juror being a cop. I also did not take into account that she may become the foreman and a possible leader of the jury. These were each mistake that compounded into the final result. The sergeant had been very responsive answering my questions and this caused me to temporarily put aside any trepidation. This cost Ramon the time he did spend incarcerated, which was, as it turned out, about one year and one half. He served his time well and with the grace of an excellent young man who was deeply upset with what had happened.

Two of the most important concerns for a trial lawyer are his natural instincts about what he hears, feels and sees from prospective jurors and the facts he learns about their separate backgrounds. My instinct told me that I had to be concerned. Instead, I allowed the Sergeant to talk me into setting aside the fact of her being a cop and prosecution oriented. Worse still, as an experienced cop, I failed to consider that she was likely to become the foreperson. Never again, on either count, did I hesitate to eliminate such a juror. It is better to go with the obvious facts whichever way they point. In that way, you never have to face the terrible anguish of a wrong choice of a juror. Years later, I actually did accept a couple of police officers on my juries in traffic cases. In doing so, I followed my instincts that were positive and the cases were misdemeanors with far less serious consequences. However, from that time forth, I would not test the principle of following the obvious in jury selection in a felony case.

Another factor that must be raised is that the trial lawyer must learn to listen to and feel the signals that are being given to him about prospective jurors from within. Our instincts of self- preservation work when we are charged with serious responsibilities such as the trial of a felony or even a misdemeanor. Our body tells us things by giving off alarms that we feel. These are unspoken signals that we all feel inside ourselves and must learn to recognize and honor. They consist of doubt, second guesses and simply feelings inside that you cannot miss. If you do, and when you do, your client is in trouble. I found myself initially not paying attention since I considered such trepidation to be just nervousness. It did not take many trials to understand that I must listen to what is ringing inside of me. When I did, the results proved that it was the right thing to do. I continued to follow the unmistakable inner signals until my last very last jury trial. Why give up a good thing?

On the civil side, everything I have stated above is valid and needs to be a part of the lawyer's thinking. However, a civil case, more often than not, involves money damages, injuries and a great variety of facts and legal considerations that are raised in the jury instructions that are not relevant in felony prosecutions. For example, a person's views about the payment of large amounts of damages or if the case is against a doctor or dentist which can cause so many other factors to be considered in jury selection. In many civil cases, you deal with far more professional expert witnesses, physicians and all kinds of experts and personnel in the fields in which the case occurs. This can also be true, but to a lesser extent in felony cases. It changes the profile of the persons you seek to hear the evidence as jurors in your cases. Since my experience in civil jury trials is far less then with criminal juries, I have limited myself to writing about what must be considered in selecting a jury in a criminal case. This is definitely a topic that can transcend both disciplines and most certainly involves understanding what you are looking for in your jurors for the case you are trying. However, the scope of civil actions and applicable law is beyond this undertaking. All I can say is that in each case I participate in, it took all of my senses, intuition, knowledge and expertise and, on occasion, what I will call, "instinct" to deciding on which certain or particular jurors I elected to keep for the trial. What I have ended up doing and thinking about the selection of jurors changed as my experience grew. Since one must inevitably face the outcome of your juror selections over and over again, you learn and experience what works for you. It took time and the agony of waiting for the verdicts of the juries selected to reach a level of wisdom and understanding about the process. Once I reached such a level, I found myself doing things during the jury selection process very differently from how I started.

Selection of a jury is a personal endeavor. It requires one to be in touch with his or her personal reactions to jurors and what you see, hear and, above all, feel. It is a process that takes time, trial and error that only experience can provide.

There is another factor involved which very much affects a lawyer's ability to select a jury that either a prosecutor or defense counsel may want. The time allowed for jury selection has become very limited due to the crowding of courts with cases, except in the most publicized and notorious cases. This very much limits a lawyer's ability to gather within himself what he thinks or feels about any given juror. A certain amount of time is always necessary and important in making the decision for or against a particular juror, including the opposing counsels' questioning and the responses given by the jurors. These can be just as important as your own. Everything counts in making your decisions. Without sufficient time, it is no better than a lottery. You are left with only your impression, face to face view and gut feelings about the prospective jurors. And then, of course, what must be factored in is the ability of the opposing counsel to pick a better selection of jurors for his or her view of the case. This becomes the ultimate question. In each case, it is a mountain that must be climbed to achieve jurors in your cases that give you a sense of confidence that they will listen well and provide a fair verdict. I can tell you flat out that trying cases with jurors you are comfortable with is far better than days of discomfort as the case evidence and testimony unfolds in front of jurors that did not make you comfortable. This brings us back to the major importance of who is selected to be on your juries. Learning the basics of jury selection and making the good decisions about whom to retain or to eliminate is something that grows inside the trial attorney as he gains experience and jury verdicts. It is really a question of understanding yourself and your immediate sense and reaction to the persons sitting in the jury box. You never lose the fear of making wrong decisions, but your confidence grows in proportion to having made the right decisions over and over again which are frequently reinforced during the trials with the reaction of jurors as the case proceeds. It is a world within a world that one experiences in each case. After all, we all believe in and cherish our jury system in America. This makes it imperative that if you are going to try cases to juries that you become comfortable with the process and the vitally important part you play when you select the people who will decide your cases. Cowards need not apply. You must reach inside, identify what you feel, decide and live with the consequences. There is no other way.

CHAPTER 7

Uncharted Waters

As my practice grew and I tried more and more cases, I landed my own first-degree Murder case that led to a trial. My client's name was Danny Lopez. His parents had heard about me from another family and made an appointment to see me at my office. Their son was sitting in the Adams County jail charged with first degree murder. Between themselves, they decided that Danny needed counsel more than being bailed out. They elected to use what money they had to pay for my fees. This was in 1969. I liked the parents and, when I visited my client in the jail, I liked Danny.

Danny was a quiet young man. He was short of stature and immediately began asking me about his parents, brothers and sister. Although he was sitting in the Adams county jail charged with murder, he wanted to know if they were ok. When I assured him that they were all well and worried about him, he was relieved and began to answer my questions. He told me that on the day in question, "After work, I went to a bar on Vasquez Blvd in north Denver, not far from highway I-25, where I could join my friends who regularly met at the bar following a day's work." He went on to tell me that, "I ordered a beer, joined the crowd and began to relax, talk and catch up on what was happening." Apparently, he was visiting in particular with two friends who were standing alongside the bar at the time he arrived. Between them, they knew many people at the bar and each of them ended up talking with different friends and persons. It was loud and boisterous. All was normal until a cab driver known to many of the people present came into the bar and ordered a beer.

In relaying what happened, Danny told me that, "My friend, Tony, yelled out loud at him, "You are a liar and a cheat." Other persons at the bar joined Tony and began calling the cab driver similar names and were swearing at the man. Danny said that," We all knew that he cheated in cards and everyone began to yell at him to return their money. It got ugly and a fight started with a person I did not know and others joined in. Tony was one of the men who started fighting. That is when the bartender shot a pistol into the air and told the customers who were fighting to go outside. I followed my friends and others out of the bar where the cab driver was trying to get into his cab. He didn't make it because he was grabbed by several men and, as he turned to fight back, he was hit and pushed to the ground." "Where were you at this point?" I asked. Danny answered "I was right behind Tony. Then I saw a man begin to kick the cabdriver in the head as he lay on the ground. It was bad and I stopped and did not become involved. The cab driver had stopped fighting and just lay there. It turned out that the man who was kicking the cab driver had steel tips on his shoes. I got hold of my friend and we both stepped away as a crowd gathered around the cab driver. Tony and I decided to go to our cars and so did our other friend. Everyone else went back into the bar or to their cars. When we left, we did not know how the fighting ended."

I learned from the police report and from the deputy DAs' assigned to the case that many people had identified Danny to be involved in the fighting and being right there when the final blows were being made at fallen cab driver's head and body. It appeared that Danny was well known and liked and many remembered him to be present. At the same time most people said that they did not see who did the final physical bad acts. However, those who claimed that they did see the actual punching and hits identified the kicker and his close friend and companions to be the persons hitting and finishing off the cab driver. The two men and Danny were the only persons charged with the murder. Everyone knew Danny and he was positively identified as being present by several witnesses.

Over the year that it took for the case to go to trial, I would regularly visit Danny in the Adams county jail. He was always polite and as responsive as he could be with me. His recollections never changed. He admitted that he would have struck the victim if he had been able to in support of his friends, but he never got close enough to do so. He did not see the actual assailant with the pointed shoes before the fighting started, and once that person plunged in to the fray, Danny simply stayed back in the crowd and watched. Among the people around the fight were at least three other persons who knew him and where he was positioned and standing. He told me, "I didn't do it. I could not have done it. Believe me, Mr. Mike. I would never have done such a thing." Danny called me "Mr. Mike" from the start and I believed what he was telling me. In fact, the more I thought about his case and began to investigate, meet with his friends, the bartender and some of the other persons identified by the police as being present at the time, I was sure of it. Danny Lopez was innocent. This made the case all the more serious since I knew and thoroughly believed that Danny was not one of the culprits. I had already learned that an innocent man is often the most difficult client to represent. This case provided further proof of that.

There were two DA's assigned to the case and I had cases with each of them separately before. The lead deputy was a big man, ex- football player and a loud mouth sort of guy. His name was Sam Lyons. He would mix humor and yelling at you without warning. He loved to make derogatory remarks about my defense of Danny and other clients I was representing at that time. I tried to give it back as I was receiving his abuse. However, this was not my style and after a while, I stopped trying. The second Deputy was polar opposite. He was quiet, intelligent and committed to the job. He believed thoroughly in the justice they were seeking.

Both of the DAs stayed on for years with the Adams County DA's office with the lead counsel, Sam Lyons, ultimately becoming the Chief Deputy DA and the second one, Richard Alvarado, became a Justice in our Colorado Court of Appeals. They were worthy opponents with the lead deputy conducting most of the trial and Richard Alvarado being the second chair deputy filling in with a few of the witnesses in direct and cross examinations. I asked Richard one day, "How can you stand second chairing in a case." He told me, "It is not a problem at all. There are many cases where I handle the case myself to conclusion." I guess I could understand that. We were not that busy when I was a prosecutor for the City of Aurora. After Danny Lopez's trial and even during the pendency of his case, I had numerous cases with either or both deputies in which we developed a friendship and understanding about each other that carried over for many years. When you are trying cases on opposing sides, you experience the trials and atmosphere of the battlefield together. It is a bond that develops between trial lawyers that is similar to sports and the military. It allows for camaraderie different and apart from just meeting and knowing your fellow lawyer. It also creates a willingness to hear out and listen to each side as it was advocated during the pre- trial hearings, casual meetings and conferences. This would often lead to cases being settled and plea bargains made and entered. The Lopez case was not to be resolved in that way. Both sides held to their guns and we went to trial, but not without a surprise offer of a plea bargain one week before the trial.

I prepared for this trial more than I had ever done before. I personally spoke with each prosecution witness that I was able to find at home or at work. In addition, I found one or two additional witnesses whom I was able to call as defense witnesses, not listed by the prosecution. Many of the witnesses were more than willing to cooperate, such as the bartender, who knew and liked Danny. He also gave me some leads on other people who were there and not included in the prosecution witness list. Everybody supported what Danny was telling me, even one of the prosecution witnesses listed in the complaint. However, I could see that although none of them were able to state they saw Danny hitting or striking the cab driver, each witness placed him right there where the final blows were being made.

Many witnesses remembered Danny as being together with his two friends, Tony and Armando, who did hit the victim inside the bar. They also placed the three of them close by outside in the parking lot. The cab driver was still striking back just before the man with the pointed shoes came up to him as he fell to the ground. Clearly the prosecution had Danny immediately at the scene and able to strike at the cab driver. However, they lacked an eye witness who actually saw him hit the victim. I honestly believed from my investigation that the case against him would not stand up in court. After two previous trial dates had to be continued, we finally received a trial date almost a year after the date of the killing. The other two alleged defendant participants were also waiting to be tried. However, it was the choice of the District Attorney's office to try our case first. The other two cases kept being set shorty after our case at the request of the DA's office, which requests were honored by the judge. I concluded that the two DA's knew that their case against Danny was not as strong as they were against the two actual assailants. However, by having the case against Danny go first gave them the opportunity to see and hear most of the same witnesses in a trial run. I accused both of them of this cold- blooded strategy which they adamantly and smilingly denied.

One week before the trial date, I received a phone call from Deputy Alvarado. He was authorized to make a plea bargain offer for the first time in the case. The offer was to have Danny plead guilty to manslaughter with a maximum of ten years in the penitentiary with an agreed upon reduction of the actual jail sentence to two years. The offer meant that Danny would be released from jail in just a few days because he had already served the time necessary to be released after one year in jail. Danny would be a free man. I just shook my head as I weighed what to advise my client. It was "Hobson's choice." Did he want freedom immediately after pleading "guilty" and having a criminal record or go to trial and obtain a "not guilty" jury verdict? I immediately visited Danny at the county jail to determine what we would do.

When I explained the plea bargain offer to Danny, he listened carefully as he always did and replied. "I will do whatever you advise me to do." "No. Danny," I replied. "It is your decision, not mine. You have served one year and can be free on Monday if you agree to the plea bargain offer. This is serious. I must have your decision." Danny thought for a minute and said. "My decision is to do whatever you tell me to do." There it was. He was not going to relieve me of making the final decision. I had to decide. All kinds of thoughts went through my mind, "What if one of the witnesses said more than he had already said and brought Danny into the killing? Did the prosecution have something up their sleeves I did not know? What will the judge do at the end of the prosecution case if no witness says that he saw Danny directly hit the cab driver? I already knew that they had at least three witnesses who will say that Danny was right there where the action was taking place. What if one of them was convinced by the DAs to say he saw Danny punch or hit the victim? If any one of the witnesses was also in trouble with the police, their testimony against Danny could be manipulated and changed. Everything was up in the air, changing frequently. Danny's friends were in and out of trouble. Will the Judge dismiss the charges at the end of the prosecution case? Will we end up having the jury make the final decision? What would they decide? The list of questions and concerns was endless. There was no way to avoid making a decision. I had to decide. Danny would just give it back to me to decide. Finally, I told Danny. "We will go to trial. I do not want you to plead guilty to something you did not do and have a criminal felony record." Danny said, "Ok Mr. Mike." We turned down the offer and went to trial.

My law partner at that time was involved in estate planning, contracts, and business law and development. He expressed his interest to sit through the trial with me in the second chair. I had no objection and he accompanied me to court each day as we picked a jury and the prosecution began presenting the case. Since my partner was not that familiar with the background of the case, I briefly described to him what each witness was going to say before he testified. There were no female witnesses. He later told our mutual friends that

I had been so prepared that I was able to predict most of what each witness for the prosecution had to say before I stood up to cross-examine. In truth, this is how any trial lawyer should be prepared.

For the most part, my cross examinations were limited to making sure what each of the prosecution witnesses were describing and placing Danny as far away from the actual fighting as I could elicit from the witnesses to admit. Not one of them was able to say that he saw Danny actually hit the cab driver either in the bar or outside by the cab. Each one said that he was close. However, one by one, the prosecution witnesses agreed with me that they did not see Danny hit, punch or even touch the victim. Most important, they each agreed that at no time before the mortal blows had been struck with the deadly steel tipped toes of the leading culprit's shoes was there evidence that Danny actually participated in the fight. In fact, as witness after witness testified, as expected, they all fell short of saying that Danny struck a blow. I felt good as the prosecution was finishing presenting their case. Then, I was shocked to hear the last witness for the prosecution says that, "I saw Danny kick at the victim while he was on the ground." When the Deputy asked if he saw Danny land a blow, his answer was that. "I could not see where the blow landed. There were three men immediately around the taxi driver." I looked at Danny and he looked back at me shaking his head. The worst fear had happened. This was testimony by the witness that we had never before or was stated in his interviews with the police or to me. Danny leaned over and said to me, "I never kicked at anybody. I was watching the guy as he was kicking the cab driver. That is all."

The deputy finished his direct examination. It was my turn to question the witness. His name was Sonny Archuleta. I began by obtaining Sonny's agreement that he had not previously told the police investigators that he saw my client try to kick the cab driver. "No, I did not say that when they first asked me." He agreed. "Then what caused you to change your testimony from that time to today? Was it the fact that you were recently arrested for sale and possession of drugs? He answered, "No that is not how it happened. I told the cops when it happened that Danny did not kick the victim, but I held back that Danny had tried to kick the victim. When they arrested me for the drug possession, I decided that it would be best for me to tell the whole truth when they started questioning me about Danny's case. I did not see Danny land a blow, but I did see him try to do so." I went on to ask, "Have you made a deal with the police about this testimony? "No. They told me to tell the truth and that is what I am doing." I continued, "So the truth is that you did not see Danny kick or hit the victim. Is that correct? "Yes, I did not actually see Danny kick the victim." I looked at the jury. Several members were leaning forward in their chairs. I had learned in many cases that jurors are often unable to hide their concerns or reactions to testimony by the way they moved their bodies back or forward or with their facial expressions. A couple looked at me as I looked at them. It looked as if the message was getting through to them. I decided that I had done all I could do and sat down. I was hoping that the defense had come across to the jury. No blow had landed if ever Danny had actually tried to kick the victim. Maybe, Sonny was trying to help himself with his own case and still not bring Danny down. We would soon learn what the result would be.

There were no further witnesses and it was our turn to put forward our defense. It was normal to make a motion to the court that the case be dismissed due to the failure on the part of the prosecution to meet the burden of proof of probable cause that the Defendant had committed the act or acts charge in the indictment. I strenuously argued that this was the case. The Judge had been on the bench for many years and had not given off any indication of which way he was leaning as he was listening to my argument for dismissal of the case. I believed that I had made a good argument that the District Attorney's office had failed to present sufficient evidence for the case to go forward against Danny. Often, such a Motion is made and argued in nothing more than a "pro forma" way and quickly dispensed with. It was different this time. I truly believed that we had a chance for dismissal by the court and I proceeded to attack the lack of solid evidence by the prosecution seriously and at some length.

The arguments were made during the morning session of the fourth day of trial. I argued to the Judge that "the prosecution has failed to show with any witness that Danny was directly involved in the beating and killing of the cab driver that had occurred. He was there but not as a participant." Deputy Lyons argued to the contrary as effectively as he could be repeating statements by the eye witnesses that put Danny close by and. Once we were finished with our arguments, the Judge proceeded to sum up the evidence. As he did so, I was hearing in the Judge's summation that he was accepting and adopting each of my arguments. He was verbalizing that the case against Danny Lopez should indeed be dismissed because the prosecution had failed to provide enough evidence for the case against him to go forward to the jury. He specifically found that although Danny was clearly at the scene when the victim was killed, but that there was no evidence presented that Danny had in fact participated despite being both very close and present.

As I was hearing this, I had this incredible feeling of awe and happiness. The Judge's summary of the evidence was that the prosecution had failed to show that Danny was a participant in the death of the cab driver. We had won! Danny was free! This was great news! I had planned to put Danny on the stand because I believed he would convince the jury of his innocence just as I had been convinced. Instead, the judge had granted my Motion to dismiss the case, thanked and dismissed the jury for their service. Danny was acquitted! We were free to leave the courtroom and Danny would be released from custody in the county jail immediately west of the court house as soon as they processed him out. This was really happening to Danny after one full year and a week in jail. I can tell you that there is no feeling ever just like an acquittal for murder. I will never forget it.

I was overwhelmed with the result and in a state of shock. I had believed in our defense, but still had difficulty accepting that it had all worked out for Danny. Many times, over the years following, I was reminded of the decision I made in Danny's case to reject the plea bargain offer and go to trial. I would get sweaty and clammy all over again. I had risked so much when I decided that we would go to trial. I do not know if I would have done it again in view of the safe alternative and release from jail. I was still young and was just beginning to learn about and trust my instincts. I did believe in our defense, but it could have gone wrong. Witnesses' stories change as trial approaches. My only advice is that you must be sure of your decisions inside of yourself or you will have a hard time living with them. There is nothing written to tell you how to deicide in such serious cases. A lesser plea to manslaughter and being released from jail is nothing to be laughed at. The facts are always different and witnesses are often better or worse than expected. It is also true that most clients do, more often than not, depend on your advice. God be with them. He was with Danny.

There was still another lesson to be learned in Danny's case. You can get hit with unexpected blows at any time and from anywhere. The eye witness had already told his story to the police, but he changed at trial. You can never be certain about what will be said in court during a trial until it actually happens. Things keep changing and people change. The lawyer must stay in touch with witnesses as much as he can right up to the trial and whenever possible. This very much applies to your defense witnesses and the Defendant himself or herself. They, too, are subject to change and their testimony will often fall short of what you were expecting or hoping for. Your case always needs to be nourished and developed as best as possible right up to trial itself. Surprises come from both sides again and again. The trial lawyers' work is never done.

Cases just kept coming in as my practice grew. I was trying traffic and DUIs (Driving under the Influence), many of which were very interesting. In one of the DUIs, I represented a man whose younger brother by two years was in the car at the same time and they looked alike and acted alike. Both of the brothers had been out together and drinking at their local bar when the car was stopped by the police during their trip home. The older brother, John, who was asking me to represent him, explained to me at that the time of the stop, he could withstand a plea bargain of lesser points against his license because of the minimal points he had on his license at that time. His brother, James could not. Because of this, the brothers made an instant decision at the time of the traffic stop to change places so that John was sitting at the wheel of the car when the officer came to the driver's side of the car after the stop. They had each ducked down in the front seat and changed places so that James was seated on the driver's side when the officer came up alongside. The officer did not see them as they changed positions in front seat, allowing John to accept the DUI citation from the cop.

When they told me about what they did, I told them that I could not allow them to lie to the court knowing that they were perjuring themselves. This would be a violation of our Colorado Code of Professional Conduct for lawyers. Another lawyer might go along with it, but I would not. I suggested that the only thing to do was for them to allow me to tell the truth and convince the DA to drop the charges against John and work the best deal possible on behalf of James, the guilty brother. They looked at each other, asked a few questions and, in a few minutes time, agreed to go ahead with my plan. I was somewhat surprised that the two of them agreed to tell the truth come what may. After all, they had made an opposite decision at the crime scene. However, they were decent young men and their deception had been weighing on them. I also did not expect what would happen when I first met the assigned deputy DA in the County Court to which the case was assigned.

I explained what the brothers had done when I met the deputy and suggested that the case be dismissed and another case be initiated against James who was the actual driver. James was also present in court with his brother, John, who had been charged. I offered that James was willing to speak to the deputy if he wished. The deputy DA refused to speak to James or to accept my explanation of what had taken place with the substitution of one brother for another. He explained that this was a ruse often tried by people in similar situations. It was the first time that I had met the DA in a case and he apparently felt that we were trying to pull a fast one on him and the court. I was unable to convince him that the James, the real driver, had the worst record and would suffer more than John if we worked a normal plea bargain for him instead of his brother. The deputy was not convinced and never changed his opinion. The result was that we ended up going to trial.

My defense became that brother John, who was not the driver, had switched places with James to save his brother's license. Having had a long time to think about what they had done, the brothers agreed that the truth needed to be told, even if it meant the loss of his license by James. We were asking the jury to accept that this was true and that John should not be convicted since he did not drive and drink on the evening in question. It was a far-out defense, but it was the truth. The deputy DA fought us tooth and nail throughout the case.

This was a highly unusual defense to present in court. Essentially, I ended up agreeing to all of the incriminating evidence presented by the arresting officer as to the manner and speed of the vehicle being driven and also to the fact that the driver was intoxicated. Where we differed was when the arresting officer was on the stand testifying and it was my turn to cross examine him. I put it to him in my cross examination as follows. "Isn't it true that when you stopped the car, both brothers admitted John was the driver of the vehicle. "Yes, that is true." He answered. I continued my cross exam with, "And, is it not true that at a distance you could not tell one from another?" He answered," Yes, I could not tell one from another" I went on to ask, "From the time you stopped the vehicle and obtained what you needed to get out and walk up to their truck, there was plenty of time for the two of them to switch places?" He agreed that "There was time." "And you were not looking at their vehicle all of the time." "No. I was not looking all of the time" the officer responded, "but I would have certainly seen it if they were changing places while I was walking up to the vehicle. And, when I arrived at the truck, neither brother said anything about a switch of places. The brothers acted as if he, John, was the brother who had been driving. He even argued with me that he was not going as fast as I had observed." This was a new piece of evidence that had not been raised by either brother in our prep for trial. We had to absorb it and hope that when both brothers testified, the jury would accept their version of the events. Following the exchange with the police officer," I went on to then raise the key issue by asking the officer if it was true that "When the brothers confessed to their switch and were incriminating the younger brother as the culprit, is it not true that he was the one who had the worst record and sure to lose his license, not the older brother." "Yes, that is t true." The officer replied.

At this point, I must state that under our rules of evidence in criminal trials, we are not allowed to question witnesses about what the punishment may be if the defendant was convicted. However, the deputy DA did not object and I was able to make that point at the conclusion of my cross examination by asking the officer, "Does it make any sense to you that they would admit to lying and have nothing to gain except that the correct brother with the worst record is convicted would end up with the punishment against his license?" He sat back and thought about it before finally saying? "I have no idea why they would do what they were doing." This concluded the officer's testimony. I asked both brothers to testify when it became our turn and they told the jury chapter and verse about what they had done after the car was stopped by the police officer. They each admitted when they testified that they each reversed himself from what they had initially told the police officer when the car was stopped. Each of them also admitted that they were following my advice not to lie in court. It was evident when I asked and they answered the same questions that a few of the jurors were surprised, leaned forward or straightened up in their seats. Each brother admitted to the initial falsehoods made to the police officer at the time of the stop. The younger brother explained the reason why he had initially lied was due to his bad driving record while the older brother, John, confessed to lying in order to save James's license. They also admitted to feeling better about now telling the truth, come what may, after understanding that their lawyer could not allow knowing false evidence to be presented to the jury.

The jury was out about two hours, but in the end, they decided that they believed what the brothers had each explained and that the wrong brother had been charged. A few of them, like me, were not completely sure if a trick had been played on them. However, they followed the jury instructions and because of their uncertainty about who was in fact the driver, they concluded that they were not able to find my client guilty beyond a reasonable doubt. A couple of the jurors thanked me for giving the advice I had given to the brothers and asked whether James would be charged with a DUI. I answered that, "I believe that James will be charged and I expect it to happen since both brothers testified that James was the driver." Nevertheless, I had no way of knowing at that time if a new DUI charge would be made or not against by the DA's office against the brother who had admitted to being the driver. I was unable to fully satisfy their curiosity since the deputy who tried the case was non-comital as to what his office would do. It turned out that James was never charged. I wonder to this day whether the two of them fooled us all.

This case showed me once again that the one can never predict with certainty how a case will end up. The variety of events and surprises that occur in cases are never ending. A trial lawyer learns that anything and everything is possible from the amazing and different ways that people behave. How things will actually play out in court is always uncertain and unpredictable. The jury, made up of stranger's unknown to each other before their selection to the jury, do so ways that cause us who try the cases to shake our heads in wonder. The system works and the blind lady of justice is well served over and over again.

CHAPTER 8

Court Appointments

During the next few years, I began to receive appointments from Judges to represent people who were not able to pay for counsel or where there were conflicts of interest preventing the newly established public Defender's office to represent the defendants. Most of my appointments came from Denver and Adams County where I had won the murder trial. The pay was much less, but most of us trial lawyers considered it to be our duty to accept such cases. On my part, I was also thrilled that the Judges' thought well enough of me to make the appointments. It was also surprising who the judges were that had made the appointments. In one case, it was the first woman judge before whom I had appeared in Adams County. I had been very uncertain as to how she felt about me. In fact, I thought that she did not like me. Maybe, that was true and this was the punishment! Yet, she chose me to represent an escaped felon from a California prison that had a shoot- out with a whole group of sheriff deputies in Adams County in which no one was able to shoot straight enough to hit anyone before my client gave himself up after running out of ammunition. He was facing about nine or ten charges. Including several attempted murder charges heading the list. I wondered who this person would turn out to be. He exceeded my expectations.

Dev Brock was a tough looking medium-sized man when I first met with him in the County jail where he remained throughout my representation. He had been serving a twenty-year sentence for robbery in the Chino penitentiary, California, at the time of his escape. He told me that he managed to do it by himself, without help from any other prisoner. He explained to me that he had to get out of Chino because the guards were "plotting to kill him." He was certain of that and did not want to return. This immediately placed an impossible burden on me since whatever the outcome in Colorado, sooner or later; Dev would be extradited back to California. Dev told me that "I am comfortable in the county facility. No one is after me here, yet." He told me this very seriously and added that," under no circumstances can I be returned to Chino." I left him after the first visit shaking my head." What had I gotten myself into?

Nothing in my life in law school or practice prepared me for what was waiting for me when I entered the courtroom in Dev's case. All around the walls of the courtroom and behind the Defense counsel's chairs, in one of which sat my client with cuffs chained on his hands and legs, were standing at least 20 sheriff's deputies. When I walked into the courtroom, placed my brief case on the desk, looked around and saw all the deputies, I looked at the DA who was the same one who had handled the recent murder trial of Dan Lyons. He shrugged his shoulders. I then looked at my client who appeared dazed. He had manacles on his hands and legs that were connected to ones around his waist. I then looked up and faced the Judge and said loudly, "Judge, look at this. It looks as if we are in Russia or some other dictatorship. The cops are all over this place in a United States courtroom with our flag above your head. I demand that my client be un-cuffed and unchained and that the Sheriff's deputies be ordered to leave the well of the courtroom." I meant to say more, but I was not able to finish because the Judge responded by saying, "Say no more counsel. I agree with you." She then looked around the courtroom at all the deputies and said, "All of you except three deputies' step away from the courtroom, un-cuff and release the defendant and we shall proceed." I liked this Judge! Her orders were complied with as the sheriff's deputies proceeded to leave the courtroom while three of them placed themselves around my client and busied themselves with my client to uncuff him and allow him to sit next to me at the defense table while they remained standing behind the two of us. A few of the deputies took seats in the back of the courtroom, evidently wishing to see what would take place as we proceeded with regular business in the case. I entered my appearance and we went ahead with the arraignment and set a date for the preliminary hearing. From that point on, Dev loved me and told me later in the jail when I visited him that, "You are the man!" As I recovered from the shock of the courtroom scene, I had no thoughts of being "the man ", only pleased with the fact that the Judge had reacted so well and strongly to my remarks. She turned out, to be a very good judge who controlled her courtroom. I always thereafter enjoyed being in front of her and judges like her. Not all judges would rise to same level of command and control in courtrooms as she did. I came to learn and experience this as the years went by.

As the case progressed and I attempted to work out a solution that worked for both sides, I had come to the conclusion that the answer to the case was to send Dev back to California where he would be dealt with by the California authorities with the escape from Chino and additional charges with more time in jail. I argued to the DA that we were wasting time and money on Dev that was unnecessary since all of the same would happen in California where he would be found guilty of escape and sentenced to more time in Chino. "Why bother with spending time and money in Colorado?" was my question and suggestion to the deputies involved. Of course, my client did not like this solution as he was sitting reasonably satisfied in the local county jail. In fact, he told me early on that things were much better for him in Colorado then in the California penitentiary. The lack of acceptance by my now friend in the DA's office soon caused me to turn to the only defense that existed for Dev. He was insane, temporarily or permanently. What else would motivate a man to engage in a shootout with a whole passel of sheriff deputies? Insanity!

In due course, since I was appointed to be Dev's counsel under constitutional authority that he receives counsel, the court approved the appointment of a psychiatrist to be hired to examine Dev on behalf of the defense. In response, the prosecution obtained a psychiatrist to prepare a response to the defense argument that Dev was insane at the time of the shooting. This was my first taste of the nuances of legal insanity. I began to ready myself for the court arguments that would follow the testimony of the two psychiatric doctors who had, not surprisingly, opposite opinions about my client's sanity.

Following his examination of Dev in the County jail, I was informed by our court appointed psychiatric expert in a written opinion that Dev had achieved a well-known and documented paranoid condition that was easily triggered by his prison surroundings and unbalanced fellow inmates and/or guards, to say nothing about the policemen who had been shooting to kill him, causing him to become legally insane. He was not totally insane but had achieved what the psychiatrist considered to be a state of mind causing a failing to understand right from wrong which was the standard existing in Colorado at the time. It could happen to any one of us under the same poor background, conditions and life choices. I liked the Doctor, but I was not really convinced. I began to think about what sort of jurors would be open to such thinking. Of course, the prosecution psychiatrist formed an opposite opinion and determined that Dev, who had escaped from prison and shot to kill against the posse out to capture him, was sane under the legal standard for insanity in Colorado since he knew right from wrong. The lines were drawn as trial approached and we were soon one week from trial.

Personally, as I came to know Dev in my visits with him in the county jail, and interacted with him in normal fashion, I had difficulty absorbing that he was insane. When I spoke with our psychiatrist about this, he told me that I had not read what he had received from the California prison outlining Dev's psychiatric history and behavior. When I did review the materials provided to the expert from California, which consisted of a long history of anger, defiance, outrageous conduct and danger to himself and others, this did give me pause as to who my client really was. He certainly had created a disturbing history of bizarre and questionable behavior. Indeed, I became concerned about who I was really dealing with.

With more cases under my belt, I had learned that the best offers by the prosecution generally come as the trial date approaches. I did not have much faith in getting an offer that might work. However, I was wrong. Approximately one week before the scheduled trial date, the DA contacted me with a surprising offer, or better stated, decision to let Dev return to California and become, once again, their problem. This was a good decision on their part, one that I had suggested from the beginning. It also left me without the ability to respond or counter-offer. I was told by Dan Lyons that on the date of trial they would dismiss all charges and send Dev back to California. Apparently, my initial suggestion to send my client back to California and save money for Colorado worked on the minds of the decision makers in the DA's office as the costs of the psychiatric analyses grew and the experts were divided in their conclusions. I had been able to hire one of the best forensic psychiatric doctors in Colorado with state money. In short, the DA's office decided not to risk trial and a possible loss. Sending Dev back to California ended up making sense to the Adams County DA's office just as I had proposed.

Dev was apoplectic about the decision to dismiss his case. He wanted to go to trial. More important, he wanted to remain in Colorado. He liked his current environment. He told me. "Mike. You know I am crazy. Everyone knows that. The jailors here say that to me all of the time. They can't send me back to California. They will kill me there. I know that and you know that." I could only reply that, "There is no choice to be made. It is not your decision or mine. The authority belongs with the District Attorney's office. When the DA stands up in court and tells the Judge that they will dismiss the charges, it is a done deal. The judge will not listen to me asking that we go to trial. That is the end of the story." Dev looked at me, angry and upset. I continued, "When we show up in court on Monday, the case will be dismissed. You will be sent back to California." Dev was completely bummed out as I left him and would see him again in court on the date of trial.

Indeed, the DA dismissed all charges and Dev was returned to the jail to await pickup by California law men.

By arrangement with the DA, I was to be told when Dev would be sent back to California. I had arranged to see him one last time and will always remember that meeting. He was calm as he seriously explained to me that since he would be killed by the California guards who would be picking him up to take him back to Chino, he had made a few decisions and needed my help to accomplish them. He explained that he had arranged with the Adams County jailers to have his wallet and his very few personal papers to be given to me. He also gave to me a final letter to his mother in California which he asked that I send to his mother. He told me that he did not trust that the Adam County jail guards would mail the letter if he left it with them. Moreover, Dev explained to me that mailing the letter to his mother was important because he knew that the guards sent from Chino prison to collect him would kill him. This remained Dev' thinking despite what I had previously told Dev about who would be picking him up in Colorado. It would not be the guards from the penitentiary, but rather Sheriff's deputies who would be coming to Colorado to collect him. I did not raise any argument and agreed to do as he wished when we parted.

Dev then took off his watch and gave it to me to be sent along with his belongings to his mother together with her address and phone number. He made me promise to call his mother and tell her what he thought was going to happen. After attempting one more time to convince Dev that none this was going to happen and that he would be picked up by regular sheriff deputies and not the jailers, he said, "You cannot not possibly know what lies ahead for me with the people who are his jailers in Chino. There is nothing that can be done!" He then thanked me for my services and we relived the first day in court once again when I demanded that he be freed from the cuffs and chains and have the sheriff deputies removed from the courtroom. We laughed about that and as I left, I made him, "promise me you will write and tell me that you have survived the transfer to California." He promised he would but repeated to me that "I know it will not happen. They will kill me. "And so, we parted.

I contacted Dev's mother who was very pleasant and accepting of what I transmitted to her. She understood my message since Dev had been telling her the same things. About three or four months later, I did in fact receive a letter from Dev stating that he had survived the trip back to Chino prison. He wrote that "It is only because I was picked up by regular deputies and not the killer jailers. I have to keep alert all of the time. You never know when they will strike." I never heard from Dev again.

As my experience grew, I had come to the realization that cases had a way of working out predictably. Many times, as happened with Dev, you could figure out a case from the beginning. The only solution was for him to be returned to California and so it turned out to be. In the beginning of my practice, I found myself holding back my thoughts about what may happen from my clients and the DAs. Then, as I gained experience, I found myself sharing my thoughts with the DAs since they were on parallel paths with me to the final solutions, whether they realized it or not. Often, they would disagree, but with the passage of time for each side and as the familiarity with the facts and circumstances of each case grew, the two sides would often come closer and closer to each other in arriving at a solution. It was more a matter of the accumulation of evidence and understanding of the cases by both sides. There was no harm done if they knew where I thought we were headed. It was the path we were on that would lead us to whatever the outcome would be. So, why not express my thinking from my experience to them and my clients? Sometimes, the clients would disagree or certainly have their own opinion. Nevertheless, this is how I came to the conclusion that thinking about the cases as the information and evidence revealed itself and projecting forward your thoughts about the possible solutions was the best thing I could do as the lawyer in the cases.

Little by little, I would think my way through to the final solution of the many and varied cases and fact situations. This process had a way of calming me as I would work and ponder my way to the final result in the midst of my clients' concerns and the press of the case logistics and court appearances. I also found that once I had planted the seed of what I thought the result would be that I would unconsciously work towards that result in my negotiations and presentation of the case to the other side. Believing in the final result does help make things happen. I guess this is a form of projection that operates in such legal circumstances.

CHAPTER 9

Murder Unraveled

Within a few months of the resolution of the Dev Brock case, I was appointed by a Denver District Court Judge to represent a man charged with murder in a downtown apartment building in the skid row section of Denver. The immediate facts jolted me. I was being asked to represent a man who allegedly hit the victim on the back of his head with a small hatchet before the victim was thrown out of a second story window to his death, or so it was supposed by the District Attorney's office at the time the case was filed. The problem was that when the body was examined, the autopsy found that he had also been stabbed in the chest with some kind of an instrument or pick. This made the case into two separate attempts at a murder which ultimately was successful. It was a gruesome case.

My client had a record with a history of robbery and violence. He had recently been released from the penitentiary after a long stretch. At the time of the murder, he had been sitting or standing on the second floor of the apartment building in question with other drunks from where the police believed the body had been thrown. The police report indicated that a group of men and women had been sharing an assortment of wines and liquor in the apartment before the killing. I was not attracted to the case, but since the Judge had appointed me, I believed it to be my duty to accept the appointment and render the legal services required. I went to see my new client at the Denver County jail then located near to the Denver International Airport in Stapleton field. I was not sure what to expect.

When I met my client, Caesar Diaz, he had already been in jail for a couple of weeks. He was short and thin with the manner of a man who did not reveal much about himself. He was sober and immediately attempted to put me at ease. "Don't worry about it", he said. "I did not do it. It was some of the other drunks who were there." When I told him that he had been identified by witnesses in the room with him, he held his ground, "Mr. Mike," It was not me. They are making things up." Caesar called me "Mr. Mike" from the beginning. This did not put me at ease since it was obvious that Caesar was deeply involved in the incident and lying. I received the same answers when I asked about his record of violent crimes and robbery. Caesar responded that he had been "betrayed" by the real perpetrators and had received "bum raps" by the police and prosecutors. Obviously, he was not going to give me information since he did not trust anyone, and certainly not his appointed counsel. This was a man who had been recently released from the penitentiary after serving 10 plus years for robbery. It was a sobering meeting and I was left to investigate further to learn the truth, to the extent possible. We parted amicably since Caesar understood that I was to be his front man facing the justice that lay ahead, whatever that might be. He was a veteran of the criminal justice system and was accepting of the time and delays that were built into our justice system. In fact, he made it clear to me that he liked the Denver county jail. "It was OK, far better than the Colorado Penitentiary," he said.

The police yellow markers were still in place at the door to the room in the apartment building on the second floor where the murder had taken place. It was dirty and filled with empty and half empty bottles and beer cans as one would expect. There were two windows that over looked an alley dividing the space between two apartment buildings. I could see down from the apartment windows garbage bins, beer cans, bottles and accumulated trash below, probably remaining since the time of the killing. The crime scene was also marked with a couple of police yellow markers where the body had been found. As I looked down at the scene, I concluded that it was unlikely that the apartment building occupants and passers-by had honored the police markers; the scene having been already littered and compromised. I did not know from which window the body had been thrown. It probably did not make any difference since the end result was an established fact. I left the room having learned very little except that it was a lousy place to be.

I proceeded down the hallway on the second floor, knocking on each door. Each person who answered said that he or she did not know anything about what had happened, but that I should talk to the old guy in the end apartment named "Mr. McGoo." When I knocked on his door, he answered the door and we spoke. I understood immediately why he was known by his nickname since he did indeed look like "Mr. McGoo," the Disney comic strip character with large glasses who could not see. This was a man who had similar trouble seeing through his rounded glasses. When I interviewed him and would later be cross examining him in the preliminary hearing, he claimed that he saw my client swing what looked like "an axe." and "strike the man on the, back of his head." He went on to say that he "had walked past the apartment in which the door was open and saw the blow being administered as he passed." When I asked if he stopped to help, he answered that "I just kept walking." I then asked if he saw a group of people in the room as he passed by? He thought for a moment and then said "I could hear shouting and arguments" from inside the room. I then approached him in the witness chair with a piece of paper with writing in large block letters and asked, "Can you see the writing? He answered "No. I cannot make it out." I literally had to come up to just a few feet from him on the stand before he could identify a single letter let alone, a person, face or weapon. With that accomplished, I asked and he admitted that his nickname was, "Mr. McGoo because I have a hard time seeing." His testimony as an eye witness was now fully compromised. It was clear that he alone could not identify Caesar. However, there were indeed a couple of other witnesses with better vision, one of which was in the room; a man who admitted to being a "drunk" and had been drinking when the alleged killing had taken place.

Two other alleged participants were also charged with the murder, a man and a woman. Their stories became available to me in the discovery materials where they had each spoken about "Caesar" being the, "killer with the hatchet" while denying their own involvement. All of the statements to the police that were included in the police report made the murder case very difficult with all fingers being pointing at Caesar. After being separately charged with murder of the victim and obtaining counsel, both of witnesses charged had stopped cooperating with the police. When I entered the case, it was evident that the two of them, through their lawyers, were separately seeking plea bargains. The case against Caesar was standing alone on a ledge, waiting to be pushed over by their cooperation.

We were scheduled to be the first of the three cases to go to trial for obvious reasons. Caesar was not talking, but each of the two others defendants, one man and one woman, were likely to reveal their versions about the evening of the murder. When the coroner testified at the preliminary hearing, I raised the issue of the death having been caused by an ice pick to the chest or something like one instead of a glancing blow by a hatchet because such a wound was indicated in the autopsy. He was not helpful and replied that in his opinion, "Death was the proximate result of either the hatchet blow or the ice pick. Each wound was deadly and, obviously, I am unable to separate the two either in effect or in time. The blows happened too close in time to one another." That was as far as I was able to get with the coroner. The stabbing to the chest equaled the blow to the head. Take your pick. The opinion was not comforting.

In every direction, things did not look good for Caesar. He kept to himself whatever he actually did or remembered about that evening other than the fact that he was there. "Somebody else must have done it." Was what Caesar told me, "I have no recollections about what had taken place that evening in the Apartment?" And he added, "I do not know how the victim had been dropped out of the apartment window. I did not see that happen." He simply was not going to help me with the basic facts and information that he knew and lived through. That never changed as we progressed to the date of the trial of the case.

My client remained cool during our visits in the County jail and this was not helpful. He recognized the seriousness of his position but was content to let things play out. He obviously was not frightened about jail and used our time together to catch up on current events that he may have missed on TV. He was not demanding of me and appeared resigned to the fact that I had a job to do that included seeing him from time to time. He never expressed urgency or a need to know what was happening in his case. His attitude was one of letting the chips fall where they may. He was not cheered by my visits or distressed. He was taking things one day at a time. Caesar was receiving his three-square meals each day and did not bug me about what may happen or not when we went to trial. It was obvious that life was easier for him in the Denver County jail where he had a certain status due to his conviction for robbery and sentence to the penitentiary and the murder charges. I must admit that Caesar was not a difficult client to deal with. It clearly looked as if we would go to trial and I began planning accordingly since there was no offer on the table except to plead guilty to 1st degree murder. The death penalty was not being enforced in Colorado at that time awaiting action by the United

States Supreme court. Things were better for Caesar where he was presently residing as we slowly approached the trial date.

Plea bargain discussions with the assigned DAs had lapsed since I did not have authority to settle the case or even offer a plea to a lesser offense. Some cases are like that and there is nothing to do but to prepare the case for trial as best as possible. This was my first interaction with the DAs, Rick" Daniels was that there were three eye witnesses. However, it turned out that all of the actual witnesses for the prosecution were not very reliable, such as Mr. McGoo, and the two best ones were each charged with the murder and negotiating for a lesser plea while the third kept changing addresses. We were going to go to trial first because there were at least three witnesses who had identified Caesar holding the small hatchet, although it was uncertain who may actually testify. The question was what else they would say or admit to and what could be accomplished through cross examination as to their reliability at the time of the murder. None of this was promising for Caesar but the uncertainties did give some hope. However, the addresses of the witnesses and co-defendants provided by the DAs' discovery were the apartment building or places nearby, none of which led to finding the named witnesses or any other witness. They were long gone or unknown and I was unable to find any person who may have been a witness. I was told by Rick Daniels that I would have to try to find them the same way they were doing it, by assigning a detective or private investigator to dig them up for the trial date. I did hire an ex-cop who found one of the alleged witnesses. However, He pleaded that he was too drunk to remember anything. The DA did better and had at least one signed statement. When I tried to visit the man at the address he had provided to the DA's investigator, he was gone. None of this was promising and all uncertain. There was no other solution but to keep trying over and over just as the DAs told me they were doing as the trial date approached. The DA's office clearly had the advantage since they could offer deals while I was limited by simply attempting to learn the truth.

There remained the unresolved issue that the prosecution had no good explanation for; the alternate chest/pick stabbing injury that was equally responsible for the man's death. As far as my client was concerned, the DA's position was that it did not matter. Rick Daniel's maintained that his witnesses could confirm that my client was present at the time of death and that he had swung the hatchet and that this was all they needed. As for the stabbing, they remained in the dark. It was established that the drinkers inside the room were fighting over the bottles of liquor that were quickly being drained by the arguing drunks. It was evident that the DAs were hoping Caesar would take a plea if only to provide a better understanding about what had actually taken place. At that time, they were also hampered in learning the full truth of what and how it happened. The victim was found two stories down in the alley and the witnesses pointed fingers at Caesar and another man and woman, the Co-Defendants. They all claimed to be drinking and not participating in the events that led to hatchet blow to the head and final stabbing and throwing of the victim out of the window of the apartment building. The entire scene was a mess that had only been partially unraveled as the trial date approached.

The truth was that the actual facts were a mystery to both sides. The burden of proof lay with the District Attorneys and they had only three participants in their sights, including, Caesar. The remaining two Defendants were charged while the DA's were still seeking to pin down exactly how the other two were involved. I really did not know how the trial would play out since none of the witnesses were reliable and the two other Defendants charged were waiting with their counsel and withholding information under their right to maintain silence as our case was approaching trial.

As is often the case when there are several defendants facing similar charges in a case, they are not natural allies. Counsel for each of the persons charged were cordial with each other, but did not volunteer any information, other than both other clients had reported that my client had struck the deceased with the small hatchet and that the victim was thrown out of the second story window by several unidentified people. Naturally, this information was damaging but unable to be confirmed and Caesar was not talking. However, the others who were charged were also listed as witnesses against Caesar. In the meantime, they were holding fast at remaining silent with the advice of their counsel. That was definitely why we were scheduled to go first. In the eyes of the DA, our case was the most vulnerable one with what evidence they had available and the likelihood of obtaining plea bargains with one or both of the other defendants. It was a game of wait and see. They were counting on the other two to break down and enter into plea bargains and becoming witnesses before the trial. Failing that, they were faced with the prospect of the other two hiding behind the 5th Amendment and remaining silent. This was likely to injure their case against Caesar to an uncertain degree. We were unable to make a deal and DAs were unable to bring the other two Defendants and their lawyers to agree to pleas and testimony against Caesar. We were facing trial under highly uncertain circumstances, with a possible break in the cases to occur at any time. Such is the life of a criminal defense attorney.

The deputy district attorney, Rick Daniels, had been with the office for about six or seven years. He was a solid lawyer who quietly went about constructing and presenting his cases. He was a good guy and I liked him. However, I well remember that during the jury selection process, I became very upset with him over one of the questions he had asked of a prospective juror which contained what I considered to be unprovable evidence in his hypothetical question to that juror. I stood up and objected strenuously. I literally began to rant against the prejudice being caused by the question to my client in front of the jury. In the middle of my loud objection and declarations, I could hear the Judge saying to me, "Mike, Mike, settle down. It's okay. There is a jury panel sitting and listening. Settle down!" I heard the Judge and I did settle down when I realized that I was out of control. The judge who had appointed me had been very gracious with me and I had could hear him through my anger. I got ahold of myself and stopped being an idiot. It was a moment of intense anger and, as I look back, anxiety about where the case was going. Only later did I realize that my anger had been a product of my mixed feelings arising from representing what certainly appeared to be a hatchet killer who was totally uncooperative. It was my worst display of anger ever in a courtroom. We proceeded with the jury selection process without further incident.

I have always remained grateful to the judge in how he handled my explosion against the deputy DA. With the passage of time, I developed a good relationship with Rick Daniels who went on to become a very good District Court Judge. I appeared in front of him many times in civil and criminal cases and tried several cases in front of him, including a Conspiracy to Murder case arising from a very unusual situation that occurs later in this book.

My anger was something that I had to learn to control, if not for my sake, certainly for my clients. I am happy to report that I did and even learned to use it to my advantage with humor instead of anger. This is something I recommend to any present or future lawyers to include in their repertoire. Humor is appreciated much more by the judges and the jurors then anger or antagonism, if not the opposing counsel. Humor that is appropriate always works in a courtroom and relaxes everyone for a little bit of time before everyone returns to the serious business at hand. I learned to lean more to humor then anger as I found that so much more would be accomplished with both the court and the jury, sometimes at the expense of opposing counsel. However, at the time of this trial, such wisdom still lay ahead of me. We continued with the jury selection process until the jury was sworn in and the court halted the proceedings for lunch. We would return after lunch for the opening statements by counsel.

I was eating my lunch in the basement cafeteria of the courthouse where many lawyers ate and met during breaks from court upstairs throughout the day, sometimes with opposing counsel. The cafeteria was often the place where lawyers would meet, discuss and, often settle their cases. I was sitting and eating alone when Rick approached me with a message that his boss, the Denver DA himself, wanted to speak to me on the telephone. Rick only said that there had been a "break in the case" without spelling it out. I had no idea what it may be since there were many scenarios that were possible. We did not have cell phones back then. I finished my sandwich and accompanied my opponent up to the 4rd floor of the court house where the DAs' had an office.

I called the District Attorney on their office phone. What he told me was amazing. He said that while we had been in the jury selection process that morning, the other man who had also been charged with the murder of the same victim who had been struck with the axe by my client had confessed to "aiding your client with throwing the victim out of the window after he had been clubbed by my client," This is where it became amazing. The other Defendant had confessed that he and others had then" watched as the woman defendant who had also been in the apartment room boozing with guys, went to the window, looked down at the body below and exclaimed, "Guess what, that guy is moving and he is still alive! Don't worry, I'll go downstairs and see to it that he is dead." She kept her word, left the room and went downstairs and into the alley where the man lay still moving and alive. With the people in the apartment looking down on the victim and female co- Defendant in the alley below, with a small ice pick, the woman Defendant proceeded to stab and kill the wounded man who had been thrown out of the window of the building. People who remained in the room on the second floor and stood by the two windows could see her stabbing the man to death. I was hearing the District Attorney describe the crime sequence with answers to the many puzzles that had been created by the murder involving the three Defendants at that time and place. I had never fully figured out exactly how the sequence of events had happened in the case since my client, similar to other participants, was not helpful. Now, I was being told the actual sequence of events which included a possible defense to murder by hatchet since the victim was alive when the defendant woman struck the victim with the ice pick after the man had landed on the ground following being shoved out the second story window of the apartment. The case had been turned upside down.

Caesar had not at all been forthcoming about what happened, and neither were the other defendants made silent by their counsel. The other witnesses had all pleaded that they did not know or see what had happened. My ignorance was matched by that of the District Attorney's office that was likewise limited in their knowledge and without a full understanding of the actual events that had taken place. Now, we were all learning what had taken place as one of the perpetrators, through his counsel, revealed the actual circumstances of the killing while working out a plea bargain agreement that was acceptable to his client. It finally all came together.

The Defendant who pleaded Guilty to his part of the events had relayed to the DA's office his version of the events. At the same time, the woman defendant was holding out and her case would be going to trial after my case had been completed. This never happened because she also ended up pleading to a charge of murder in the 2nd degree which was being worked out at the same time as I was speaking to the deputy assigned to the case. The DA asked me what my client would be willing to plea to under the new circumstances that had arisen and told me during our phone conversation that he would consider a lesser plea since he wanted to wrap up the entire case. We discussed at that time a possible plea to 1st degree Assault by my client in return for the murder charge being dismissed. I told the DA very frankly that I had no idea if Caesar would agree or not but said I would recommend it to him right away. 1st Degree Assault at that time had a fifteen-year sentence attached to it, and with good behavior, would normally lead to being released after five to seven years.

I left the DA's office in disbelief over what had transpired and went to the jail section on the same 4th floor of the courthouse where inmates facing trial and court proceedings were held waiting for their court appearances. Making things more convenient was the fact that felony trials all took place on the third or fourth floors of the court house. What would Caesar say when I told him about the amazing offer I had just received?

There were three separate rooms available for lawyers to meet with their clients, before, during and after court appearances and trials. This was a place that I had already been spending a lot of time since, like so many of my fellow lawyers, I frequently met with clients before their court appearances when they had not yet been able to bail out before or during trial. It was better than driving out to the county jail, if it could be arranged. Such was the life of a defense lawyer.

When I met with Caesar and explained the change in circumstances and the fact that there was now a defendant who would be telling the jury exactly what had happened, he listened quietly and took it all in. I discussed 1st Degree Assault and the fifteen-year sentence that had been offered in his case. Even as I was telling him the news, I was not feeling good about such a result. Caesar would be walking away from a murder charge with what would end up being just a few years in the penitentiary with good behavior. This was hard to swallow. But there it was, and it was my job to take the offer to my client for his decision. He thought about it and asked, "What will be done with the trial and Jury?" I explained, "The jury will be asked to wait in the jury room while you and I will stand before the Judge and agree to a plea of guilty to 1st degree Assault and the DA will agree to dismiss the murder charge. Also, and this is important, you will be asked to admit before the judge in court that, in fact, you committed the assault. Can you do that?" Caesar carefully considered this and I waited expectantly. He had never admitted to doing anything except drinking at the apartment building. In fact, he had told me. "Mike, don't worry. I did not do it." Caesar then said to me, "Okay, I'll do it." To which I replied, "That is not good enough. You must be ready to tell the judge in open court that you committed the assault with the hatchet. Do you understand? This is the procedure whenever a plea is being entered by a defendant to any charges. As your lawyer; I need to know when I stand next to you that you did commit the crime." Caesar took a few seconds before he replied, "Yes, I did it." With this affirmation, he had admitted to me for the first time that he was indeed guilty of the hatchet assault. He also admitted that with a couple of other people in the room, he had thrown the victim out of the 2nd floor of the apartment building.

Caesar was calm and composed as he was telling me that he had done the deeds with which he had been charged. There was no change in his composure as he spoke, certainly no remorse. It was a fact. He had done it, all of it. With that, I left him and went back to the courtroom to advise the deputy and the Judge that we would be entering the plea to the agreed upon lesser count of 1st Degree Assault. When my client was brought back into the courtroom, we went ahead with the plea of guilty in front of the Judge and Caesar admitted under questioning by the judge that he had indeed participated in the man's death with a hatchet in support of his plea of Guilty to 1st Degree Assault.

The jury had been waiting for us in the jury room attached to the courtroom. They were waiting for the trial to be continued with more questioning of the panel in the jury selection process. Instead, they reassembled in the courtroom and the Judge informed them of the entry of the plea of "Guilty" by Cesar to the agreed upon 1st degree assault plea bargain. The Judge then thanked the jury members for their service and dismissed them in a procedure that regularly takes place in courtrooms around the country each day. I never saw or heard from Caesar again following his entry of the plea of guilty to charges before the Judge and his receipt of the agreed upon sentencing of fifteen years in the penitentiary.

I left the courthouse that day somewhat stunned. I knew that if we had proceeded with the trial, the jury result was likely to find Caesar be guilty of murder. This would most likely have brought about a life sentence. The punishment did not fit the crime. Yet, all three culprits were going behind bars. I guess we had achieved approximate justice. Still, I found myself continuing to carry this case in my mind and memories. It totally juxtaposed the entire criminal process and the results stayed in my mind and left an indelible print that would not go away as I continued to represent people charged with serious crimes. I think I became soberer minded and lost some of the excitement of the previous years. This was a serious business. There was no getting away from that. As time passed, and as I became involved again and again in an amazing variety of cases that walked into my office, the Diaz case would periodically reenter my consciousness as one of the more lurid examples of how we arrive at justice in our system.

Several years later, I began to give annual and sometimes semi-annual lectures at my law school at Cornell to students at the request of the Dean who had been both the Dean and my professor in several classes when I was a student. I would meet with the Dean before my talks and seminars to discuss various cases I had handled since we last met. He would then select which case or cases he wanted me to speak about with the students. We would review the recent cases I had handled or tried from the standpoint of what could be learned by the students from the cases themselves. I would cover the lead up to the trial or the trial itself, the ethics, professional responsibilities and the procedural and criminal process involved. He selected the Diaz case for me to speak about in a three-hour seminar class to interested law students in addition to the separate regular talk I gave to all of the students about the ethics of practice and trial work. At that time, Cornell law school was admitting around one hundred and fifty students for each class. The number of students would whittle down each year as students transferred or dropped out. For example, we were advised by the Dean my first year in law school that the class had one hundred and fifty students. By the time we graduated, the class was composed of approximately one hundred students.

The seminar class was held in the same seminar room set aside for smaller groups that I had attended with about eighteen fellow students as a third-year law student. The class taught by the Dean was called" Constitutional Procedural and Criminal Law Problems" At that time I had been mesmerized by a prominent Washington, DC lawyer, Edward Bennett Williams, who spoke to us about one of his cases from the initial conference with his client to trial and an appeal that went to the US Supreme Court. The case became a milestone search and seizure case. It was an honor to be asked to do the same thing at Cornell Law school about the Diaz case from my first conference with Caesar in jail to the unexpected turn of events during the trial and the ultimate entry of the plea of guilty to 1st degree assault. It certainly provoked many questions and concerns from the students, just as the Dean had predicted. I have also used the case as a tool for learning when I was teaching classes on Constitutional Criminal Law and Professional Responsibility and Ethics at the University of Denver law school as an adjunct law professor many years later. The process of obtaining justice is always full of surprises and often, perplexing. No one enters this field without being wounded.

Chapter 10

Texas Justice

My practice both in civil and criminal cases began taking me out of Colorado occasionally for cases occurring in other states. This was mostly due to Denver people being involved in serious problems outside of Colorado who necessarily had to seek help from their family in Colorado for whom I had done legal work. In one such case, I was asked by the family in Denver to represent their son, Rick Rondeau, who had been arrested in El Paso, Texas and charged with murder. They were very concerned since their son was now in a Texas jail which did not have a good reputation among black people for how they handled blacks in their jails. They were very worried and hoped that I would be able to help alleviate his situation. I accepted the case with more concern then normal due to my total lack of knowledge about how things were done in El Paso. I prepared immediately to travel to El Paso the next day after confirming with the El Paso DA's office the date and time of my new client's court appearance.

The basic facts turned out to be that their son, Rick, had gone to El Paso to purchase marijuana for resale in Denver. His parents were good, religious and hardworking people who were very upset that their son had become engaged in such criminal activity. When they learned of his arrest for murder, they were deeply alarmed before seeking my help and advice. It was a $100,000 bond and was beyond their means to pay for a bondsman in El Paso where the best they were able to work out by phone was a $12,500 fee to post the bond. I learned from the Public Defender's office that no one had yet been assigned to Rick's case because they were overloaded with work and had very few lawyers to handle all the cases. There was indeed a bond hearing scheduled in two days and, according to the lawyer I spoke to, their son's chances for a reduction of the bond was not good. Rick's parents wanted me to go to El Paso and attend the hearing, see their son and figure out what should be done. They decided that their money would be better spent on obtaining counsel then the release on bail of their son. We agreed on a retainer and I immediately prepared to fly to El Paso the next day.

This was a very serious undertaking. However, I could not say "No." This was my job and they and their son needed my help. It was a challenge and it was what I had signed up for. The scary part was that I did not know anyone in El Paso and had no familiarity with how Texas handled such cases. In Colorado, there were always differences in how things were handled from one county to another. This would be another state entirely. Nevertheless, I found myself looking forward to the unknown that I was about to enter. The only information we had was that their son had shot and killed a man in El Paso. I was unable to learn much more other from a deputy DA in the office since a deputy had yet been assigned to the case. As I boarded the plane to take me to El Paso, I found myself leaving on an adventure into unknown territory and Texas justice.

I had previously represented Rick Rondeau in a speeding case where he faced the loss of his license. He was a fun loving young man and easy to get along with. I had been able to work a deal in which I saved his license just a few months before he was jailed in Texas. This is what allowed him to drive to El Paso and meet what turned out to be the drug dealer who had been shot. Naturally, Rick's car had been impounded upon his arrest. One of the tasks I had taken on was to pay off the impound fees for the vehicle and to drive the car back to Denver after the court hearing.

I had my hands full when I arrived in El Paso the day before the hearing and went about obtaining all the information I could before the hearing set for the next day. I started by visiting the Public Defender's office to obtain whatever background information they had which was skimpy. They had a file which contained only the charges and none of the discovery that the prosecutors were bound to provide to the defense. No one in the public defender's office had yet been appointed to take the case and I was informed that they did not know for sure which one of them in the office would become responsible for the case when it was called the next day. Of course, if I presented myself as counsel, the public defender's office would happily be out of the case.

Next, I visited the District Attorney's office and was informed that they would give me all of the discovery material the following morning when I entered my appearance. Unfortunately, the DA assigned to the case was in court so all I could do was to try to catch up with him if I were to visit the courtroom which, fortunately, was in the same complex with the DA's office next door to the Court House. It turned out that the county jail was also nearby to the courthouse. This allowed me to be able to get far more accomplished the day I arrived then I had ever dreamed possible. Had Rick been in a jail many miles away from the courts and the DA's office, I would have had to spend far more time and travel before achieving any real knowledge about the case.

When I visited the Public Defenders' office, I found it to be in a small set of offices a few blocks from the Justice complex where my client was located. Same as in Denver, the public defenders in El Paso were the stepchild in the justice system. All around the country, public defenders can be found in lesser quarters then DAs, paid less and further away from court then are the DAs' offices. That is something that goes with the job. Many real good trial lawyers earned their chops defending the long unending line of criminal defendants who were being represented without charge under the auspices of the Supreme Court decision that everyone is entitled to counsel under our Constitution. The Public Defender in charge, after learning that I was prepared to enter the case, happily showed me their file which contained the police report and other data related to the shooting incident. At that time, no one in the office had been able to get started in the case. What stood out immediately was that the victim drug dealer had been shot in the chest at close range and that his gun was found near him as he lay sprawled out in the entrance way to his home with the front door open. It was evident that self-defense was in play in view of gun found by the victim. This was good news. The public defender went on to tell me that the dead man was well known to the police in El Paso as a bad dude with a violent history and reputation in addition to dealing in drugs. Apparently, Rick had rid the community of a known violent criminal and drug trafficker. This was good to know. Since I had already made appearances in court in civil matters in the states of Wyoming and Texas, I asked him "Would you or whoever may be present in court tomorrow be willing to present me and my credentials to the judge so that I could be admitted to represent Rick Rondeau? The head of the office told me he would be there in the morning and was more than willing to move for my admittance before the Judge. I had accomplished all I could and we parted with me having in my hands copies of the very limited public defender's office file since they had not yet entered their appearance and did not have the all-important prosecution discovery. We would meet again tomorrow in the courtroom.

After seeing the police report and meeting the public defender at his offices, I decided that I should next speak to my client before meeting with the DA assigned to the case. Since the jail was located close by, it was just a short walk. It made sense that I learn my client's side of the story before I met with whomever would be assigned to the case in the morning. I proceeded to enter the jail and show my credentials as a lawyer in Colorado and was admitted to visit with Rick without any problems. He knew I was coming and was eager to tell me what had happened. It turned out that Rick had decided to try and make some additional money outside of the job he had been working in a grocery store in Denver. He had flexible hours and had watched other people go down to the border such as El Paso, obtain marijuana at a good price and then sell it in the Denver area for a profit. He learned the name and phone number of the dealer in El Paso, called him and set up a date and time for a pickup and the amount of money to be paid. He had never done this before.

Rick decided to arm himself just in case. He borrowed a .38 caliber pistol from a friend and took it with him to Texas. When he arrived in El Paso on the agreed upon date, he found his way to the home of the dealer, parked, left his gun in the car and went to the door of a regular looking home at the address in the neighborhood. Rick rang the doorbell and a tough looking man answered, told him to wait, went back into the house and came back with what appeared to be the agreed amount of marijuana. Rick gave him the agreed money, took the marijuana and returned to his car. Once in his car, Rick placed the marijuana on a scale he had brought for that purpose and discovered that he had been shorted.

Without thinking about the consequences, Rick put the .38 into his back pocket and returned to the home. When the same man answered the ring and opened the door, Rick told him he had been shorted since he had checked on his scale. He said "I want the rest of the marijuana." The dealer immediately shouted at Rick, "Fuck you! Get the hell out of here or I will kill you!" and reached for what Rick believed to be a gun. Rick instinctively did the same. He beat him to the draw just as the dealer was drawing his gun. Rick reached shot the man in the chest, causing the dealer to fall in the entrance way of the home with his gun falling to the ground beside him. Rick ran away immediately and high tailed it out of El Paso only to be stopped and arrested by Sheriff's deputies just as he was leaving the city. Witnesses had seen his blue convertible sports car racing away from the scene since it was daylight. Rick was charged with first degree murder and possession of drugs, another felony same as it was in Colorado.

On the bright side, Rick did have a defense to the murder charge. It was also clear from the police report that Rick was the only witness to the shooting. Since the police had his gun, forensics would verify that he was the shooter of the fatal bullet. The dealer's weapon was found by his body and it was loaded, which certainly gave credibility to Rick's version of the events that had taken place. He had been arrested with the marijuana in his car and told the police at the time of the arrest that he shot the dealer in self-defense upon seeing him reach back and pull out his gun. He also admitted that he had purchased the marijuana from the dealer that was confiscated by the police at the time of his arrest. The money that Rick told the police he had paid was found in the pocket of the victim. In his confession, Rick had nailed himself to the drug purchase and sale charges. He now faced the result of a mixed bag of bad choices and only the hope for a reasonable solution.

My interview with Rick made clear what I had available to negotiate with the deputy DA assigned to the case. I would be seeking a lesser charge then murder due to the fact that Rick acted in self-defense. However, since he was undisputedly in possession of the drugs and had admitted to receiving them from the victim, *I could only hope that some accommodation would be made by the DAs* resulting from the gift of the elimination of the drug dealer. A trial of the case would place the jury in the position of knowing that Rick was armed and had shot a known drug dealer when he appeared at the dealer's home. There was no escaping the bad facts around the killing. Still, the gun having been dropped by the drug dealer gave us a strong basis for self-defense. The down side to that was that Rick had armed himself when he returned to the door to argue about the amount of marijuana he had received. This showed intent and anticipation of the worst. As in most cases, there were many problems to be faced and worked out.

I was pretty certain that Texas was just as tough on the drug charges as was Colorado at that time. This turned out to be true. However, when I met with the deputy DA who had been assigned to the case, we immediately hit it off when we discovered that we had both served in the Air Force and I had spent three years in Texas at the Amarillo Air Force base in a SAC Wing that was attached to the base with B-52 bombers. During the tour of duty, I had even visited El Paso and Juarez, Mexico across the border. I was able to relate to him how much I liked Texas and that I had served as an Air Police officer in Amarillo, AFB, where we also had to deal with drug problems. This connected us immediately as we began to try to unravel the pros and cons existing in the case and circled around each other's arguments as I was accustomed to doing in Denver on a daily basis. It was obvious that we were enjoying the give and take of the negotiations. I could see that a deal was in the making. I found myself on common ground with my adversary.

We soon agreed that we both needed to put together more information about what had happened, me with my client in a longer visit with him in jail before he would be brought before the Judge the next day for the bail hearing. The DA informed me that there would be a room available in court for me to speak with my client while he and I could work out the details of any agreement that may be reached. He too, needed to speak to his supervisor to see what he would be authorized to do. We parted amicably and, following his recommendation, I found a place to eat and stay overnight close by the courthouse and his office.

When we met the next day after the DA had completed his docket and I had visited once more with my client, I argued that Rick was clean of any record other than traffic tickets and worked in a grocery store. The El Paso DA's office had already checked my client's record and the Da confirmed that Rick was clean. I stressed that he had done a great favor to the El Paso community when he unwittingly shot the drug dealer. The deputy replied that with Rick having a gun," he created the problem." I responded that, "It was only because he had the gun that he was able to save own his life, allowing us to have this conversation about his gift to El Paso of the dead dealer. This has made everyone's' life better in El Paso." Our arguments went back and forth as we attempted to work out a fair and reasonable solution. I told him about the Dev Brock case where the Colorado DAs had decided to just send my client back to California and avoid the costs of a trial that could have been lost. I suggested that he was facing a similar problem since I had an excellent defense to the shooting and a candid and believable client. I told the DA that, "You face a serious risk of losing the murder case if we go to trial and will be left only with the drug deal. This will put an unnecessary egg on your office's face. My client did El Paso a big favor." We had put our positions on the table and, as happens in such talks, we were each considering the pluses and minuses of each side. Both of us recognized that the either side could win or lose on the issues raised. It actually made sense to reach a compromise deal.

The negotiations continued for quite a while. Most of the other cases had been worked out and there were just a few lawyers left in the courtroom as we continued to play out our cards and arguments. Finally, we reached a tentative agreement of a plea to manslaughter with the murder charge being dismissed but were stuck on the sale of drugs charge and probation or not. After going back and forth with different possibilities, we agreed that the deputy needed to speak with his boss and I needed to consult further with my client. It was the end of the day, so we agreed to meet again in the morning before the re- scheduled hearing on the bail that we had jointly agreed upon and entered before the Judge in the case. The siting Judge accepted our agreement to carry over the case to the next morning and the case was being continued accordingly. Both sides informed the Judge that we were trying to reach a final agreement on all issues in the case. This made the most sense since we wanted to make the best use of my time instead of flying back and forth from Denver to El Paso at more cost to my client's 'parents. There was also another issue we had been unable to agree upon. His office had a stern policy about bail and this was a murder case. I had not been able to move him on a lowering the bail. We shook hands and each of us left the courtroom. I immediately went to the jail to meet again with Rick.

My meeting with Rick provided an unexpected request on his part. He was not happy with the treatment he was receiving from the jailers as a young black man and was very concerned about serving time in Texas. He recognized that if the plea bargain was made and entered, that meant jail time in a Texas penitentiary. This was not a pleasing consequence for the young black man. What he did was to plead with me to somehow arrange an agreement that involved serving his time or probation in Colorado instead of Texas where, he believed, he would receive better treatment in jail and could see his parents and family members. He and I had discussed the alternatives when we had met earlier. Rick did not have a record which ordinarily gave him a decent chance at probation, except that this was also a drug case. I had seen such deals being made in cases where pleas would be entered in another state and probation served in Colorado. It was possible if both sides agreed, but nothing was certain. I was unable to provide Rick with any assurances as our conference ended. On that note, we parted knowing that we would find out what was possible in the morning. If we were unable to reach an agreement, I would be arguing to the court for a bond reduction in view of the self-defense evidence that existed which Rick's parents might be able to meet. This was a longshot at best from what the deputy told me about the Judge's leanings towards high bail bonds, particularly in drug cases.

The next morning, the deputy and I met before court commenced. We came together outside of the courtroom and he offered manslaughter and one count of felony drug sale. It looked to me that his office was concerned about losing the murder charge due to evidence of the drug dealer's weapon but wanted to keep the felony drug charge in place. I felt I had to concentrate my argument on my chances of winning the murder case and pointed out to him once again that my client was the only witness to what happened. If I was right, they would be facing a bad loss with or without the drug charge. We went back and forth for a few minutes and then the deputy said, "Okay, we are willing to take a misdemeanor possession of the drugs and probation for the manslaughter. His immediate response made me believe that his office had been prepared to accept a misdemeanor for the drug case all along. Otherwise, the DA would have had to speak with his superior once again. I then said, "We would agree if the probation is done in Colorado." He looked at me, shook his head and stuck out his hand which I grasped and shook. We had a deal. Obviously, this had been their fallback position coming in to the hearing that morning. I had already learned after countless of negotiations with the District Attorneys in Colorado that you do not make a deal until you know you have reached the bottom line with the other side. Our bottom line was probation Colorado. Their bottom line was the drug charge. This was how deals were made in Colorado and Texas.

As soon as the case was called up, the deputy introduced me once again to the Judge and informed the court of the terms of the agreed upon plea bargain, which I confirmed. Next, the new lesser charges were presented to Rick with me at his side and he entered pleas of guilty to manslaughter and the misdemeanor drug possession charges. The court accepted the pleas and the granting of probation in Colorado, which I had confirmed earlier by calling the Denver county probation department and learned who would be taking responsibility at the Colorado end of the deal. The court then ordered the bond to be dismissed. I shook hands with the DA and left the courtroom. The fact of the death of the drug dealer was an important disclosure to the court in the presentation of the agreed upon plea and dismissal of charges. It certainly did help our case some bad rubbish had been eliminated in El Paso. Both sides used this information in their support of the plea bargain to the Judge. The court readily accepted the deal and following my client's plea to the charges, authorized his release from jail and probation in Colorado in accordance with the terms of the plea bargain.

I found myself leaving El Paso with Rick in his vehicle in a semi-shocked state, having accomplished a final result much sooner than I had ever expected. In fact, the immediate return to Colorado was beyond my wildest imagination. It was like shooting a last second basket in a game that swished through the net as the time ran out. Rick was free and we were looking forward to leaving El Paso for Denver as soon as possible. The family was obviously thrilled with the unexpected result that he was free once again and returning home.

After Rick's release from the jail, we collected the keys to the convertible and paid for accumulated fees for towing and storage. We then got into the car, which was a convertible, and drove happily out of El Paso due north through Texas and New Mexico to Denver. As you can imagine, it was a welcome and enjoyable ride in decent weather back to Denver. Rick successfully completed his probation in far less than ten years and never had any criminal problems or arrests again in his life. I continued to represent his family of two brothers and a sister in various less serious traffic and domestic problems as the years went by. Rick would occasionally stop by my office to say "hello" as time passed and the case faded from memory.

What I learned in Rick's case was that you can never tell in advance how things will work out in a case because there are always things that are beyond your control. What you can control is how you act in the face of the problems and facts as they arise, particularly in dealing with the other side. Preparing for whatever the changes of circumstances or surprises is difficult and, in some cases, not possible. However, you can to some extent control how you get along with the prosecutors. You do not have to become friends, but the prosecutors must learn that you know and understand the facts and circumstances that are in play for both sides. This is essential to establishing a good and even trusting relationships in order to get results. The success in negotiations is dependent upon the acceptance by the other side about what you are suggesting and/or proposing is fair and workable. For this to work, everything comes into play; the facts and circumstances, your relationship with the DA, even if it is short; your take on the facts and circumstances and the manner in which you can use or diffuse them to cause the DA to agree to the negotiated plea bargain. This always means fast thinking on your feet and reacting well to the character and foibles of the DA as you come to know him and them. At the same time, you must use whatever charm or persuasive skills you have. To make things even more interesting, this is all accomplished on the run, often in quick discussions or agreed upon meetings. More often than not, you do not know the opposing counsel or had only an occasional contact. This makes for the need to decide on your approach quickly and decisively and to rely heavily on your immediate instincts in dealing with the lawyer on the other side. It happens in every case and the results rest on what you are able to accomplish during the short discussions that take place. It is all part of a lawyers' daily life.

I never considered plea bargaining to be a game of dare. Rather, it is an honest exchange of what you know the facts and provable evidence to be, good and bad, and likely outcome of the trial if everything is placed before the jury. It is vital that you know as much about your case as is possible, but you are necessarily dependent many times on what the other side has available that can be verified. This must be gauged, understood and countered in the negotiations. I have found that honesty always works best as you feel your way towards the solutions of the cases as they develop. It can be a satisfying process where you have to be ready to filter in any new facts as they are learned by both sides. Remember, police reports do not always contain all the facts. Certainly, I never knew from the report that Rick had shot a notorious drug dealer. However, my visit to the public defender's office brought this important information to my attention which I was able to use in making the deal. And so, it goes. Discovery of facts and information never stops.

There are always important facts that are revealed as the case unfolds that will sometimes go your way. More often than not, both the client and your normal investigation and review of the facts bring forth new, important and, on occasion, game changing information. However, one must always be careful accepting a client's statement of facts and remain open to what future discovery will reveal. The truth unfolds slowly, and sometimes, out of the blue, new and important facts come to life as the case progresses. You have to remain alert to these possibilities and respond accordingly. It is always an ever-changing scene when it comes to resolving and absorbing the facts in a case. Clients do not always tell the truth. It is one of the reasons they are in your office facing criminal charges. Stay alert and focused. Do not be afraid of raising different issues as you learn about the cases existing against your clients. You and the DA involved have a common goal, to serve your clients; you the paying client and he or she, the state or federal government. Each side must respect the commitment of the other side to his or her client and keep looking for information and possible solutions, if at all possible. Since the percentage of plea bargaining is so high across the board, it is well worth the time and efforts of the lawyers involved.

I learned that working out a case in Texas was pretty much the same as it was in Denver. In fact, this turned out to be the truth in all of the various states I ended up having cases. It always involved give and take, same as in Colorado, and flexibility during the negotiating process. Above all, whether you liked the person representing the state or not, you needed to find a way to get along in order to promote the best interests of your client. After all, he or she was facing criminal charges with the state and its resources lined up against him or her. It was your job as counsel to work things out as best you can. This all starts with getting along with the prosecuting attorney, whom ever he or she may be. That person held the keys, literally, to whether your client's future included jail time or not. These were the people who mattered to your client's future. Often, it helped if you had prior dealings with the DA, since it would provide a basic trust and understanding for any future negotiations. In any case, the object was to have fair and honest exchanges in the hope of working things out in the face of the criminal charges. Almost all of my court appearances in criminal cases involved meeting with the prosecutors with whom I had previously met on behalf of other clients. If it was for the first time, then a short feeling out process was necessary before getting down to the business at hand.; Negotiations, offers and counter offers were normal and sought after as lawyers met and mingled in court awaiting the calling of the docket or Motions hearings. We would be speaking to one another as cases were called to be heard by the court. A surprising amount of work in the case at hand and others was accomplished in the midst of the court hearings as counsel would sit, stand or meet outside the courtrooms. I always found myself looking forward to the docket calls since one never knew who you would meet or what cases you might be able to work out while waiting to be called in your case.

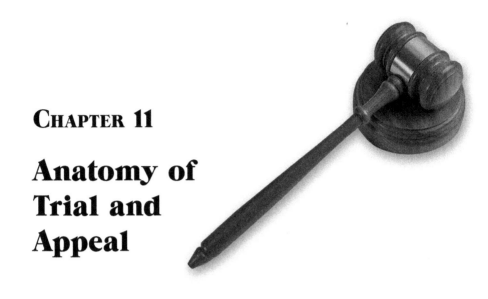

Chapter 11

Anatomy of Trial and Appeal

I was fortunate in not having many cases that required an appeal during my years in practice. In particular, this was true on the criminal side. As a criminal lawyer, most of my cases were resolved with a plea bargain. The remaining cases that went to trial were very much dependent upon making a sound judgement about how good the chances were of obtaining a not guilty verdict versus a conviction as result of the known facts and circumstances. This is the question that every trial lawyer is carrying around in his head in each of his cases as they unfold and come closer and closer to the trial date. My judgment was getting better as the years went by and I became smarter and wiser in convincing my clients that it would be better for them to avoid going to trial when the odds were stacked against them. As a result, I was rarely facing an appeal after the trial. However, sooner or later, appeals had to be made with differing results.

My first experience with an appeal was when my first boss asked me to take over and argue a case for his client that was set to be heard in the Supreme Court of Colorado just a few days after I had been admitted to practice. The decision was made immediately after I had learned that I passed the Colorado bar and was about to be admitted to practice. He came into my office with a file carton containing all the files and history of a contract dispute between his client, a moving and Storage Company, and the plaintiff company that hired their services. It was not a very complex case, and I was able to get a handle on the facts and legal authorities in dispute pretty quickly. I saw right away that our client's chances were not good. This may have been my bosses' reasoning in giving the case to his newly initiated and inexperienced associate. He ended up sitting with me at the Appellant's (The litigant filing the appeal) long desk in the Colorado Supreme Court as second chair while I made the opening argument to the Justices for our client. I was thrilled to be there and presented our case as well as I could on such short notice. During the hearing, while I was making my opening oral argument to the full panel of Justices on a factual point that was in our favor, the Chief Justice turned to my opposing counsel and questioned him about his side of that certain point that I was making. I will never forget the lawyer's answer to the Chief Justice as he stood to speak and said, "Why sure, your honor. It happened just as we have stated it in our pleadings." The lawyer was a plain old country boy who was very likeable and I knew instantly that we had lost the point and the appeal. My boss argued the rebuttal after the opposing counsel made his argument to the court, but to no avail. We did indeed lose the case. Yet, I had appeared and argued in the Supreme Court of Colorado as a fresh new lawyer. I left the courtroom thrilled that I had participated in the presentation on behalf of our client. But we were still the losers and, I concluded, my boss had anticipated it. That was why he had given to me what I considered to be a great opportunity to argue the case in the Colorado Supreme court with the client watching.

Soon after I had opened my own law practice, I signed on with the United States Court of Appeals for the 10th Circuit to represent indigent clients on their appeals. At this time, the public defender's offices for state or federal courts had not yet been started. I wanted to have more experience with appeals, particularly on the criminal side. To accomplish this, I learned that appointments of counsel were available and sought by the Federal Court of Appeals. I signed up on the list of lawyers willing to accept such cases free of charge. My wish was soon rewarded when I was appointed in a case on behalf of a woman who was convicted alongside her husband as a participant and the alleged lookout for her husband in a bank robbery in Oklahoma City. She and her husband were tried and convicted together in the Oklahoma Federal District court which was also in the 10th federal circuit that included Colorado. The two of them were represented by the same lawyer. This was something that I had seen happening in many cases in Colorado. It was an issue that had been receiving a fair amount of attention nationwide as defense lawyers and legal commentators were writing and talking about the inherent difficulties and conflict of interests involved in representing more than one person charged with the same criminal episode or case. Moreover, the issue raised in the case was that this constituted a violation of the 5th Amendment of the Constitution, the right to counsel.

I was excited to become involved in what I believed was a cutting edge of criminal constitutional law in America and immediately began to study the current decisions and cases that referred to this issue in various states and federal jurisdictions. There was a growing amount of legal material available to help me prepare my brief and the ultimate argument on appeal. I put together a brief that I thought was convincing and looked forward to appearing on behalf of my wife/defendant client before Justices of the Court of Appeals who were located at that time in Wichita, Kansas.

It turned out that the federal prosecutor assigned to the case, Dan Banner, was on the same plane to Wichita as I was. We did not realize this until we landed in Wichita and headed for a taxi to take us to the Federal courthouse for the scheduled argument before three Justices of the Court of Appeals assigned to hear our matter. We got along well and ended up returning together to Denver later the same day. In between, we watched and waited for two other cases to be argued before it was our turn to proceed. As I watched and heard the lawyers present their arguments, I became more and more excited to be soon standing before the three Justices and presenting my argument on behalf of my appointee client. These were the experiences that young lawyers go through in their initiation to the practice of law in our courts and it was exciting.

I went first since it was my appeal and delivered my arguments fully believing that I was correct that my client was entitled to a separate counsel under the circumstances of the case despite the limited law available in favor of my position. My argument consisted of pointing out to the Justices all of the many different times during the trial that my client was compromised and even harmed by her lawyer either looking out solely for her co-Defendant husband at her expense or failing to protect her separate rights and independent interests with objections during the trial. We all had available to us the stenographic record of the trial. I had described each of the conflicts of interest or failures to look out for my client's interest that had occurred in the brief I filed on her behalf with the Court. Sadly, all of this was done in the face of long established law and precedents in the 10th circuit and almost all of the other circuits in America that held contrary to my argument. There were a few cases in different federal jurisdictions and several state courts that pointed in the direction that I was asking the court to follow. However, those cases were in the clear minority. This was evidenced in the Justices' questions to me which indicated that they were not ready to strike new constitutional ground. As Dan Banner and I flew back to Denver after the argument, sitting together in the plane, we agreed that based on the questions that were put to us by the Justices, it was likely that the Court of Appeals would rule against me and that the only hope for my wife- client was to file a Writ of Certiorari with the US Supreme Court.

The Court of Appeals did rule against me and I soon found myself preparing the Writ of Certiorari seeking the US Supreme Court to hear the case. My brief for Certiorari consisted of the same arguments and cases that I had made in the Court of Appeals including a rebuttal to a couple of the cases mentioned by the Justices in the Court of Appeals opinion that they had written. I asserted my belief that the time had come for the courts to recognize the significance of a defendant's rights being violated when the lawyer represented more than one client at the same time in a criminal case. My argument included many of the instances that I had referred to in my brief which were contained and verified in the transcribed record of the trial. The Justices listened and raised a few questions but did not show much interest in my argument. All I could do was to hope and wait.

I had been writing to my client as she continued serving her time in the federal prison in Oklahoma City as the appeal was progressing and remained hopeful that if we were denied by the Court of Appeals, the United States Supreme Court would hear her case. In due course, we were indeed denied by the Court of Appeals and I immediately filed a Writ of Certiorari to the Supreme Court setting forth the arguments why my client was being denied her constitutional rights. I was petitioning the Supreme Court of the United States for relief less than two years out of law school. It was a thrilling prospect. However, in a few weeks' time, the bubble was burst. I received a Denial of Certiorari signed by our fabled Colorado Supreme Court Justice, Whizzer White, who had starred in football at the University of Colorado and had become an All-American. I was informed in a short one-page Order that the Supreme Court did not achieve the requisite four votes for the case to be heard. The issue of separate counsel for defendants such as mine had to wait for a few more years to become the law of America. I was definitely on the right side' but the time and momentum to change the law had not yet arrived

I hated to lose. However, not long afterwards, the courts did indeed recognize that a lawyer representing both the husband and wife in a criminal prosecution was indeed in a conflict of interest position which constituted a denial of the right to counsel per the 5th Amendment of our Constitution. It became accepted as a matter of law and practice that any defendants who are charged with commission of or participation in a crime or incident together with other defendants was entitled to separate counsel. It was a fight worth making and waiting for the change in law to occur. In constitutional law, this is often the case. It takes hundreds and even thousands of different cases and circumstances across the country to push the courts to new, changed and, hopefully, better understanding of the Constitution rights intended by our forefathers.

As a law student at Cornell University, I had listened in rapt attention to the previously referred to lawyer from Washington, DC, Edward Bennet Williams, when he spoke to a seminar class I had taken as a third-year student on Constitutional Criminal Procedure about the problems in a case he had taken from the first interview, trial and appeal to the US Supreme Court, hoping to bring about a change in the law of search and seizure. You never know when you can succeed in such ventures. In his case, it required the case to be tried, appealed and ultimately taken to the United States Supreme Court. At that time, it took the passage of almost two years. Edward Bennett Williams succeeded in causing a change in the Supreme Court's position when he successfully argued the case of United States vs. Katz. This case became an extension of the law of search and seizure at the time that he lectured to us at Cornell law school. The same thing happened when the Supreme Court decided a few years after I had argued the Oklahoma case in Wichita before the Court of Appeals

that all persons charged with a crime are constitutionally entitled to separate counsel representing them in the criminal proceedings. I was able to take pride in the fact that I had been part of the growing cadre of voices that called for this change to the constitutional interpretation of the 5th Amendment.

Our Constitution has weathered over two and one quarter centuries of changing circumstances, historical expansion, intellectual and constitutional battles, unexpected problems and legal tribulations. In large part, in America, we are both sustained and empowered to survive the legal turbulence engendered as a result of our long-standing belief and tradition of following the rule of law. This includes purposeful and thoughtful advocacy of what was intended by our founding fathers when the Constitution was promulgated. Not all interpretations or changes were good at the time they were made, such as the Dred Scott case favoring slavery, but as time passed, such monumental errors and glitches were resolved and will continue to be resolved in our legal process. My lifetime experience as a practicing lawyer has strengthened my belief that we live under a legal process that works so long as we remain vigilant and fight to the end the battles that come into our offices raising serious constitutional issues.

I believe the best approach to the legal and constitutional issues is one of pragmatism in determining what a fair and just decision is in any given circumstance. The time I have spent deliberating over what is the right solution to my clients' legal dilemmas in their cases was often the most important thing I did as a lawyer on their behalf. Invariably, the time spent was rewarded by the results obtained, including the final jury verdicts. As our forebears have done before us to the best of their ability, counsel must present and argue the best arguments possible under the unendingly changing facts and circumstances of each case. This makes me neither an originalist nor a believer in adjusting our law in accordance to the social and changing mores of our times, such as is loudly advocated today. Increasingly, this thought process has become the basis for the more liberal minded Justices now serving on our federal courts. I do not agree with their thinking.

The benchmark should be what is right, moral and appropriate and how it aligns with court precedents, not a designated political, ideological or economic structure or mandate. More recently, such thinking has led to changes in our constitutional law that are not tied to the basic precepts and understanding of our forefathers who created and interpreted our constitution. Under the Constitution, any newly created right would have been lawful and proper had it been considered and made into law by Congress and signed by our President. Instead, for example, the right to gay marriage is a fiction totally disconnected from the legal rights that had been created by Congress or the Constitution. It makes our Supreme Court a law maker over and above our legislative branch of government. This is not what our forefathers created in our three equal branches of government. Therefore, to my mind, it has become questionable law which will ultimately have to withstand the test of time and thought by our ancestors in the normal ebb and flow of history and changes in thinking that find their way into our constitutional law and judgments. This is what I hope for in many of the most recent Supreme Court pronouncements that have opened windows and rights never before imagined by our founders or the lawyers and scholars that followed. I will leave this issue at this point since this book is intended to deal with the practical problems and dilemmas faced by practicing lawyers' and not the ultimate pronouncements of our Supreme Court.

In my experience, what works best in accomplishing justice is that the result be fair and evident from what is known to the deciders of the given case facts. This is something that juries, randomly selected, are very good at. I believe that good ideas and well thought out law can always be argued successfully to the trier of facts. Unequivocally, my experience is that this applies best to juries. Appellate Judges are another matter completely. Sadly, they are now becoming prone to legislate their thinking to resolve legal problems instead of upholding existing law and leaving it to the legislative branch to determine new or different law in accordance with our Constitution. It remains an ongoing tension and battle that is played out in the states and federal courts each day.

I found myself having to appeal a verdict rendered against my client for arson when I thought that he was innocent and did not receive a fair trial due the rulings by the judge over the objections I had made during the trial. I believed that the court rulings seriously and erroneously affected the outcome of the case. This happened only one time in my career and I have written about this case in more detail in Chapter 13. Due to the highly unusual circumstances of the case, it took another twenty years to pass before I experienced another case equally difficult and exhausting which took practically the same amount of time and energy. I also believed in the second case, same as the first, that I represented an innocent client. One thing is certain. If a lawyer believes fully in his client's innocence, then trial is exponentially more difficult since you unavoidably feel personally compelled and responsible for the result of the trial. If the case ends with a guilty verdict, then it must be appealed.

I have spoken with many lawyers who have had varying degrees of success with cases on appeal. In large part, success is based on how well the legal issues raised during the trial were handled by the Judge or counsel as they occurred. This is a product of protecting the record in the trial as it is happening by the lawyers trying the case and, similarly, by the Judge, each with different motives. The lawyers must see to it that he or she has objected when he or she believes errors are being made by the court so that there is a record in the trial court for the appeal. The trial Judge has a similar motive to protect the record and to keep the trial record error free and protected for both sides. All of this is taking place instantaneously as witnesses are testifying, counsel and the court are speaking and arguing with one another and court orders are being simultaneously issued and or debated. There is no time for reflection or second guessing. As counsel, you immediately stand up and object and voice your concern about any legal impropriety or error that may be occurring as the case is unfolding. That is an integral part of trial work. The rub is that this is all occurring as the lawyers on each side are attempting to weave together and build his or her cases in the best light possible to win.

However, the goal of victory can also mean that, sometimes, the lawyer must refrain from voicing concern about error. This is largely the result of what you are feeling about your case as it is unfolding before the jury. If your instincts are telling you that you are winning, raising objectionable issues is not as important. It is more important that the flow of the trial not be interrupted. This is being decoded instantaneously by the trial lawyer each time an objectionable event occurs. You can decide to ignore errors being made and or go ahead and raise the objection. Believe me, the many instances and the decisions that trial counsel has to make during his days and time in court can often cause headaches as you drive home after a long day in court hoping to rest your mind so that you can be ready for the next day of trial. Such brain trauma is an integral part of a trial lawyer's life.

Another way to look at such developments during trial is to weigh the value of protecting the record with objections for appeal on the one hand if your instinct is that you are losing versus the simultaneous and important value of allowing for development without interruption of the story you are developing through the witnesses for the prosecution or defense. Are the objections and creation of a record more important than the development of the defense as it unfolds? Some lawyers view the creation of the record for appeal as both essential and necessary, no matter what. Other lawyers, myself included, believe that the object is victory, not appeal. We make our decisions accordingly. In between, are lawyers who are in the trial knowing that they will lose and simply have to make the best record possible for the inevitable appeal. This, of course, raises the issue of whether the correct decision was made to go to trial, except when there is no other choice. As I have previously written, I learned to be more careful about objections as I gained experience trying cases. I also noted that more experienced trial lawyers I faced, civil or criminal, would also let objectionable matters go without rising to the bait. Testimony would tend to flow without interruption as we came closer to the end and the trial or court decisions. This was an unspoken alliance between trial lawyers as they were seeking to reach the final decision to be made in the given case.

Not to be forgotten is that if you think that you are going to lose, it is best to find a way to resolve the case with a plea bargain. All one has to do is to speak up to opposing counsel in a civil case or the prosecutor during the next recess. As a result, in meetings with my clients before trial, I would explain that I would not always be objecting just because the question asked was objectionable. It was more a determination of what was happening in the courtroom as the testimony was unfolding and how things were going. I preferred to follow my gut as to whether an objection would stop the flow of the testimony that was going our way. This takes immediate processing and decision making on the spot that could not be planed or discussed beforehand. It was solely my decision and without the time to even think about it; just to react or not as the case may be. Often, a lawyer must decide and act or refrain from acting instantaneously. It is impossible to know ahead of time just how you will react when the objectionable questions occur. For the most part, clients would often tell me that they understood. However, only the final verdict would let us know if I had acted correctly.

As counsel, you always try to keep the plea bargain option on the table since people, your client or the witnesses, often change their stories or what they were expected to say while they are on the stand. Moreover, your own investigation often develops previously unknown facts or circumstances that change the picture in your case. A good case gets worse and conversely, a bad case gets better. The final outcome is always up in the air, but with the passage of time, most cases show where they are likely to end up. More often than not, you alone must decide on the way you will construct or reconstruct the defense. Clients cannot possibly grasp all the variables that occur during trial. Essentially, this becomes a process of accumulating the known facts that will be displayed before the jury and what is likely to be the probable outcome. These are always tough decisions that lawyers must make together with his clients, whenever possible. However, experience will teach you that it ultimately boils down to what you personally believe you can do with the facts in the case in trial as they unfold. This is where your innate ability to grasp and translate what is happening during the trial takes over and causes you to make the immediate and necessary decisions. Take the deal or go to trial? Keep trying the case or decide on a settlement? It becomes your call and the client will almost always follow your lead

My practice experience led me to try cases protecting the record only when the errors by the court or counsel were obvious and glaring. Instead, I preferred to remain focused on the presentation and cross-examination of the facts, evidence and the story that would win the case. This worked for me because I went to trial almost always when I thought I would win. It ended up happening over and over again. One grows in confidence with the decisions he or she makes over and over again in the cases that are tried. This is the consequence of a complete knowledge of the facts and issues of the case and belief in your own ability gained in court experience to convince the jury or trier of facts with your version of what took place. After all, trials are a recreation of the facts and circumstances of the events leading to the charges or complaint in the case. You win if you can convince the Judge or jury of your version of the events. The result was that I have had few cases that required an appeal. The object was to win. When you win, appeal is not necessary and if you kept the record clean of unnecessary objections, so much the better.

Another point comes to mind as you try to successfully turn the jury's thinking into your favor. This involves showing the jury why you are objecting. This is because if you try cases, you will learn very soon that juries are both interested spectators of the trial as it unfolds and forming opinions as they hear and experience the evidence from the witness stand. Objections often give you the opportunity to bolster your case by adding to the information that the jury will be attempting to unravel into its' verdicts. For example, if you stand up and say, "Objection your honor. Hearsay, "Most jurors may not understand exactly what that means. I soon found myself saying to the court, "Your honor, I object to counsel asking for evidence that comes from somebody else. Hearsay." or "Objection, I am unable to the cross examine what is not before the court." When the Judge grants your objection, the jury recognizes that opposing counsel has tried to pull something over their eyes. It is a teaching moment that helps your case. Another example often happens when the objection is, "Your honor. I object to the leading question." Again, some members of the jury may not understand. It is far better to object and flatly state the issue. "Your honor, I object to counsel putting words into this witness's mouth. He is leading the witness." Often, the judges are quick to say, "Granted. Rephrase the question." Or. "Do not lead the witness." Either way, the jury becomes better informed if they understand and hear your objection in detail. They will then knowingly look at the opposing counsel or the deputy DA who raised the question. It is all part of building your case and the story you are projecting. It also has the result of adding to your credibility when the judge rules in your favor.

The same goes for hundreds of other ways in which objectionable questions continue to occur as the trial goes on. The lawyer must decide on the fly to object or not, raise a fuss or let it pass. Then too, I often found myself standing to object, look at the jury, shrug and sit down. Their looks showed me that they understood. The points had been previously made and the witness's answers were likely to be tarnished. This is all part of the art of trying a case. You are an actor and director of the scene that is unfolding. However, as the questions and answers take place, an immediate response or not must be decided and/or acted upon, depending on what is taking place in the court at that time. To object or not to object is the question; to refrain from objecting or posturing is your decision to make over and over. It is always in your hands to use and mold as the trial unfolds. This is why we trial lawyers get very tired when we are trying cases. It is the mind and body together that are in constant use and abuse.

I almost always went to trial believing I would win. The more experienced I became, the more deeply I believed in my ability to win the cases I tried. In particular, I had learned that the more I was able to show that I believed in my clients' causes or the fact that there existed a reasonable doubt and portrayed these feelings to the juries, the more likely I was to win. The confidence I showed was an instrumental part of my success. Clearly, this mattered and it was not something I had to make up. It was a part of me and how I thought and operated. It was real. It also mattered to my clients who would be questioning me due to their fears and uncertainties. I learned to be positive with them in addition to myself. We were going to win! This was important because there are many cases and clients who are incapable of feeling positive since their life experiences were often negative. When I would tell them to keep their heads up and to even smile at the jurors, they would think I was crazy and were unable to comply. However, if they too could show confidence, this was a plus. In fact, most clients experienced difficulties and I ended up continuing to project my positive feelings and beliefs to the jury. There is no choice but to proceed and follow through with what you believe in the trial. It made me a lawyer who concentrated on winning and not giving much concern to establishing a record for appeal. This suited me fine and kept me out of the appellate courts for most of my years of practice of criminal law. I did indeed have an appeal now and then in both civil and criminal cases. Fortunately, they were rare and unnecessary, especially when the verdict was "Not Guilty."

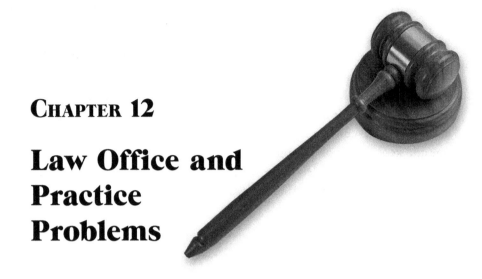

CHAPTER 12

Law Office and Practice Problems

A ny trial lawyer is dependent on the people he hires and how well they perform their assigned tasks on behalf of his clients. During my years of practice, I had two wonderful secretaries, one following the other. Each of them remained with me for many years; the first for close to fifteen years and the second for twelve. Both were great with clients, dependable, loyal and self-starters. As each of them grew in knowledge of my clients, practice and foibles, they often were able to predict my needs and those of my clients. This gave me a feeling of security about the phone contact, correspondence, legal pleadings and other necessary paperwork involved in the practice of law and, most importantly, the feelings and needs of my clients and their cases. I wish for all lawyers to have secretaries or assistants such as they were. After each one retired, I had great difficulty replacing her. As time passed with each of them being as capable as they were, they each adapted well to the changing forms, pleading requirements and procedural changes that kept occurring in addition to the unending repetition involved in doing and redoing the paperwork and pleadings necessary to litigate in both the criminal and civil sides of my law practice. Even more important, they both connected with my clients. They were in touch with the difficulties being experienced by the clients emotionally and legally. Each of them was able to help them work through the issues while also passing along information and developments in the cases as they occurred. This added tremendously to my being able to effectively communicate with my clients.

If you do not have such persons up front in your office, it should become your goal to do so. It is an integral and extremely important part of representing people with legal difficulties. There is only so much time in the day to take care of the needs of your clients in their cases, particularly if you find yourself under court deadlines, endless court appearances or in trial. Your secretaries and office staff are your only connection to the rest of your practice while you are tied up in trial or the existing deadlines, emergencies and regular court appearances that keep occurring. Knowing that your back is covered and your clients' needs are being taken care of is vital to any successful trial practice. On top of that and unavoidably, there exist the problems that you bring upon yourself that will most certainly take place as the years go by.

I had filed a civil case for damages against a local Police Department and three of the city police officers for the manner in which they handled a female client of mine when she was arrested for a DUI causing an accident. She was taken by the officers into custody and to the city jail. During the process of the arrest and transportation, she had been badly treated and physically harmed. In filing the case, I asked a young lawyer who was doing work for me to carefully review and double check the police report and investigative data we had available as to the identity of the officers and their participation in the alleged poor treatment of my client. This was a necessity before we filed the case. When she reported back to me, she said that she had reviewed all the information and affirmed that we had the correct three officers named in the complaint and they were each culpable. I signed off on the complaint and arranged for the case to be properly filed with the Clerk of the Court and served on the officers involved. I then waited for the expected Answers to the complaint to be filed.

I did not have to wait very long. As I was starting to read the Denver Post one morning about 2 weeks after the case had been filed, (Our Rules of Civil Procedure called for Answers to be filed within twenty days.) I noticed a headline on the second page that stated, "Wrong officer Accused of Assault!" I quickly read the article and saw my name prominently mentioned as the lawyer who had brought the complaint against the "wrong officer." The other two officers were mentioned but without any accusation of being wrongly accused. Here I was, exposed to the world as negligent and falsely accusing a police officer who had not participated in the alleged wrong doing. The article quoted the lawyer for the police officer saying that I had "willfully exposed his client to shame and public humiliation. "The article went on to say that all the officer had done was to arrive at the scene of the incident afterwards to aid in the investigation of the scene of the accident following my client's arrest and delivery to the city jail for lock up pending bail and drying out.

I proceeded to my office as quickly as I could and tried to put together in my mind what to do to straighten out the situation if the allegations against me in the Denver Post were correct. Along the way, I stopped to pick up the Rocky Mountain News and found the same accusations facing me prominently in that newspaper as well. This was getting worse by the minute. I was both worried and upset. What had my young associate done, if anything at all, to double check the facts and circumstances of the officers involved? I did not know the answer and it was not a fun ride.

At the office, I double checked the file. I found all the investigative work we had in the file and many other documents and papers, including my notes and a few made by my young assistant. The contents of the file left me in doubt as to the third officer, same as I felt when I assigned the problem to the young lawyer. My next step was to call and speak to the lawyer who represented the police officer involved. He proceeded to lecture me on my carelessness and on how badly this had affected his client to be so publicly humiliated. He was arguing his case against me as I listened and digested his venom and the steps he had taken by contacting the press and letting it all hang out. When I said to him, "Why didn't you call me and I would have straightened things out immediately?" His reply was, "Why didn't you call my client or the Police Union before you filed the case against him." This raised a good point but did not bring us any closer to solving the problem. I told the lawyer that I would get back to him once I had double checked on everything. The first step was to speak to my young associate who had just arrived in the office. It did not help when I learned that all she had done was to re-read everything in the file and speak to the client who could not remember the specifics of what had taken place or the names of the officers who were involved. This was a lawyer who ended up eventually being a County Judge in an outlying county in Colorado several years later. All she could do at that time was to apologize for not having more seriously double checked and investigated the actual facts and circumstances of the case. This too was no help to me at the time.

As I was working my way through the storm that had fallen on my head and also spoken with my client by phone, a plan was forming in my mind as to how to approach the problem of my own doing. My client understood and approved of the direction I had decided to take once I pointed out to her that things could be later changed and corrected if it turned out that the facts did in fact support the complaint raised by counsel for the officer in question. In other words, if the named police officer did actually participate in the physical harm my client had suffered, we could later amend the complaint based on the new information learned and bring him back into the case with the additional evidence that had been found. It would not be fatal if the officer was dismissed from the case at that time. It was not a matter of double jeopardy same as a criminal charge.

I then did the following: First, I wrote a letter of apology to the police officer through his attorney for the mistake that had apparently been made and included with the letter a Motion to Dismiss the Complaint and Order for signature by the court to dismiss him from the case that I had filed with the court. I sent a copy of the letter, Motion and Order to both the Denver Post and the Rocky Mountain News requesting that they place them into their newspapers in the next editions in order to publicly exonerate the police officer in question. I mailed copies of everything to opposing counsel, both newspapers and to my Client. The Motion to Dismiss and my letter stated that I was simultaneously filing the Motion, Order and correspondence that day with the Clerk of District Court in the case file. I then drove down to the courthouse and personally filed the pleadings in the Clerk's offices. Then, I waited for the results.

The results were beyond my expectations. Both the Denver Post and the Rocky Mountain News printed my letter and noted that I had filed the Motion to Dismiss and Order. Soon thereafter, as I would be walking through the corridors of the Denver courthouse or other counties, lawyers came up to me and praised me for what I had done. Several of them joked with me about how busy I must be to have let the problem develop. A few even figured that I had turned the tables on the police officer's lawyer who had raised the fuss by going to the papers. They agreed with me that the best thing he could have done would have been to contact me immediately to resolve the issue without any publicity. After all, we all knew and understood that there would have been far less publicity if the officer's counsel had simply called me. Effectively, I had squelched the issue before it had burst wide open and made our profession look worse than it really was. A couple of Judges took me aside and lauded my response as good publicity for lawyers. I was able to walk through the hallways of court with my head up and smile about the incident.

In the weeks that followed, I gave this incident a great deal of thought. I was learning that if you left yourself wide open, you could be hit very hard and publicly. One could not depend on lawyers being willing to call you and raise the issues before pouncing on you or in the press. As a younger lawyer, I had in fact experienced many lawyers being considerate and sometimes offering help and understanding even if they were opposing counsel. We were still a small community of trial lawyers in Denver at that time and knew each other by name and reputation. However, as I grew in time and experience, not every lawyer would rise to the occasion when his opposite lawyer had blundered. I had just met up with one of such lawyers. He and I did not know each other before the case had been filed. In fact, there were many more like him in our profession and I began to keep running into such lawyers as the number of lawyers grew in the Denver area. This brought me to the inevitable conclusion that I had to be more careful than ever before about bringing civil cases against defendants due the pain and discomfort that it can cause. This was especially true when it came to suing police officers since their public position could create immediate publicity. I not only had to be more careful, but as certain as I could be that the allegations that were to be made in my cases were true and correct. These were sobering thoughts. It also involved who I would be depending upon for the work to be correctly turned out. The young lawyer who let me down in her review and double checking as to which police officers were actually involved did not meet the standard of due diligence. Soon afterward, she left my offices for other pastures. Fortunately, and in large part due to this incident, I became better and wiser in the hiring of young attorneys to work for me.

There was another side to the issues that each of us who practices law in court must face. How to deal with the press? Far more back then than now, the newspapers covered what was happening in the courts regularly and in considerable detail. It was done in large cases and small and you never knew when you might have a case that would draw such attention in the press. Even in smaller and unexceptional cases, reporters would often turn out to obtain copy for their newspapers. It was not unusual for a reporter to speak to counsel after a court proceeding, preliminary hearing or jury verdict in a case. This also applied to civil cases that had a compelling story behind them or unusual facts. I found myself being talked to by reporters on numerous occasions. My cases were appearing in the newspapers more than I had ever anticipated. What I learned very quickly was to be careful about what I said when I spoke to the reporters in court or by phone about the facts and circumstances or what the judges had actually said or ruled. If you are stopped by a reporter or are called on the phone and agree to speak, you must understand that you need be careful and take the time to allow the reporters to both understand and correctly note what had taken place. It does not help your client to have things quoted incorrectly or somehow harmful to them. You have to be ready to spend whatever time it took to make sure your side was well presented. It is not pleasant to read incorrect and or unfavorable comments in the papers about your cases.

I was learning that not all news is good news. In future instances, I found myself taking time before I spoke to reporters, speaking slower and more carefully about what had taken place in court or had led to the court action that had been filed. In truth, you never knew when the newspaper or, in later years, radio or TV coverage would occur. It became a matter of understanding what was at stake and responding appropriately. We trial lawyers are used thinking on our feet. However, in such circumstances, the audience grows immeasurably larger and the reporter you are dealing with becomes very important as the conveyer of information and facts in your cases. It was one more problem that, as the lawyer in the case, I needed to learn to deal with on behalf of his clients.

The assault case cited by the newspaper articles, once it left the glare of the immediate newspaper coverage, ended with a reasonable settlement for the injuries and permanency involved. More often than not, such a case becomes a whimper without coverage or with only a line or two as the case proceeds to its legal conclusion. Cases like the police assault generally take quite a bit of time before a settlement or verdict is achieved, particularly where it was necessary to obtain the consent of a city council to the settlement that is achieved. In the meantime, the newspapers or other media lose interest as new incidents or news become more important.

The case itself was eventually settled and the lawyers on both sides, acting together, appeared before and had to convince the City Council to pay the amount of money agreed upon in the settlement to my client. This meant both opposing counsel and I were required to appear before the city council and argue that the facts of the case called for the proposed settlement and that the settlement amount was appropriate since the city was at risk that a jury verdict could cost the city even more money. Effectively, both sides were joined together in the task of convincing the City Council to do the right thing. This is another good reason for lawyers never to burn their bridges with opposing counsel. You never know when you end up having to work together to achieve the goals of your separate clients.

It should also be noted that as the years went by and the competition and rising costs of publishing newspapers increased, their coverage of cases decreased as radio and television became more prominent in reaching the public. Such coverage grew and prospered but was concentrated on the most thrilling and explosive cases. This left the more routine and regular cases alone since television coverage and time were limited to minutes and seconds. Actually, this was a relief for counsel and client and our judicial process, except when the sad and explosive cases were given the focus and time necessary to catch the imagination of the viewers. Lengthy or even thoughtful articles would appear after the cases had happened in magazine type journals and TV coverage. Although newspapers attempted to follow up by giving space to more facts, info and personal follow up data, I found myself talking to newspaper reporters far less in my last twenty years of practice and did not miss them at all. Justice continued to be accomplished in the courts same as before.

There is always a good reason to fight hard but to not, at the same time, destroy communication between the counsel involved in the cases. The need for good communication is ever present since cases have a way of turning in directions never before considered. I admit that I did not always have my eye on the ball of maintaining good communication as I fought and litigated with opposing counsel in both criminal and civil matters. I was easily angered, and it was a trait hard to shed. However, duty to clients, facts and the ever-changing scenario in the life of cases as they would unfold requires that counsel on both sides maintain open communication with each other. In fact, I learned as a young lawyer that often, opposing lawyers would refer clients to me. After all, who is in the best position to know what kind of a job you do for your client then the lawyer on the other side. As the years went by, lawyers became a great source of business and I, too, would refer clients to the lawyers who most impressed me with their work and abilities. You never know what the next day will bring. It is such equanimity and flexibility that is incumbent upon trial lawyers to maintain with one another through each case to the ultimate conclusion.

I began handling another very interesting case about this time. I was contacted by the parents of a man who had parachuted out of a private plane into the midst of a large gathering of bikers from many different states in an open area within the county. They informed me that after their son had landed on the ground and disrupted the bikers where he landed. Fighting and scuffling had occurred and a man was stabbed to death. Their son was being held as the chief suspect in the homicide. The parents had had little other information and once I was retained, I drove from Denver to the city jail in Colorado where it happened in in order to see my client. As I was speeding to the city where it happened, all kinds of scenarios were racing through my mind from a decided intention to find and kill someone to an argument and self-defense caused by being suddenly in the wrong place at the wrong time. When I arrived at the jail, close to the court house it was too late to attempt to meet with someone in the DA's office. I proceeded to visit my client in jail.

Roger Winters turned out to be an ordinary young guy who loved motorcycles, cussing, drinking and chasing women. He was a drifter, having traveled to and through many parts of the United States. He held jobs only long enough to accumulate enough money to get away and ride around the country some more. His only purpose in hiring the plane to parachute from was to make as big a splash as possible when he landed in the middle of the biker convention. Well, he certainly accomplished his goal. But his exuberance backfired in his face with all eyes having turned on him as he floated down and landed in the middle of a group of bikers out of California. They were upset with his unexpected interruption of their enjoyment with his parachute, accompanying paraphernalia and Roger himself. He was greeted by jeers, slurs, serious swearing, personal threats and physical pushing and shoving as he and they tried to disentangle themselves from his parachute equipment. Several men started attacking and hitting him and it got worse when he did the same back at them. He was bloodied and injured in the melee that took place. The entire area became crowded with shouting and boisterous bikers attacking and arguing with each other.

From what Roger told me, someone in the midst of the crowd was killed. He said that, "when the police arrested me they kept asking why I had knifed the dead man." He said that he told the cops," I did not know the man and I did not have a knife on me. I did have a .38 revolver, which the cops took away from me. I want that back." He went on to say that he had been told by the cops that "many of the bikers identified him as the killer". He said, "To the best of my recollection, I did not see the victim or was even close to him when he had been stabbed." He believed that the blood located on his person was his own or somebody else's with whom he fought, and there were several such guys. Roger spoke to me very excitedly and clearly wanted out of the jail. This was not why he parachuted into the crowd. I believed him. How do you make such things up? However, I could see that it was going to take time to unravel this mess and told him so.

The next day, I had a long talk on the phone with the deputy DA assigned to the case, Henry (Hank) Bancroft. He confirmed that many witnesses had seen Roger land among them and soon thereafter thought he may have fought with the deceased. None so far had seen a knife during or after the slaying, but two or three remembered Roger to be in the immediate vicinity after the body had been discovered. The DA's office was awaiting the test results for the blood on the deceased and any finger prints on his clothes, watch, belt and shoes and those of my client. At that time, no bloodied knife had been found. Roger was the only suspect while the police were continuing to investigate the victim's record and background for any additional leads. The victim had a reputation among the California bikers of being a tough dude according to the detective I spoke with once I was on the case. A couple of the bikers said that my client had enemies among those who had attended the convention. Also, the deceased was a large man, definitely bigger than my client who, nevertheless, was a muscular and strong guy. It was a mixture of some good news and bad. There was work to be done by both sides. We ended our conversation and agreed to speak further when we appeared in court for the initial hearing, advisement and bail hearing.

I started my own investigation with an ex- cop, Keith Lambert, who had been a Detective for many years before he retired. He was a devoted biker and knew a lot of people who had attended the bikers' convention. While Keith had not been there, he had heard about the biker killing that had occurred and agreed to look around and speak with people he knew and find out whatever he could. I had established a relationship with Keith after being introduced to him by a lawyer friend of mine who was working at that time as a deputy DA. He said to me that, "Keith was one of the best cops on the Denver force." My friend had worked with Keith in several cases and was impressed with his hard work and dedication. I knew that he had a good idea as to Keith's abilities and trusted his judgement. Once Keith retired and opened his own investigation agency, I became one of his clients with great results for my clients over many years to come.

I highly recommend to any would be trial lawyers that they hook up with people with similar skills as Keith had to work on the investigations or defenses for their clients in criminal or civil matters. As a lawyer's workload increases, he cannot possibly do all the investigations himself as I did for many years as my practice was growing. Moreover, the skills and experience and contacts of former police detectives, including their instincts developed over their years on the police forces are invaluable. As the years went by, Keith became a valuable aide in arriving at the truth in so many cases. In fact, in one case where my client was the owner of a warehouse where stolen goods were found, Keith's investigation discovered that the true culprits were the owners of a warehouse next door to the warehouse owned by my client. He learned that they would stash stolen goods in the warehouses next door and, on occasion, in my client's warehouse. It turned out that the nefarious neighbors and their cohorts were able to easily open and use my client's warehouse for additional storage of their stolen goods. My client lived in California and depended on a paid overseer who ended up being a part of the criminal enterprise next door. Essentially, Keith ended up solving the crime and pointing the police in the right direction which led to the solving of many additional crimes and thefts in and around that commercial area. This is the kind of investigator all attorneys need to have available to aid their clients.

Once Keith's investigation was completed, I was able to present the District Attorneys' office with a detailed summary of how and who were the true culprits which completely exonerated my happy California warehouse owner. He later sold the warehouse after figuring that it was not in his best interest to own and run the warehouse in Colorado as an absentee owner.

I went ahead and appeared in court on behalf of Roger Winter for the entry of appearance and plea of Not Guilty and setting the case for a preliminary hearing for determination of probable cause of the murder. I had little success in having the bail lowered but did argue to the court about the improbability of my client parachuting openly into a Greeley biker convention with a motive and intent to kill someone in a public gathering. The Judge acknowledged my line of thinking but was not persuaded to lower the bond. Sadly, Roger remained in jail as the case progressed.

One or two days later, my move to hire Keith paid off. He found a person who had seen my client land his parachute and become involved in the yelling, shouting and fighting that took place as my client tried to get his parachute, himself and his things untangled from the parachute. Soon thereafter, the witness heard shouting from the other side of him about ten yards away that he later learned was where the knife killing of the victim had occurred. He did not see it happening, but did see the person lying on the ground, apparently dead. When the witness turned the other way, he saw my client walking in his direction at least five yards away. He was carrying his parachute and paraphernalia wearing a black jacket with blood visible on his face and white T-shirt beneath. He did not look like a person running away from a crime scene. On the contrary, my client was headed towards where the body lay. It never occurred to the witness that my client could have been in both places at the same time since he himself was in the middle between the two events which clearly were not related. I went to see the witness at his job located halfway from Greeley and Denver. He confirmed all that he had told to Keith. This was all good and I was soon on the phone with the Greeley deputy telling him about my witness and how he could be reached.

Nothing happened. When I called the deputy again a few days later, I was told that they were "investigating" and that he would get back to me. There was nothing to do but to inform the family and my client and to prepare for the now vitally important preliminary hearing where the judge would decide whether or not there was probable cause that my client had committed the murder. I had a good feeling about our position. However, I had already learned over the years of going through preliminary hearings, that it was very rare for a judge to decide that a District Attorney's office failed to show probable cause. For the most part, preliminary hearings were good for the defense to learn as much as they could from the prosecution witnesses who were called through cross examination. Still, it was rare that the prosecutors exposed their best witnesses and, certainly not all eyewitnesses. More often, they put the police officers or a detective on the stand who would testify to heresy evidence, (what other people said or saw) that they had received from witnesses or even heresy upon heresy by witnesses who heard things from other people. This is even more difficult to attack and cross-examine, but the courts permit the use of such evidence for determining probable cause. Moreover, such limited testimony almost always led to the finding of probable cause and court orders to go forward to trial.

In my entire career, I can only remember a few times that I was able to accomplish a dismissal of a case in a preliminary hearing. In fact, the last time it happened and the only time in the twenty first century for me was when a Judge found insufficient probable cause to go forward in a kidnapping case. As the very good and capable deputy DA and I were walking out of the courtroom, she turned to me and said, "You know, Mike, in eighteen years as a DA, this has never happened to me. I am in a state of shock." I tried to comfort her by saying that it had only happened a few times for me and "I certainly did not expect it here today." She has gone on to become one of our very best Denver District Court Judges.

The minimally low probability of dismissal of a case in the preliminary hearing very much affects the strategy of both the prosecution and the defense in the use of the witnesses. Since hearsay use is rampant, prosecutors limit the testimony of their witnesses to a minimum to cover the basic elements of the crimes charged. This leaves the defense to try to gain as much as they can from each witness even though much of what they are receiving is hearsay and unreliable evidence with limited hard evidence. Still seeing and hearing what is revealed can be positive as more of the facts become known. As for calling witnesses to present opposite views or evidence, defense lawyers rarely even try, except where they feel that some benefit could be gained later in the case in support of motions or defenses to be filed or raised. For the defendant to testify is almost nonexistent. Even if I were to call the witness who confirmed that he was in the middle of the action to testify, since he did not see the knifing itself, this was unlikely to be enough for the Judge to decide that the prosecution had less evidence then necessary to meet the low bar for finding that probable cause existed. There was little to be gained from exposing the witness to cross examination, while at the same time I would still be unable able to cross-examine the prosecution's chief witnesses. These were the back and forth considerations that normally led to withholding our cards at a preliminary hearing.

I went about preparing for the hearing and did serve a subpoena on the witness who was nearby to the crime scene and waited for the date of the preliminary hearing. The final decision to use that witness or not would be made at the hearing itself. Upon receiving the prosecution discovery, I saw that they did have what they considered to be two eye witnesses. However, when Keith interviewed them, it became apparent that their views of the crime scene were flawed in different ways. One was way off on his description of my client while the other placed my client near to the murdered man but without his parachute or noticing that he was himself bloodied by the events that followed his landing. Most likely, he had seen a suspicious person who was not my client. In fact, both sides were continuing their investigations. It was hard to tell just exactly what lay ahead. Keith continued to seek more witnesses and the DA's office was doing the same. Would either side turn up more evidence? It was now thirty days after the homicide and nothing was certain. I really had no idea what to expect.

As no doubt readers have come to expect in the development of cases, the unexpected happened. No sooner had I arrived in Greeley, entered the courtroom and the deputy saw me, he motioned to me and took me outside the courtroom and into the corridor. He then told me that his office was split on whether to proceed with the case or not and that the DA himself had decided that the best course of action would be to vacate the hearing at that time and allow my client to go free while his office continued to investigate. In this way, there was no prejudice to the state or my client. My opposing counsel admitted that he was himself uncertain if they had the right man and favored the dismissal at the time. There were too many questions that needed answering. We shook hands and returned to the courtroom where the deputy proceeded to tell the Judge that his office wished to drop the current charges and continue its investigation of the murder. I walked out of the courtroom happily to await the release of my client together with his parents.

To my knowledge, the crime was never solved and Roger never again parachuted into a biker convention or anyplace else. Once more, I was struck by the reality of criminal charges sometimes being shaky and subject to further information and facts that may develop one way or another. It was not unusual for prosecutors to change their minds and, to their credit, withdraw cases against wrongly accused defendants. This is an imperfect business requiring both sides to keep working to ensure that justice is done. I found myself proud of my profession as I walked out of the courthouse after another correct result.

There were unexpected consequences from the dismissal of this case. I had received a great amount of publicity in Greeley and Denver among bikers. I found myself being asked by many bikers to become their lawyer in cases ranging from DUIs to assaults, robbery and drug offenses. I had developed a reputation in the biker community and soon, had many such clients. As the cases mounted, instead of being pleased, I began to feel uneasy. I was meeting and dealing with men who were often dealing in drugs in addition to the charges against them. Many had criminal records and staunch views against cops, courts and our system of justice. The persons I was representing at that time considered themselves to be outside the law and society to a large degree. They were tough, belligerent, foul mouthed and often lacking in the normal courtesies of life. I was continuing to receive quite a few calls seeking my services. My secretary was complaining and I was unhappy with what was taking place. As cases were going through the normal process and in various stages, I found myself in the company of people who lacked respect for the law and our system of justice. For the first time in my practice, I did not like or look forward to representing such clients. My heart was not in it. This is a dilemma that we all face sooner or later and I was facing it big time. What to do?

Dean Thoron at Cornell had discussed this very issue in classes at Cornell and told us that when it occurs, "Each lawyer must decide for himself what he is to do. It is an absolute that every person is entitled to a defense and counsel, no matter the charge or the circumstances or how odious the client may be. However, in the end, it is a lawyer's personal make up and choice as to whom he will represent." I had been saying this to myself and believed it thoroughly in my years of practice up to that time. However, I had never had the personal and direct bad feelings toward a client or clients, let alone several at the same time, as was now taking place.

It was clear that I needed to take stock of the situation and figure out how it should be resolved. The answer lay in how far each case had gone. A couple were close to resolution with plea bargains and the remaining ones all had strong evidence existing against the clients which had to be faced, making trials unlikely. I could deal with these circumstances and get through them with my current clients. As for future similar cases, I simply decided to say, "No. I am too busy to take on another case. I am sorry." Having said that a few times afterwards to prospective new biker business, the referrals stopped and it was a long time before I represented another biker. In fact, I took this position to another level when I also decided that I would no longer represent people who were charged with drug dealing or selling except for the end users caught in the terrible nightmare of addiction. Such persons, I continued to help and represent in the hope that they could break out of the terrible cages they had put themselves in. Thankfully, some did and this was worth the time and effort spent.

Often, I would convince the client to seek professional help which would often accomplish the best results in court when we appeared. In such cases, I was able to inform the court about the steps that were being taken by my client. Moreover, in Colorado, special drug court proceedings were established where clients could help themselves by attending drug rehabilitation classes and participating in trying to lick the drug addictions to which they had become prey. It worked in some cases, but not all. I must state that since I turned down the biker's years ago, I have met and represented many bikers with a much better opinion of law enforcement who were just as enthusiastic about riding as were my previous clients. Times have indeed changed.

Dean Thoron was right. Each lawyer must decide for herself or himself who he or she will represent or not. It is always a tough decision, particularly with the money that could be made in fees. One can easily forget that what might be financially lucrative can at the same time take his or her practice to a level that affects ones' ability to sleep well at night. Making the right decisions about whom to represent and where to draw the line is very important for each of us who practices in the criminal defense field. These are very personal decisions which need to be faced and decided upon. They include not only the types of cases and people involved, but one's own ability to deal with the raw and disturbing reality of the people and the crimes being committed by them who seek your legal help. It is a personal choice about where to draw the line. A lawyer can act ethically in the middle of the horror of what his clients have done and, more often than not, continue to do so while they are out on bail awaiting trial. However, the proximity to the unforgivable acts, the actors themselves and the stink of the crimes is more than many of us can tolerate. I have lived this dilemma. I started to draw the lines after about 10 years of practice. I have never regretted or looked back on the choices I made not to handle certain cases. Each of us must face what we see and what we can personally deal with in arriving at our decisions. There is no escape. It goes with the territory.

CHAPTER 13

Burned by Arson

T he most difficult case I tried during my first twenty years of practice was an arson case. It was tough on several fronts. My client was a man in his thirties with a wife, children, home and mortgage. He and his wife were separated and she had left him with the home and had taken their children out of state, I believe to Kansas, where her family was located. He was doing the best he could to handle all the accumulated obligations, child support and alimony while working in the construction business on a crew that was responsible for a job located about twenty-five to thirty minutes away from the home depending on traffic. A fire occurred in his home that was first seen and reported by the next-door neighbor who was the mother of three children. She reported that she saw the fire at approximately twelve thirty and remembered that she had seen her neighbor, my client, leave the home about one half hour before she noticed the fire. She was confident of the time because she always watched Sesame Street on the TV with her children and it had just ended at noon when she saw my client leave the home.

It turned out that right around noon time, my client was in a lunch break at work on a construction site together with three of his co-workers, all of whom remembered him to be at work and with them and at lunch at the same time and date that the neighbor claimed she saw him leaving his home. The home and construction cite were miles apart. He could not have been at both places at the same time. By the time the fire department trucks arrived, the home was significantly burned and ended up a shell of what had once stood as his residence. The home was insured, but any monies to be obtained were clearly dependent upon what could be worked out with the insurance carrier as they investigated the cause of the fire. It was evident from the beginning that this would be a very difficult case, and so it was.

My client, Dan Unger, was soon charged with Arson and destruction of his property for insurance purposes. The District Attorney's office attributed to Dan the motive of cashing in on the home owner's insurance in order to pay off all of his bills and marital obligations so that he could get out from under the huge pile of financial problems arising from his deteriorating marital situation. It was claimed that the fire department investigation showed that the fire had been set manually by someone based upon evidence that they had accumulated after the fire was put down by the fireman. The report certainly supported the theory that indeed the fire had occurred in the manner that was indicated. However, as the case proceeded and after the preliminary hearing and a finding by the judge of probable cause that my client had started the fire, there was a surprising development. My opposing counsel and deputy DA, Richard Sanders, informed me that the fire department had lost the evidence that had been accumulated in support of the findings of the investigation of the Arson. As a result, Rick Sanders advised me that he was not able to provide the discovery materials that previously existed. This explained the unusual delay by the DA's office in providing me with all of the prosecution discovery materials and information, most important of which were the actual reports and physical evidence and findings by the fire Department arson experts. We had battled about this delay at the time of the preliminary hearing, but the Judge decided, based upon the proffer (A statement by counsel of the evidence that would have been offered by the firemen and experts who attended the fire) that he was still able to make a determination of probable cause. The DA, Richard Sanders, argued that heresy evidence was sufficient in a preliminary hearing to find probable cause. The Judge agreed since this was the basic law in Colorado. This was a setback, but I was not particularly concerned because, as previously noted, the prosecution rarely reveals more evidence than necessary for a case to be bound over for trial. So, this was nothing new. However, the DA's notification of the loss of evidence gave the case a new direction and a fistful of issues I had never before encountered and, most likely, neither had the DA.

The trial date was fast approaching. I decided that what had to be done was to file a Motion to Dismiss all the charges based upon the fact that the District Attorney's office had since acknowledged that the fire department had, in fact, lost all of the evidence that had been accumulated after the fire was investigated. They were unable to find any of the actual accumulated evidence of the fire upon which they had intended to prosecute the case. Effectively, my Motion argued that the case cannot be proven without back-up and real evidence of arson. If you lose the gun in a shooting and the bullets, you cannot connect the act of shooting with the results. It was the same for setting fire to a home. Without the evidence supporting the conclusion of fire being set by a person instead of instantaneous combustion, then the case must fall of its own weight. In this case, I argued that, "the state of Colorado is unable to prove the case beyond a reasonable doubt due to the missing evidence. The state has the burden of proof and we are entitled to a hearing on this issue before the trial date since the state has admitted that it is without the evidence to support a finding of guilty." The judge agreed to set the matter for hearing on my Motion for dismissal but surprised us by deciding that this would be done immediately preceding the date of the trial. He proceeded to set the date of the hearing to be on Friday before the week in which the trial had been previously set. My argument was that this would effectively force both sides to go through the same evidence and arguments twice, in the motion hearing immediately before the trial and, then again, during the trial. This would cause both sides to have to spend additional time and hours in preparation for both the hearing and the trial unnecessarily. My argument fell on deaf ears and the motion hearing was docketed to occur on Friday immediately before the trial was to commence the following week.

My client had been able to pay a bail bondsman so that he could be released from jail and was free to keep working and attempting to keep up with his mounting bills and attorney fees. However, he soon fell behind in payments, and as often happened in such cases, my fees and costs were soon behind and getting more so as the case progressed. To his credit, Dan would occasionally bring a small amount of money and apologize for his inability to keep up. This was far better than most clients facing the same problems, but I was not about to give up on the fight to win or have the case dismissed. The fact that we had eye witness co-workers ready to swear that Dan was at work meant that there was a full-fledged defense regardless of what the next-door neighbor was saying she saw. This was not a case I could walk away from. Plus, I had grown to like Dan, who had been raised on a farm and had agreed to do some work on my property rebuilding fences and other repairs that I had been putting off. In this way, I was able to credit him against the fees for work that he accomplished at the going rate. My daughters, who were teenagers at the time and my wife came to know and like Dan as we grew familiar with him while working on our property and saw that he was a man of his word. I had never done this with client, particularly in criminal cases, but it worked with Dan and he did reduce his debt to me as the expenses continued to grow. On the down side was the fact that my wife and daughters liked and enjoyed Dan, which made winning the case all the more important and personal.

The deputy DA was a man I had met and dealt with on several occasions in other cases. Richard Sanders was young, brash and spoke his mind without any censorship. We all called him "Rick." He was blunt, direct and sarcastic with counsel and the court. Things could be said in better ways and tones, but his fellow prosecutors, defense counsel and the Judges were accepting of his direct and, sometimes, outrageous comments. You could hear him ranting during huddled conferences with other defense lawyers who would give it back to him in the same manner while the rest of us would wait for our turns to work out our cases with him and other DAs during docket calls. I found myself looking forward to exchanging insults with Rick. He had a thick skin and so did I. Still, he always surprised me with how far he would go with his insults and arguments. Nevertheless, in my previous cases, we would invariably arrive at the correct disposition and I would leave court having enjoyed the pushing and shoving. Rick was smart, funny and quick to decide on the State's position in cases. However, he adamantly would not agree to a dismissal in the Arson case. He took the position that he would prove the arson by my client with the testimony of the firemen and experts with whom he would put together their recollections and findings without the actual lost evidence. I responded, "You cannot do that without the evidence. Each of your witnesses would be without the back-up proof of the evidence they were talking about. You are going to lose." I also assumed that the Judge would ultimately decide that without the lost evidence to bolster and confirm the state witnesses' testimony, the court would be forced to dismiss the case. I was wrong on both counts.

When the hearing on my Motion to Dismiss began with both sides ready to go to trial immediately after the weekend, it was my burden to show to the court that without the incriminating evidence the state could not prove their case. I called as my witnesses, the fireman deputy in charge of the evidence room and one of the firemen who attended the fire. I also called to testify the fireman investigator who had responded to the home location at the time of the fire and collected the evidence to support the theory of arson. As each of them testified, it became clear from their testimony that it was indeed based on the evidence that had been seen by the attending firemen and obtained from the remains of the fire on the home and property which was subsequently stored. This was the normal procedure for the purposes of being retained and saved for trial, if necessary. No one knew how or why the evidence had been lost. They grudgingly admitted that the lost arson evidence was intended to be preserved as back up exhibits in support of their testimony if there was a trial. They refused to admit that the case could not be substantiated without the evidence. Each witness, having been well prepared by Rick Sanders, testified from memory exactly what the lost evidence looked like as if it were still available. Deputy Sanders also kept referring to the witness next door, the mother of the three children who identified my client to be leaving the home one-half hour before the fire had been noticed. Sanders argued that the, "the jury would hear more than the evidence necessary to support a finding of guilty from each of the state's witnesses even without the specific evidence which was lost. It became apparent that the position of the District Attorney's office was that even without the lost fire remains and evidence, they were confident that a case of arson could be proven to a jury together with all of the witnesses. He certainly believed that he was entitled to go ahead with the trial.

My argument was, "that a fire without the residue collected by the investigators and firemen was not arson. Arson was the basis for any charges against my client. This is simply a fire without proof or evidence of any crime that may have been committed. Why else would the firemen and investigators accumulate and save the evidence that has since been lost except to verify and show the residue to a jury of the fire consisting of what remained. What is the point of keeping and accumulating evidence except to support the finding of "Guilty' that they sought? Without the evidence, the jury would have to rely solely on witnesses who had not actually seen the fire or the accumulated residue until they arrived at the scene." I submitted to the court that they were likely to be coached and filled with observations that they had never actually acquired when they were present at the scene of the fire and were attempting to put it out, which was their job. As for the experts, it is fundamental that when they testify, they are always asked to identify the real hard evidence that supports their conclusions to the jury. In this case, I argued that, "There is none of that evidence other than the alleged observations of the firemen attending the fire which is a different matter from investigating the fire. Finally, Mr. Sanders does not take into account that the defense has been denied seeing, feeling and actually examining the real evidence of the residue showing the nature of the fire in support of the state's' charges. We have been blocked and denied the ability to put together a defense. This case must be dismissed."

Rick Sanders argued vehemently that his witnesses were actually saying and demonstrating how the fire took place and what the normal and correct conclusions were from what was seen by them and their experts. In addition to that, he argued that he had been able to present sufficient evidence from the next-door neighbor which, "Standing alone shows that my client had been present at the time that the fire had most likely been started due to her recollections of when she viewed him to be at the home at 12 noon." We argued all of these issues long and hard after the state testimony unfolded before the Judge that Friday afternoon. My position was that to proceed to trial placed an impossible burden on the defense since we had never had the opportunity to properly view, test or examine any residue or other evidence or to obtain even our own expert review of the evidence that had been accumulated and lost. An opposing expert was both normal, fair and to be expected in such a case. Yet, we were being denied since it no longer existed. This argument did give the Judge reason to pause since it was common to have defense experts view the scene of crimes and provide counter arguments to the prosecution expert witnesses. I explained to the court that "We would have no such examination. "What were we supposed to do in response to their expert's opinions without being able to review and test the back up evidence? Paper alone was not enough," I said. I could see that the Judge was concerned.

I also argued that, "even if it were true that my client had been present in the home before the fire started, this did not preclude someone else from coming to the home and causing the arson after my client had left and before he had returned to the home. Also, we must not forget that we have three eye witnesses at his job who swear to him being at work and at lunch with them at the same time."

Rick Sanders forcibly argued that he could demonstrate my client's guilt even if he were limited to the memories of the firemen and fire expert witnesses who could put all of the assorted information and recollections into more than enough proof of guilt beyond a reasonable doubt that arson had occurred. He also repeated over and over that the court must remember that he had an eye witness that my client had left his home right around the time the fire had been started. He would say over and over, "Judge. Do not forget. We have an eye witness, his neighbor next door, who saw him leave his home just before the fire started."

At the conclusion of the prosecution evidence and the arguments, pro and con, on my Motion to Dismiss the case, the Judge adjourned and took some time to consider his ruling as we waited outside of chambers. Finally, the Judge informed us that he was ready to rule and we returned to his chambers. His decision was to deny my Motion to Dismiss because he found that there was sufficient evidence presented by the prosecution to satisfy the test of probable cause required in a preliminary hearing. At the same time, he entered orders that the prosecution was not to be allowed to refer to the lost evidence in support of their case during the trial. I was very disappointed with the court ruling, but I felt that the case could still be won with the prohibitions put in place by the Court. The case was adjourned to start the trial Monday. Both sides left with a weekend to continue to prepare and sort out how the prosecution would present the case and how I would counter with our defense and use of objections in the event the prosecution crossed the line set by the Judge regarding reference by witnesses to the lost evidence prohibited by the court; I thought that we still had hope for a fair trial and that the prosecution case would die a natural death despite losing the Motion to Dismiss.

The jury was a typical one for that time in Arapahoe County consisting of white collar workers, male and female, farm, ranch dwellers and retired people. Once the jury was selected and the prosecution witnesses began to testify, I began to see what the deputy DA had in mind. Each fireman witness who attended the scene of the fire was asked to describe what he saw at the scene including the debris and burnt remnants of the fire. Each of them was allowed by the court to describe and identify everything that they saw, both in color and texture to the jury. It was as if each of them had become an expert in viewing and describing the nonexistent evidence. I found myself objecting over and over again that the witnesses were providing hearsay testimony beyond the scope of their ability and capacities and which was, in fact, written in the textual reports they had ultimately been provided but not available at the time of the trial. I argued to the court that "the witnesses had been prepared beyond their true knowledge and understanding at the actual scene of the fire since it was their job to fight the fire, not examine it. Moreover, the evidence itself does not exist and cannot be personally examined, inspected or cross-examined as it was being stated by the witnesses in their testimony. "With all due respect, your court order of prohibition of the lost evidence is not working. Mr. Sanders is proceeding as if the evidence is real and exists." This is what I found myself arguing over and over to the Judge. I never was able to convince him to stop the flow of damaging evidence during the trial.

We would go into the Judge's chambers each time I objected on this issue because it was not appropriate to make such arguments for and against the evidence in front of the jury. The judge understandably did not wish the jury to hear or be contaminated by what we were arguing about. We found ourselves each making the same arguments to the Judge in chambers over and over. The Judge kept upholding the testimony he was hearing in the belief that it would all be tied together in the end as promised by the deputy. This was Rick Sander's argument which I was losing before the Judge. What I had previously predicted when I had argued the Motion to Dismiss was now actually taking place and I was unable to stop the hemorrhaging. My case was sinking and I found myself unable to right the ship.

It all became worse when the lady next door testified. I was unable to affect her credibility due to the fact that the time was pegged by her to be at the conclusion of Sesame Street which was indeed being shown between eleven and 12 o'clock noon on all TV sets. She did admit that it may have been a few minutes before noon, but I did not think that helped very much. The arguments and hearings in chambers continued from Tuesday to Wednesday as I would repeat my objections over and over and the Judge continued to uphold the DA's position that he was complying with the court orders. My case was drowning and my client was losing as the jury would hear over and over from each fireman and prosecution witness all the details of the crime scene evidence being presented as if they were real facts and really existed. To make it worse, the DA's two experts opined that the fire had actually started but had not yet been noticed as taking place inside my client's home about a half hour before the approximate time that the lady next door said she saw my client leaving his home. She also testified that she was one of the persons who later saw and reported the fire about twenty to thirty minutes later. The case was being re-constructed on evidence that did not exist and could only be opined.

The testimony was being presented by the fire department witnesses as if it were real and reliable. It was from the non-existent evidence that the witnesses gave testimony upon which the jury would rely in its verdict and finding that the fire was created by my client. To make matters worse, each time I objected, both counsel, my client, stenographer and the judge had to leave the courtroom for the chambers to renew our arguments. It was evident that the jury was not happy with the frequent and lengthy delays. This was not good for Dan Unger since I was causing the delays with my continuing objections. I could see the concern in the eyes of jurors as we would return from chambers to the courtroom with the judge having ruled against my objections. It is not hard to see distress and boredom in the jurors. Then we would restart and soon I was objecting again. However, since I was conscious of the effect of the repetition of the objections on the jury, I would simply state that I was renewing the previously stated objection and sit down. The trial would continue. I was not bored, but I was certainly distressed.

Finally, as I was objecting to the testimony for the nth time, the Judge became upset with me and ordered us into chambers because he clearly had had enough of my objecting. Still, I felt that I had no other choice. I remember walking into chambers realizing that anything I said would be later reviewed and read by Justices on appeal in the Court of Appeals. Of course, this was always the case, but it felt different because it became foremost in my mind and I knew inside myself that we were losing. I decided that I would consciously direct my words as if I were speaking to the appellate Justices, not the trial Judge. There was nothing to lose, so as I began to speak to the trial Judge, I felt myself directing my argument to the appellate court of three justices about my inability to properly defend my client. In doing so I listed all the ways in which my job as counsel for the defendant was being hampered by the court rulings and the actual lack of real evidence.

The Judge told me once we were seated in chambers that "I am about to hold you in contempt of court if you do not stop interrupting the proceedings with your objections. I have made it clear in my rulings and you must follow them whether you like them or not." I responded to the Judge slowly and politely, thinking about the appellate Justices who would read what I was saying for one of the few times I have ever considered this in my oral arguments in court. I had always been focused on winning the trial and not the possibility of appeal. Appeal was rarely in my thoughts. However, in this case it was and I proceeded to tell the judge that "I appreciate what you are saying, your honor, but I must continue to object to the court rulings as they are made, come what may. I find that my client is drowning and I am unable stop objecting and repeating the objections as each of your rulings are being made. As counsel, I have been placed in an impossible situation where he is being repeatedly burned by evidence that does not exist and cannot be produced or validated except by your rulings of admission as unreliable heresy. It is all non-existent evidence. My client has no other recourse, Your Honor. I am his only hope and I feel duty bound to keep objecting. I wish now that I had never made the Motion to Dismiss. Your decision and rulings are killing my client and I have nothing that I can do to except to keep standing up, objecting and fighting for him. The DA is being allowed to proceed as if the evidence was never lost. This is a total miscarriage of justice. It is something I have never said before in a trial and I hope I will never have to say it again. If the court believes that I should be held in contempt, so be it. I must remain true to my client and my calling as a lawyer in Colorado." After my statement, the Judge was silent for a few minutes which gave me a chance to become composed. Looking back, perhaps he was doing the same since I had asked for the contempt order to be made. When the judge spoke, he ruled against me one more time but did not raise the issue of contempt. Rick Sanders stayed silent. After all, he was winning as I was losing. I could feel the three of us, lawyers and Judge, holding ourselves back and in check.

We went back into the courtroom and, thankfully, the Judge never pursued finding me in contempt of court. Despite a few other objections which I limited to simply stating that "I am continuing my objections to the evidence being admitted for the same reasons as I have previously stated before in chambers." I would sit back down back down and listen to the damaging testimony that was being permitted without the court having to call us to go in to his chambers. I was left to depend on what had been argued and stated to the court in the previous objections and arguments for review by the Court of Appeals once the case had been appealed.

The Judge had previously been an Assistant City Attorney in Aurora before my tenure as a prosecutor for the city and we had always had a good relationship. I think that this may have prevented him from pulling the plug on me. This was not the first time I had been threatened with contempt of court. Sometimes, it does come down to being ready to face the consequences of your honest and legally held views as to the law applicable to the decisions being made by the court. God help me. In the end, the Judge's discretion prevailed and I was spared being held in contempt of court.

We finished the trial on Monday or Tuesday of the following week. For the defense, I had called each of my client's fellow employees who totally supported my client being present at the job sight during lunch time on the date and alleged time of the fire. The jury was left with both sides having witnesses saying under oath that he was in two different places at the same time. I also had my client testify to being with his fellow employees at the time of the fire and without motive or intention to set his home ablaze. He stated that, "I had nothing to gain from burning my home and placing my family's future at risk. The insurance was not enough to have covered the losses that were likely to occur. And that is exactly what happened. In fact, our lives and welfare were turned upside down with the fire, insurance troubles, debt, bankruptcy and, as you can see, prosecution for something that I did not do." He testified that he "first learned about the fire, when he was contacted by the police on the job that afternoon." This had been corroborated earlier by the police officer who had made contact with him at his job site when he testified. Dan went on to testify that "They informed me at work that my home had burned down. I left immediately to drive home and see what had happened. It was terrible when I saw that we were homeless and everything we owned was lost. It was the worst feeling I had ever experienced. It made me sick." I could see that the jury was watching him intently and hearing his pain and suffering and that of his family. It raised my hopes since it was further buttressed by the very good eye witness testimony of his fellow workers that he had been with them at work during the lunch break when the fire had started and was taking place. The co-workers were several men without any motive to lie verses the lady next door, also without motive, but very possibly mistaken. Despite a long, spirited and accusatory cross examination by Rick Sanders, I felt that Dan had held up well under cross-examination. Overall, Dan demonstrated to me that when a witness is telling the truth, it comes out, one way or another, or so I thought.

I considered that both Dan and his work mates to be credible witnesses and, later, on Monday when the trial was resumed, I argued in my closing statement to the jury that," whoever caused the fire had to have come into the home after the lady next door saw my client leave the home or she had mistakenly identified that person to be my client." I was asking that the jury accept that, "my client could not possibly be in two places at the same time as the DA was arguing for them to accept. Some other person had time to do it which I believed had been established by Dan's workmates, none of whom had reason or motive to testify to anything but the truth. Dan was not connected to the fire except his ownership of the home itself and all of the family belongings. Why would anyone start a fire with no hope of obtaining enough money from the insurance to cover the losses?" I had hoped that we had achieved some head wind going to the jury. However, because of my continuing objections during the trial and the regular adjournments to the Judge's chambers, I was very worried about how the jurors viewed all of this as the trial neared the end. After our closing statements and the judge reading to the jury his instructions, we adjourned for lunch and later returned to the courthouse to wait for the jury verdict. This was on Monday, one week after we had the jury selection and beginning of the trial.

Within an hour after I had returned from lunch, we were summoned by the Judge's clerk and informed that the jury had reached a verdict. After receiving the case late in the morning and eating lunch, they had deliberating only a short amount of time, just over one hour. Could this possibly mean a quick decision of Not Guilty? This is what I was hoping for as I waited in the courtroom with my client very anxiously. However, another voice inside me was telling me that this is not good. When the jury verdict was read, what we heard shook me very badly. The verdict was "Guilty" of the Arson after deliberating for the shortest amount of time I ever remembered in a felony case. I was shocked since the quick decision by the jury meant that all my efforts were in vain and Dan was facing an uncertain prison sentence. I felt terrible for Dan and his family. Making this worse was that I totally believed that he was innocent. We set the case for sentencing and I left the courthouse deeply upset with the outcome.

When I returned home, both of my daughters, who were teenagers at that time, were already home from school. They were aware of the trial and the circumstances and immediately asked if the jury had reached a verdict. When I told them the verdict, I was unable to hold back my emotions and started to cry. This had never happened before. Whatever had been my emotions upon the receipt of a verdict, I was generally in control of myself long after I had received the news and returned home. In this case, the courthouse was less than fifteen minutes away from my home and enough time had not passed for me to gain control over my emotions.

My daughters have never forgotten that day when their father cried after receiving a verdict. I never meant to show these feelings, but out they came. Well over twenty-five years later, I can still feel the sorrow of that verdict and the afternoon in my home with my children. I recently had a visit from my oldest daughter and she mentioned how she still remembers Dan and my reaction that very sad day. I can only say that in the profession I practiced, it is hard not to become involved and to personally feel the wins and the losses. This was a loss of the highest order and, soon thereafter, I went about filing the necessary pleadings to begin an appeal.

Dan received a five-year sentence which he began to serve immediately. The Judge turned down my Motion to Delay serving the sentence until after the appeal had been decided. This caused Dan to be unable to pay any balance of my fees as he made whatever final arrangements he could to put his deteriorated financial circumstances in the best order possible. He had arranged with his wife's family that she and the children join them in Kansa where they lived. In the meantime, I decided to try to obtain the help of the Colorado Public Defenders office to take over the appeal of his case since Dan had become indigent and unable to support his family. I visited the main Denver office and spoke with their appellate staff describing the issues. They quickly decided that they would take over the appeal and entered as counsel on his behalf. Two or three months later, I received a phone call from the Public defender lawyer assigned to work on the appeal and he told me that he had, "received the trial transcript and had been reading and re-reading it." He sympathized with the problems I had with the trial Judge and told me, "I respect how you fought for your client. Based on what I have read, I believe we have a good chance to win on appeal. You made a great record for me to work with." This certainly made me feel good, but Dan was serving his time and appeals always took a great deal of time. I thanked him for the phone call and returned to my practice and the ongoing cases heading for settlement or trial.

About four to five months less than two years after the verdict, the Colorado Court of Appeals did indeed reverse the trial court. The grounds for the reversal were that Dan had been denied his basic rights under both the US Constitution and the Colorado Constitution. The burden of proof always lies with the prosecution. The rulings of the trial Judge, according to the Court of Appeals, ended up with placing on Dan the burden of proving a negative, the lost evidence that weighed heavily in the trial against my client. This burden never belonged to a Defendant in a criminal trial. As the lawyer who tried the case, I can flatly state that, "such a burden of proving the negative is beyond difficult." When I contacted Dan to congratulate him on the reversal, he was already on parole in a Denver Halfway house, having been released for good behavior after serving less than two years of the five-year sentence. He and his wife had reconciled and he decided to move to Kansas to join her and his family as soon as possible. He had already been advised by the Public Defender's office that the DA's office had no intention of retrying him for the alleged arson. That was the good news, but it hardly made up for the injustice of the conviction that had occurred.

I believe to this day that my client was in fact innocent. However, I recognize that had the evidence not been lost, he probably would have been convicted unless I had found some other way to show that the next-door lady was wrong about seeing Dan that day. It was her testimony that the jury found had overcome the testimony of his fellow workers who each swore under oath that he was with them and not setting the fire. We will never know who or why the fire was set or started. This case adds to those accumulated over the years where the final truth is indeed unknown even at the end of the legal process. Dan Unger did come out of it all without a criminal record since the guilty verdict was nullified and he was cleared of the felony conviction. Of course, there was no way to make up the time served. I never saw or heard from Dan again.

This case happened in the first twenty-five years of my practice. The problems presented were equal to some of my more serious cases already reviewed in this book. However, the difficulties I had with the rulings of the judge were greater than anything I had ever encountered. Nothing in my past experience prepared me for the drama and setbacks of this trial. As it occurs in in all of our cases, the judges and the lawyers are different, each with his or her personality. The witnesses are often unique in their differences with each one creating a different set of problems and ways to be tackled individually. As the trials progress, each jury develops its own fresh personality. And finally, there is a huge difference in each Judge as he or she conducts the cases, each with his or her own manner, demeanor and personality or even a lack of personality. The Judge in the Unger case was steady in his demeanor and rulings, never openly upset before the jury. In chambers, however, he began to display impatience with my conduct and endless objections which did, in fact, keep interrupting the progress of the trial. He and I were both victims of his rulings because I had no choice but to object over and over again to which he kept ruling against my arguments. There is no question that this took the regular continuity out of the trial and was upsetting to all of us, the judge, witnesses, lawyers and the jury. In fact, I believe the jury reacted with anger to what it saw with the very quick verdict it rendered. It ended up about six days in court for each of them. The two or three jurors I spoke at some length told me that it was a matter of believing the next-door neighbor and against Dan's co-workers. They obvious felt that Dan's co-workers were covering for him. They all agreed that too much time had been taken with the legal arguments and too many trial interruptions.

In the end, the Judge never did impose a sanction of contempt on me. I believe it was due to the fact that despite my continuing objections and arguments in chambers, I did so honestly and without rancor. I was upset with the rulings and not the Judge personally and he knew that. I liked and respected the judge. He proved to be wrong. However, as it turned out, I did not push him to a limit of his patience. For that I was grateful. Sadly, the judge never did learn the final outcome of the appeal because he contracted meningitis and died during the first year after the trail. He was a great loss to his family and children and all of us who knew him, enjoyed him as deputy prosecutor, practicing lawyer and respected and well-liked District Judge. He was a very good man and a credit to our profession.

CHAPTER 14

Wrong Place at the Wrong Time

I had previously met David Valerin when he accompanied his father to my office. The Valerin family had immigrated to the United States from Belorussia during a large flow of immigrants from Russia in the early 1980's. Being a Russian immigrant myself, I related right away to the Valerin family and was pleased to be asked to help them. As a result, I became counsel for the family until I retired from practice. I advised them on the legal problems implicit in doing business in Colorado and numerous other issues. Many years later, a more serious problem arose which involved another Russian immigrant from California visiting Colorado for reasons unrelated to the Valerin family, but who knew David when he had lived with his family in LA.

One day, I answered a phone call at the office and spoke with the wife of a Russian man who lived in Los Angeles. She told me that her husband had called her and said that he was in jail as a result of being arrested by the Denver police when he viewed a man being assaulted and killed with a knife. She went on to say that "My husband did not do it. The other man had done it. My husband would never do such a thing." I told her that I would visit her husband in the city jail and learn what I could and get back to her. Her husband's name was Boris Rasilkin. I confirmed with the City and County jail that Boris was indeed incarcerated and went to the jail to see him.

In Denver, we always had to make sure that the arrested persons had not yet been moved to the City and County jail located east of the then Denver Stapleton International Airport from the jail located next to the police department and courthouse. Such a mistake was always costly in time and travel. I confirmed that Boris was in the city jail in the same complex as the police department, kiddie corner across street from the courthouse. I soon met with Boris in the city jail.

Boris told me that he had come to Denver together with his friend, Alex Shisnikov, who wanted to collect money from a Russian man who owed him the money. This gave Boris the opportunity to visit friends in Denver. He did not know the man who owed money to his friend. Boris was the person who had been acquainted with David Valerin when David lived in LA. For Boris, it was a chance to see Denver and to visit with a couple of his friends while Alex took care of his business. Their first stop after arrival in Denver was a Russian owned bar which was not far from my office at that time. When they arrived at the restaurant/bar, they located the man that Alex was seeking right away. In fact, the man was sitting at the same long table as was David Valerin, who was with his wife enjoying drinks, music and talk among friends. Alex confronted the man he was looking for and an argument followed that grew with insults going back and forth between them. This caused people around them to tell the two men to leave the restaurant and take their argument outside, which they did. As Alex and the Denver man left the restaurant to finish their business, Boris followed them outside the restaurant. David Valerin had also decided at about the same time to step outside to smoke a cigarette. He had wanted get away from the arguments then taking place in the restaurant, unaware as to what would soon take place outside when the other three men came outside and stood nearby. Their actions were independent of David wanting to have a smoke. Remaining inside the restaurant, at the large table, were the wives, girlfriends, husbands and single men and women who continued with the drinking and talking that had been taking place in the restaurant.

The man Alex Shisnikov was seeking was named Roman Dubinsky. He was sitting with his wife in the restaurant close to the bar. Upon spotting Roman, Alex immediately confronted Roman and then began arguing. It was al about a debt that Alex wanted paid. David did not know anything about the issue between the two men as he was peacefully having a smoke standing outside the restaurant. Alex and Roman walked out of the restaurant together as they continued their arguing and stopped a few yards away from where David was standing. Boris explained to me that once the two antagonists were outside with him having followed, the talking swiftly became belligerent and, without warning, his friend, Alex, whipped, out a knife and shoved it into the other man's stomach. He remembered that David Valerin and a couple of other people were also standing in front of the restaurant, but apart from Alex and Roman, who was stabbed. There was no chance to stop the assault from happening. Alex went back to the car he had rented with Boris reluctantly accompanying him as they drove away. The police found the two of them at the airport while they were waiting for a flight back to LA. Both men were arrested at that time. On the way to the Denver city jail, they were told by the police that the man Alex had assaulted with his knife had been taken in an ambulance to the emergency room of the Denver City Hospital. It was explained that he and Alex were possibly facing aggravated assault or attempted murder charges. This was a serious situation for Boris who had not been a party to the arguments between Alex and Roman or the actual assault. He had never contemplated, intended or participated in the actions and reactions between Alex and the soon to be dead man. However, he had accompanied Alex and had witnessed all of it, including what was said between the two men. He was asking me "What should I do?" The answer was simple. "You must tell the police detectives the truth." I obtained his consent to do so and went to speak to the detectives involved in the police headquarters next door.

When I did so, the detectives arranged for me to meet with them and Boris in a conference room in the city jail. However, there was a problem. There were no Russian interpreters readily available at that time in Denver, so the detectives asked me if I would interpret while they also made a recording of the interrogation and my translation. As the Russian community grew in Denver, I often found myself in the position of being the only one to understand what was being said by a Russian. I was not concerned about my ability to translate but told them that I had to check with my client first. When I checked with Boris, his main concern was to get out of jail as soon as possible and return to his family in L.A. He reiterated to me the basic facts of how quick the incident had taken place that there had not been any warning, Also, that he had done nothing wrong. He had been unexpectedly a witness to the assault. As I was hearing his story, I explained that there was danger in what he would reveal to the police since he had accompanied his friend knowing that he was collecting a debt and, worse still, saw the assault with a knife by Alex. This would cause the police to think that he was an accomplice. Boris denied any discussion with Alex about taking physical action. He explained that, "I was along for the ride and to meet with friends in Denver." He had not yet had the opportunity to even call them and set up meetings. Neither he nor Alex expected that he would meet up with Roman right away in the Russian restaurant/bar. He did not know about the knife and was, himself shocked and surprised at what Alex had done." He assured me that there had not been any talk about what Alex might do except to collect a debt. He was not involved or had an interest in the debt recovery. He was just accompanying Alex as a friend and hoping to see a couple friends while they were in Denver. Boris not only agreed to be questioned but was hoping to be freed from jail and allowed to return to LA as soon as possible.

During my conference with Boris, I learned that he had not sensed or believed that a fight would occur from the collection effort. When Alex actually pulled the knife and stuck it into Roman's stomach, Boris was both shocked and distressed. Also, Boris was not close enough to stop him, even if he had been able react. The most incriminating evidence was that he was there when it happened. That could not be changed. However, there was no blood on him and he had never met or known the victim before. The quick meeting in the Russian club before they had stepped outside together with Roman was the only contact Boris had ever had with the victim. Once Boris and I had provided this information to the detectives, we learned from the police that Alex had told them that Boris had nothing to do with the killing and that Alex had claimed self-defense as to what had become a murder charge against him. The victim had died in the hospital. They wanted to know everything that Boris had seen and heard. What they ended up hearing from Boris would certainly seal the case against Alex.

Boris wanted, above all, to get out of jail and to return to L.A. I explained to him that cooperating was the best way to get this done. Soon after the detectives had everyone in place, I found myself in the unusual position of interpreting for my client what he was saying in response to the questioning by the detectives while the interrogation was being filmed and recorded. It was strange, but actually not that difficult since I had spoken Russian all of my life and had been over all of the facts and circumstances with Boris a couple of times. It worked out very well. The following day, I was informed by one of the Detectives that a certified Russian interpreter had double checked my interpretation and found it to be accurate except for one or two words which did not detract from the statement. I had never claimed to be 100% accurate as a Russian translator since the Russian language had changed somewhat under Communist rule. However, my translation of Boris's answers to the interrogators did lead to his release from jail with no charges being filed and the promise to return for the trial if it became necessary as a witness.

Upon his release from jail, I took Boris to the airport to once again wait for a flight to LA. He had not signed off on the vehicle that had been rented by Alex, so I advised that we inform the rental agency so that the car could be picked up where it was left nearby to the Russian restaurant. In view of the homicide, it did not look as if Alex would be released from jail since a bond, if any, was ordered, most likely would be too high to be met. All of that would be up to Alex's counsel when he or she was obtained. I received payment for my services from Boris within a week of his departure. However, that was not the end of my work as a result of the murder he and David Valerin had witnessed in front of the restaurant.

Before the criminal trial of Alex Shisnikov took place, I found myself, once again, deeply embroiled in the facts of the knife killing. David Valerin, who was unlucky enough to be standing and smoking outside the restaurant about six or seven feet away from the knifing, had been civilly sued as a co-Defendant together with the restaurant/bar outside of which the killing had occurred. He asked me to represent him in the case. The complaint was brought by the dead man's wife, Valeria Dubinskaya, who accused David with the commission of conspiracy to murder her husband, Roman, together with Alex Shisnikov. The restaurant was also sued in the same case for gross negligence and failure to safely provide for its customers as a drinking establishment under Colorado law. Because David had known the deceased in Los Angeles and was himself involved in a financial dispute with him in Denver, same as Alex, the victim's wife believed that David had conspired with Alex and set up her husband's death. It did not help at all that David had coincidentally been at the restaurant and gone outside the restaurant and was standing on the side walk having a smoke at the same time and place as the killing occurred. In fact, David had watched as the killing occurred and was also a witness in the criminal case that was brought against Alex after his arrest. Alex was ultimately convicted of 2nd Degree murder. All of this was an event in which David happened to be in the wrong place at the wrong time that would not go away.

The legal theory against David brought by the wife of the Alex was that he was friends with the killer and had accompanied Alex and Boris as the three of them went outside together before the knifing had occurred. On top of that, incidentally, David and the dead husband had also been arguing in the restaurant about a longstanding debt to David, hence the premeditated assassination that had occurred. The dead man apparently owed a number of people money and David was caught in the same circumstances that had happened around him. The theory was that David had planned the appearance of Alex and threat of slaying as a means of getting his debt to be paid at that time. There were many loopholes in this theory such as the fact that my client, Boris, knew nothing in advance about the impending killing or any connection between Alex and David. In fact, Boris turned out to be a real good witness on our side. Neither he nor David had planned or conspired to create a fatal meeting since they did not even know each other. On top of that, Alex, the knife killer, had told the police that there was no connection with the deceased to either Boris or David. I was quickly able to confirm these facts since I had been Boris's counsel before I had been retained by David in the civil conspiracy case. It was pure chance that David had stepped outside the restaurant. Boris had never spoken to Alex about David before the events had taken place. Moreover, Boris confirmed in his deposition in the civil case that when he, Alex and the victim went outside, David was not with them or known to them. He only saw him on the sidewalk nearby after the death of the victim. There were also other witnesses outside at that time. It was true that David was standing nearby when the man was killed, but David was not conversing with Alex, Boris or even saying "hello." However, these facts were all to be developed during the course of a large amount of discovery and depositions that were taken in the civil case against David. The depositions included many of the persons who were sitting in the restaurant where the victim and his wife were seated together with David, his wife and about a dozen other Russians. It turned out that David and his wife were actually seated at another separate table in the restaurant than the one in which Alex and Boris approached Mr. Dubinsky. No deposition was ever taken of Alex since he was criminally charged with murder, facing trial and had taken the fifth Amendment.

During this case, I became friends with the counsel for the insurance company representing the restaurant on the liability and damages questions that arose from the killing. He was a Japanese American who was a good guy and a hardworking and skilled lawyer. His name was the same as mine, Michael Nicosabi. We bonded during the taking of the many depositions together of the witnesses who were in the party at the restaurant on the evening in question and in or outside the restaurant when the killing occurred outside. Most of the witnesses were not good in English, so Russian translators were being used by the insurance carrier. The problem with that was that a couple of the Russian translators were themselves weak in English, so I ended up informing my fellow counsel and the record of the appropriate English words for translation whenever it became necessary. This caused the record of the depositions to be full of corrections made by me. However, I was able to clarify for the record what the Russian witnesses were actually saying. We ended up taking about eight depositions over a period of two or three months. It all paid off for my client because I was able to successfully put together a lengthy brief in support of a Motion to Dismiss David from the case that included enough deposition testimony and evidence to fully exonerate David from planning or participating in a scheme to kill Roman. About six months into the case, I received an Order of dismissal of David from the case. Many months later, the restaurant and Mrs. Dubinskaya achieved a financial settlement of all issues. We were not privy to the settlement amount and, as occurs in so many settlements involving insurance companies on behalf of their clients, the parties were forbidden to announce the amount involved.

The Judge who granted the dismissal had been the prosecutor in the Diaz axe killing murder case I had tried many years before and referred to in Chapter 9, Murder Unraveled. He had brought the message to me as a deputy District attorney from his boss, the Denver District Attorney, that led to the 1st degree Assault plea bargain. Michael Nikosabi, in the instant case, became a very good District judge before whom I successfully tried a couple of felony cases, including the Reed case that occurs in Chapter 17 later in this book. He went on to become an excellent Federal District Court Magistrate dispensing wisdom and justice on a daily basis. He has always been regarded well by the bench and the bar of the state of Colorado.

All of this points out the necessity of having even handed and good relationships with opposing counsel, prosecutors, clerks, law office or court staffs or any lawyers that a practicing lawyer comes into contact with. A legal career takes a long time. You cross paths with your fellow lawyers over and over again. Many become judges and you appear frequently before them as the years pass. Lawyers and judges talk to each other and each of us develops a reputation that follows him around the courts from county to county in his state and in the Federal courts. Whatever is happening in a case, a lawyer must keep in mind that there are more days ahead with each of the participants. Make your points, argue to the best of your ability, but do not burn the bridges with opposing counsel since they will have to be crossed again and again. It is not just for your own sake that your reputation matters, it counts for the legion of clients that you represent, particularly when important decisions, plea bargains, settlements and trial results are at stake.

We lawyer each embody within ourselves our past cases and impressions into the present disputes and trials. Sadly, this is often forgotten by lawyers who give in to the hyperbole and nasty advocacy of the case at hand. There is always another day and another case that is just as important as the present case is to your client. Each case contains a fair number of ups and downs, curves and off-speed strikes that need to be absorbed and placed into the total structure and understanding of the people and events involved. The final picture of a case forms as the case develops. To be strenuously voicing conclusions and accusations at the beginning can be foolhardy. This is well known to experienced lawyers, prosecutors and defense counsel alike. Withholding final judgement pays dividends for both sides and, most importantly, allows for civil and rancor less exchanges between counsels on both sides until they each achieve the necessary full understanding of the cases. That understanding, once it is achieved by both sides, is what leads to the final dispositions and plea bargains in most of our cases.

On the criminal side, more often than not, prosecutors have the advantage of seeing the evidence, witness statements and police reports before the defense counsel. Defense counsel often only knows what they have been told by the client which is likely to be much less than the total picture. This is particularly true at the time of the initial court appearance or appearances. My opening remarks to the DAs in cases I have just entered were often," I have not read the discovery yet and do not know the full picture. What can you tell me about the case?" Many times, the deputies would fill me in on some facts and details, some more than others. They would generally understand and be as helpful as time would allow. Many of these conversations would occur in the middle of docket calls in which many defense lawyers and a much lesser number of deputies would be milling around waiting for their cases to be called. At times, the deputy would know as little as you or even less then you, not having even opened the file that morning. This is how the very important relationships between the prosecutor and defense counsel begin. As both sides came to know their cases better, there are phone calls between counsel informing each other of important facts or evidence that has been learned. The better the relationship between counsel, the sooner each side is able to make sound determinations about the strength and weaknesses in their cases. This allows them to decide whether to plea bargain or go to trial. It is a time-consuming process and definitely does not happen overnight. Justice does indeed work slowly and this is not necessarily a bad thing.

Your reputation in court also grows slowly and is the most important thing you have. It is not something to be messed with. Yet, many lawyers do exactly that and often fail to realize what damage they have done to themselves, their reputation and by extension, to their clients. Your reputation follows you wherever you go. You become a known quality who meets and greets his fellow lawyers in court or their offices. You learn a great deal about other lawyers. How do you think people learn about you? It is very simple. What you do and say and how you act under pressure marks you as it happens. It cannot be escaped. It is always best to leave good, ethical and sound impressions.

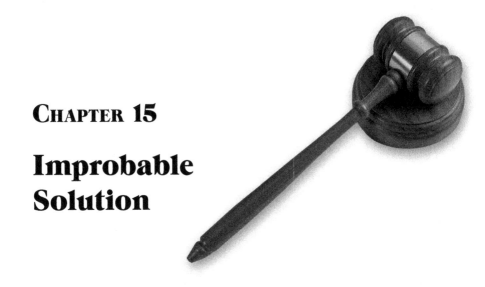

Chapter 15

Improbable Solution

W hen Dr. Ronald Strong walked into my office, I had no idea that he was a physician. He had a weather beaten, but friendly face. He was clearly upset as he settled into one of the chairs in front of my desk. He was dressed in a heavy wool shirt, baggy pants and a hunter's like cap that had ear muffs attached for use if necessary. He spoke in a raspy voice and was obviously unhappy to be visiting my office. I took him to be over sixty years old and having been around the block, very possibly a drinker since I viewed a redness that was often caused by excessive use of alcohol. I figured this to be a DUI case as I asked him to sit down and tell me what I could do for him. He immediately surprised me when he told me that I had been recommended to him by one of the judges in Adams County who was a friend of his. I had often appeared before the Judge he mentioned and liked the way he handled his courtroom. With my interest having been peaked, I sat forward in my chair and listened to Dr. Strong's recounting of events that led to him being charged with 22 counts of felony theft, 14 counts of falsifying documents and 1 count of conspiracy.

I began reviewing the criminal complaint that the Doctor has given to me as he was speaking. As Dr. Strong was relaying to me the history, facts and circumstances of the criminal charges I was reading and scanning the Complaint, I learned that they were the result of a Medicaid fraud investigation conducted by the Medicaid fraud unit of the Colorado Bureau of Investigation, (CBI). It was immediately apparent that this was a case to be reckoned with since we were dealing with a Colorado state investigation that had been meticulously investigated and prepared with dates, events and activities laboriously laid out in chronological order. This was, without a doubt, the biggest case I had ever been asked to handle and without question, one that would take more time and effort than anything before. It made me wonder whether it was something I could handle as a sole practitioner. I listened intently to what the good doctor was telling me as these thoughts were running through my head.

I slowly began to like the doctor as he started to recount his long time general medical practice in Westminster, located contiguously north of Denver as a separate city. The case was filed in the Adams County District Court in Brighton, Colorado where I had both the Lopez and Brock cases many years before. Dr. Strong had been in private practice for twenty-eight years and had a huge following of patients in his practice. He was indeed a hunter and fisherman in his spare time, but that time was limited by his very busy general practice. I learned that his practice included a part time receptionist, secretary and two full time clerks in addition to a part time semi-retired elderly nurse who met and spoke with patients in order to learn the essential medical background and symptoms that brought them to his offices. Because of the length of time that he had been in private practice, the practice included many patients who had remained with him for years. This caused the Medicaid portion of his practice to grow considerably and consequently, the need to deal with the endless computer and paper requirements of compliance with the state government rules and regulations for treatment and billing of Medicaid patients.

Doctor Strong's business was thriving, but vacations, hunting and fishing trips were limited and the criminal charges were weighing heavily on the doctor, causing him to be despondent and weary. This is exactly how he looked as he was relaying to me the facts and circumstances of his case. He reported to me that he had a heart condition that required him to be careful with his diet and mental state. It was a disconcerting picture before I had absorbed and come to terms with the details of the actual charges.

I was working with a man at the peak of his profession and service to society desperately in need of peace of mind and contentment just to handle his medical and professional obligations. His life had been torn asunder with the accusations of wrongdoing by the state of Colorado. He told me that, "I do not know what to do. Nothing like this has ever happened to me. I always tried to do whatever the law required." My heart went out to him and I was just beginning as his lawyer. I was holding in my hands a compilation of a mountain of charges, evidence and facts that needed to be sorted out, reviewed and rebutted.

I told Dr. Ron, which was the name he asked me to call him since that is how he was known by his patients, friends and acquaintances, that I had never represented anyone charged with the offenses he faced. He replied, "That is not a problem. The Judge told me that no lawyers in Colorado or the courts have a background in Medicaid cases since they are just beginning to appear. He said the Judge had told him that." you were up to the challenge and would become as well prepared and knowledgeable as was possible. This is how you work. That is what I want in my lawyer. As for myself, I do not know anything about the filing and keeping of the Colorado Medicaid records. I left that completely up to my two filing clerks and nurse." He went on to tell me that the two filing clerks' "spent almost all of their time on recording and filing the necessary documents for Medicaid payments. They are so busy that I have agreed to let them work during into the evenings when necessary since they also handle, together with my secretary receptionist, all the paper work for the non-Medicaid patients. They let me know how much money was being charged when they provided me with the documents that must be signed and forwarded". My instincts told me to ask whether he "checked the documents for accuracy of the reporting?" His answer was, "Not very often, unless they had a question about a specific procedure or if they had properly read my notes and scribbles on the medical charts. They have been doing it for a while. They actually know them better than I do."

It was immediately apparent that the two clerks were vitally important witnesses since they were the principal participants in the required reporting process. I reckoned that a lot depended on these two ladies since they were likely to become witnesses for the prosecution if the case were to go to trial. It also occurred to me that it may be that they had already spoken to the prosecutors or their investigators. I made a mental note that I needed to meet with the two clerks right away.

I asked Dr. Ron "Has any one in your office staff been spoken to by an investigator from the DA's office?" He said "No." but then remembered that a few months before, "I had a visit from the State Medicaid office by a representative who said he was doing a routine review. He had questioned my two clerks about the office procedures including the entry of the Medicaid records." Dr. Ron continued by telling me that, "they told me about the visit and that the inspector had been very nice and explained to them how some of the entries should be made. They said that he had been very pleasant and helpful." I wondered about the true motives of the representative as I heard this and realized that my first task was to visit Dr. Ron's office and speak to the two lady clerks.

Since the initial court appearance was scheduled in a couple of days, I decided to see the two lady clerks before I made that first appearance. Because of Dr. Ron's reputation and the cooperation of his office, the DA's office had decided to allow a personal recognizance bond from the time he was arrested and charged. This is what we called a "PR bond" in Colorado, whereby Dr. Ron personally certified that he would appear in court whenever he was required to do so. He gave me all of the paperwork from his office that he thought I needed to have, subject to further disclosure as necessary. The case was growing rapidly with the promise of more paperwork than I had ever had in a case.

The next day, I visited Dr. Ron's offices and met the two ladies who handled the paperwork and submissions to Medicaid. They were friendly but reserved. We spent over two hours going over the procedures and entries on Dr. Ron's medical charts to the Medicaid forms. It was clear that this was a laborious process locating and placing into the state forms all the necessary patient info in support of the money charged for the professional work being performed by Dr. Ron. There was a shorthand involved that had been provided, in part, by the visiting Medicaid state inspector. This had been newly initiated but offset by the fact that more info was required to be imputed in order to make the filings correct. The ladies informed me that what they learned had only increased the time necessary for them to do the job correctly each month. For that reason, they explained that they were negotiating with Dr. Ron to increase their pay and had already received his consent to work two or three evenings a week to keep up. This increased their hours and overtime pay came into play. Since, Dr. Ron had little time to double check them and never returned to the offices once he left for the day, they told me that they tried to double check with the part time nurse without much help being provided. As I was listening to them, I was definitely feeling that the two ladies were covering up for themselves in describing their work and circumstances. The question was, what else were they hiding

My former surgical nurse secretary had explained to me that many drug companies made deals with entry clerks in doctors' offices to add their products to the Medicaid claims for patients and provided kickbacks. Was this happening here? I asked about the overtime pay and they responded by telling me that "payment depended on whether Dr. Ron had a good month or bad. If it is a bad month, he would pay their regular salaries. Good months meant more pay or bonuses. They were obviously working unattended and not being double checked. I put all of this in the back of my mind as I was hearing about totally unsupervised time creating records that were the basis of the criminal charges. This was not good and I decided to speak to Dr. Ron about it in view of him confirming that they used a stamp to place Dr. Ron's signature on the forms. What I was seeing was an out of control system that was easily subject to false entries and reporting unknown to my client. On top of that was the possibility of fraudulent entries in support of higher pay.

At the time I appeared in court for my first appearance, I learned that I would be facing the same two deputy DAs who had worked the Lopez murder case. Both of them had remained and grown in their roles in the Adams County District Attorneys' office. They appeared together in court for the initial hearing, which was unusual, but was soon explained. They greeted me with the news that they had an open and shut case against Dr. Ron. In our discussion before the Judge had appeared in court, they had told me that not only was the case against Dr. Strong well-documented and voluminous, but it was going to be corroborated by both of his employee clerks who had just been arrested and were cooperating. This was not good. However, it turned out that they did not know that I had already spoken with both of the employees and that I now fully understood why they were walking a tightrope when they were speaking to me. The case was changing colors and severity almost on a day to day basis. This was similar to many other cases I had handled. Criminal prosecutions often had a way of growing and changing mid-stream as new evidence and witnesses appeared, mostly for the prosecution, but sometimes for the defense. To be flexible and open to the ups and downs of cases was part of the trial lawyer's life that you become accustomed to. However, it particularly hurt to learn about the culpability and cooperation with the DAs by the two clerks as I was just entering this case and so liked my doctor client. What other surprises would there be in this case?

In reaching an agreement to represent the Doctor, I asked that he not only pay a retainer but also, a monthly stipend that would pay for a lawyer to work part-time solely on his case for me. This young lawyer would be asked to search deeply into the details of the Medicaid fraud allegations and help me to cope with all the medical information and payments that would have to be digested concerning each patient involved. Fortunately, my secretary had been a nurse in her previous career and was also be able to add to my knowledge as I became more familiar with the facts and documentation in the case. Dr.

Strong had agreed to my terms since it was apparent to him that there was much work and voluminous paperwork ahead to be learned and mastered.

As I began my preparations for the preliminary hearing, I ended up speaking with each of the prosecuting attorneys based on who I was able to reach when I called and who called me with information or response to questions or concerns on my part. Both sides were preparing for what ended up being the longest preliminary hearing I had ever experienced up to that time. It lasted two full days. Since we lawyers were well acquainted as a result of the Lopez murder trial and other cases that followed with each of them, the DAs each gave me some additional important background that Dr. Ron had been unable to provide. This is because it was apparent to the three of us that there was so much information to be digested and learned. It made sense that they would point the way to what I needed to know. This was clearly a product of professional courtesy as a result of working together in other cases over the years.

I was told that some of the records had been falsified principally by the clerks, who said it was at the doctor's direction. This, I knew would be immediately denied by Dr. Ron when I told him about their accusations. Many of the accusations included charges for prescriptions and treatment that their experts had told the DAs did not fit the patients' illnesses or diagnoses or were unnecessarily changed and duplicated. Other charges were the result of Dr. Ron's office being unable to provide the required back up notes or history to support the entries that were being charged at the time the Medicaid representative had visited the doctor's office. This was something that the two clerk ladies had not mentioned to me when I had asked them about the Medicaid man's visit with them and the questions that had been asked and answered.

All of the information I was receiving directly from the DAs was disturbing since I was convinced that Dr. Ron was not the kind of man who would knowingly falsify records or order that they be falsified by his staff. I already had worked on a number of criminal cases in which the owners or chief operating officers of the businesses faced criminal charges for acts done by their employees with or without the approval of their boss. This may be the situation that Dr. Ron found himself in. I knew and understood that the motive most likely was money but could not yet fit in the details and whether or not drug company salesmen were involved. It had to be money, but how? More and more, I was concluding that the clerks had done the doctor wrong. The problem was that I did not know how they were profiting over and above their hourly and overtime pay. The two DAs were not forthcoming about their case against the two clerks since they each had separate counsel. I knew that this would have to wait until the preliminary hearings took place in Dr. Ron's case and those of his secretaries.

When the time came for our preliminary hearing, we learned that Dr. Ron would be standing alone to face the charges. This was not a surprise since the secretaries had been cooperating when I had entered the case. Both of his clerks ended up admitting to committing fraud as their preliminary hearings were reset to enter pleas of guilty and sentencing, most likely, dependent upon testifying against Dr. Ron. I had been expecting them to both say that the doctor would only check on their work occasionally and had allowed them to use his signature stamp to approve the reports and claims for money. In this way they would be claiming that they had unwittingly made mistakes due to his lack of supervision. His was indeed a very busy in practice, causing him to concentrate on the needs of his patients and not his own business needs like so many other overloaded doctors. The result was that we found ourselves to be standing alone to face whatever accusations and charges the clerks were making in their confessions and admissions as part of their plea bargain agreements. The case jeopardy was growing exponentially. I found myself waiting to review the admissions and confessions made by the two clerks as I was attempting to shift gears on the spot as the preliminary hearing began with the testimony of the Medicaid inspector.

The preliminary hearing lasted two days with only one of the two clerks being called upon to testify, making it the longest preliminary hearing I had experienced up to that time. It took a very long time for the prosecution to present the testimony of the Medicaid inspector about the alleged charges, one by one. It was clear that the DA's office was saving the other clerk for the trial since a determination of probable cause by the Judge was inevitable and there was a great deal of ground that had to be covered by the clerk who was testifying explaining the details of the alleged wrong doing by Dr. Ron as to each count of the criminal complaint. This was compounded by the time it took me to cross-exam the investigator as we laboriously reviewed the evidence, count by count, and went through each exhibit in support of the separate charges.

The one clerk who testified stated that the two of them had been really concerned with Dr. Ron because they knew that there were errors being made and that he would not listen to their pleas or pay close attention to their specific concerns. As a part of the testimony, the DA had asked about specific entries that had been made during several months when they knew mistakes were being made that led to Dr. Ron receiving more money than he should have billed. These allegations had not been contained in the initial charges and counts. These were later to be added as amended charges and additions to several of the counts against Dr. Ron that I would receive a few days after the preliminary hearing with the deputy's apology. It was explained to me that this was due to the last-minute pleas that had been made and entered by the clerks while admitting their guilt to reduced charges against them. It became clear that we would need to have another preliminary hearing to cover the additional charges. The Judge obliged me by granting a delay to absorb all of the new information we had received before the second additional preliminary hearing was set.

In my research and review for this book, I came across an article contained in my case records in the Westminster Window by the editor dated, April 22, 1982. She was one of many spectators who attended the hearing on both days. She stated in her article as follows:

"After two witnesses testified for more than 10 hours during a preliminary hearing in Adams County Court, Judge Thomas Ensor found "probable cause" to continue with the case against (Dr. Ron) in District Court.

"The principle witness for the prosecution was John Hadden, a former investigator with the fraud unit. He said that (Dr. Ron) first came to his attention as a possible suspect in Medicaid fraud following a conversation in December, 1980 with a former nurse and bookkeeper for (Dr. Ron). She alleged (Dr. Ron) was falsifying Medicaid forms, he testified. Two other former employees of the doctor supported the claim, Hadden said.

"Hadden testified some of the tests for which Medicaid was billed by (Dr. Ron's) office are seldom performed in a doctor's office, that equipment found in (Dr. Ron's) office when it was inventoried April 8, 1981 by the law enforcement officers was insufficient to perform the suspect tests and that (Dr. Ron) was seldom billed by any outside lab for the tests in question."

"(Dr. Ron's) attorney, Mike Makaroff, pointed out all of the claims submitted to Medicaid bore the physician's signature stamp, not his personal signature. He also stressed many of the patient charts used to conduct the evidence graph were written in the handwriting of (Clerk who testified), not in that of (Dr. Ron). Makaroff also established that police had never inventoried the doctor's home for laboratory equipment, and in cross examination of Hadden it was determined that law enforcement officers could not identify what equipment was actually required to perform the various tests in question."

My cross examinations of all of the other witnesses raised questions but did not dent their testimony and with the standard of proof being less than a reasonable doubt, the Judge ordered the case bound over to a trial. This added more stress and despondency to the good doctor as he left the courtroom knowing that he now faced a trial in which he could be convicted of numerous felonies. The case had clearly become of utmost seriousness. He alone was in the direct line of fire from the testimony and plea bargains obtained by his clerks. My concern with their motives and access had now risen with the expressed and known facts.

As Dr. Ron and I were leaving the courthouse, he was began experiencing chest pains once again and we decided that I would drive behind him to his doctor's office in Denver to make sure that he arrived safely, which he and I did. I learned the next day that Dr. Ron was hospitalized with a full amount of testing being done to ascertain his condition. When I spoke to his doctor the next day, I asked him to give me his opinion about Dr. Ron's ability to withstand a jury trial in view of what had taken place after the preliminary hearing. He told me he would do so once Dr. Ron had been fully examined and checked out of the hospital. In the meantime, I decided to go back into the case and review everything to see if I could find something, anything that would cast further doubt on the two clerks and their credibility. A suspicion was not enough, but I still believed that there was an ulterior motive behind their pleas and testimony. They were covering something up and I had to find it.

I had expressed my concerns about the direction Dr. Ron's case had taken to my secretary, Jackie, once I had returned to the office following the preliminary hearing. Jackie was the best secretary I ever had working with me. I lost her as a full-time secretary only after I moved my offices to the west side of Denver, making her trip to the office impossibly long and difficult as the traffic flow worsened in Denver over the years. However, she did continue to help me part time for many additional years, allowing her to travel during the non-rush hour traffic. Jackie had been a full-time nurse for years before she became a legal secretary. Her medical knowledge and expertise was a great help in my practice since, at that time, I was handling personal injury cases in addition to the criminal and divorce matters. I often needed such expertise and knowledge to understand the medical issues. Her presence made everything better and easier.

In the Dr. Ron case, Jackie came up with the answer I was looking for. In reviewing the Amended Complaint and going back over the counts, she discovered the pattern of duplications of treatment that led to the accusations which failed to correspond with the correct timing of the administration of the medicines. In other words, they were being over prescribed. These were different medications than the ones that had been raised in the preliminary hearing. It looked to her that the two clerks were receiving kickbacks from the drug companies for the use of their drugs on behalf of the companies. Jackie was well aware of the common practice at that time to reward similarly situated employees in doctors' offices for adding use of their products into the patient cases. This was the motive for which the employees received separate compensation unknown to the doctors whose patients were being administered their products. This information raised the prospect of a complete defense on behalf of Dr. Strong in view of the guilt already established by the clerks in their separate cases. We had become aware of the inappropriate behavior taking place in Dr. Strong's offices. This became a vital part of the defense that I was constructing and would definitely help produce a more accurate understanding for both sides.

One day, a month or so later, when Dr. Ron came to my office, he once again experienced heart difficulties as we were speaking. I called Jackie into the office. She spoke with him, looked at him and checked his pulse. She said he needed to see the doctor. We called his doctor's office and an office mate and I accompanied the good doctor to his car so that he could drive to see his doctor as soon as possible. The doctor's office was not that far away. It was clear that Dr. Ron was not in good shape. We had already obtained a continuance of the first trial date because his slow recovery from the heart incident after the preliminary hearing. Recovery from the last episode had been slow and now, we were about to experience another hospitalization. I had already received a letter report from the heart doctor stating that Dr. Ron's heart condition exposed him to the danger of dying if he were to go to trial.

When I informed the prosecutors about this, they had not yet taken it to heart as a serious obstacle to trial. They proposed Guilty pleas to many of the counts and we were unable to make a deal. In the meantime, Dr. Ron looked terrible sitting in my office. He had been downcast and just plodding in his manner and mental responses. He described to me that he felt weak and unable to cope with even the lightened practice that he was still conducting which included cutting down on his staff and one of the newly hired filing clerks. He was not earning what he had before and was feeling that he could not provide for his patients in the manner that he should. He asked me, "What should I do? I feel terrible, physically and mentally. It will just not go away. Is there some way to end this nightmare?" I answered that I would ask his doctor to send me another letter after he saw him that day and will go back to trying to work things out with the DA, s office in view of what we now understood to be the reason behind the false entries by his office clerks. I told him that, "I will do everything I can. I can see that you are really ill and with your doctor's help, we will figure out a way to end this."

At some point in my regular mental review of my cases, often while driving to or from court in other matters, I remembered a US Supreme Court case, North Carolina vs. Alford that had been decided recently. It held that a lawyer could accept and work out a plea of Guilty for his client even if his client was innocent if the benefits of the plea bargain outweighed the downside of trial, finding of guilt and punishment. Under such unusual circumstances, a lawyer could act within the boundaries of ethical behavior and work out a plea of guilty ending the case and exposure of his client to life threatening repercussions. That case, once again, came to mind after I had received an even stronger written affirmation from Dr. Ron's doctor that his heart condition was absolutely not strong enough to sustain the physical and mental stress of a trial. With that in hand, I was ready to reopen negotiations with the DA's office. However, this time, I was also armed with the motives and harm done by the Doctor's clerks which gave me the ability to argue that the bad deeds had been done by the two clerks for money, unbeknown to the Doctor. I could not prove it at that point, but the billings from his office could now be read in ways that supported the theory. More important still was the fact that the actual physical and mental condition of Dr. Ron had become undeniably worse since it was fully documented and supported by the heart physician.

The next time I was scheduled to be in the Adams County, I called and set up a meeting with the two deputies in their offices about the case before the court hearing. I had already sent them the latest distressing opinion by Dr. Ron's doctor. When I raised the Alford plea with them, they objected at first, but as our meeting continued, softened their stance as we went around and round on the amount of counts to which my client should enter his plea. They argued that the doctor should plead to a large number of counts while I argued that one count was enough as long as he would receive an agreed-upon sentence of probation with the Judge's approval. The effect of the plea would be that that Dr. Ron would have to leave the practice of medicine which was now greatly diminished due to his medically deteriorating condition. This caused us to have to consider the time necessary to close down his practice and transfer his patients into the hands of other doctors which he had already started to do on his own. We went back and forth after not reaching a final decision in the meeting. However, we continued the negotiations by phone with one or the other of the deputies until we finally reached an agreement.

It was agreed that Dr. Ron would plead guilty to two counts of felony theft and all of the other counts and Misdemeanor would be dismissed. I would make a record before the judge as to the doctor's medical condition and that the case fit within the parameters set forth in the North Carolina vs. Alford case in entering the pleas of guilty to the two counts. The sentence would be for two years and no jail, with probation to begin immediately. We made phone contact with the court, spoke with the judge's clerk and set up a date for the plea on the judge's schedule in a couple of weeks. The Judge assigned to this case was well known to the prosecutors and defense counsel as a maverick judge who went his own way sometimes, even if a plea agreement had been made. We knew that both sides had to convince the judge to accept the plea. No one involved had ever done such a plea before. We were joined together to bring about a conclusion to the case.

When the court date for the hearing arrived and we appeared in court, the chief deputy of the DA's office and one of the two trials deputes, Dr. Ron, I and the court clerk were invited by the judge into his chambers for the hearing. It turned out that the Chief Deputy had informed the judge ahead of time about the proposed plea and the judge decided to have the matter heard in his chambers instead of the public courtroom. I hoped that this was a good sign as we filed into his chambers and seated ourselves around his desk with the court reporter setting himself up with his equipment alongside the judge's desk. This was common practice at that time and has been replaced with microphones in all court venues and chambers during the past years.

The trial deputy began with a statement of the intention of the parties and the consent of the DA's office under the circumstances to the plea bargain. He handed the Judge as evidence the two letters written by Dr. Ron's heart doctor and sat down. After the Judge read the letters and looked up, I told the Judge more specifically about Dr. Ron's heart problems and difficulties. I also informed the Judge about the defense that had been developed which caused me to believe that the good doctor was not guilty of the charges. I advised him that Dr. Ron was experiencing shortage of breath and weakness and what I had myself witnessed when he had twice experienced heart difficulties in my office and immediately after the preliminary hearing a month or so later. I also stressed to the Judge my belief in the doctor's innocence which had developed from my investigation of the facts and circumstances. However, since I was convinced that he may die if we went ahead with a trial, I believed that the Alford case provided the best solution and asked the judge to consent to Dr. Ron taking the "Alford" plea. When I finished, I handed the Judge a copy of the Supreme Court case. He accepted the copy and placed it alongside the case file on his desk. The Judge then proceeded to ask Dr. Ron if he understood the nature of the plea and the acceptance of guilty pleas to the two counts. Dr. Ron replied that, "I do and I believe that there is no other choice for me but to enter the plea that we are requesting you to approve," The judge then told us that he had read the Alford opinion beforehand and was prepared to accept the plea. I relaxed as we went through the formalities of the plea being entered by Dr. Ron to the two counts and dismissal of the remaining counts. The court sentenced the doctor to the two-year agreed upon sentence and granted probation. It was over. Dr. Ron walked out of the courtroom never to return. He completed all of his probation requirements without incident and lived another five years.

I have always remained grateful that we were able to resolve this case in the manner we did and allowed Dr. Ron to live out the remaining years he had without rancor or trouble. It was my understanding that Dr. Ron's two clerks, after they had entered their felony theft guilty pleas and completed probation, both found work with other doctors and neither had any further difficulties with Medicaid. Hopefully, the clerks had revised their ways and had been thoroughly watched.

It goes without saying that the case could not have been resolved without the work and cooperation of both sides. It was not just my defense work that sealed the deal. The two deputies in the case had done their due diligence and taken into account what I had raised and considered to be the way in which the crimes were accomplished by his clerks which led to the accusations against them and their ultimate entry of pleas of guilty. That, taken together with the doctor's condition made the plea bargain inevitable and allowed for what turned out to be a just resolution. What needs to be remembered is that once counsel assumes the role of defense, he must remain open to all the possibilities that are raised as the facts and circumstances unfold. When things occur that raise questions or you doubt statements or testimony, you must keep searching. All of us in court can feel it when witnesses are not being forthright, but it is not always possible to show that when you first confront the lies. Investigation and continued questioning of the known and unknown facts of a case must be pursued from whatever source possible. A trial lawyer's work goes way beyond the courtroom and into the scenes of the crime and beyond, wherever the case takes you. We all know that people lie and cover up all the time. But how do you show this? It takes time, energy and a will to pursue the paths that are opened or found by the case investigation. Sometimes, you find evidence. Other times, it can be what other people saw and heard. Finally, it can boil down to what a jury sees, hears and feels same as you or not. The more you can put together in support of what you believe to be the best-case result to be, the more likely it is that you can obtain a just solution.

CHAPTER 16

Perils in Tennessee

One again, I was given another opportunity to represent a client in jail who was facing charges in another state. This time, it was in the state of Tennessee. From what her parents told me, their daughter was charged with conspiracy to murder, theft and receiving. Apparently, her husband was also in jail and facing charges of murder and grand theft over $5000. This was certainly very serious and I made arrangements immediately to visit the daughter, Angel Porter, in Tennessee as soon as possible. I had been in Tennessee once before when I travelled by car home to my home in New York while I was in the service and stationed in Texas. I remember falling asleep during at night somewhere in eastern Tennessee and waking up just in time to catch myself as I was going off the road during a curve. I had come to a screeching stop and it took some time to gather my wits about myself and settle down before continuing my drive home, wide awake at a slower speed. I took another route back to Texas on my return trip. This experience should have warned me that there were perils ahead in Tennessee.

Once I was retained, I made arrangements to fly to Knoxville, Tennessee, rent a car and drive north to Bristol where an Army base was located in the vicinity where Angel's husband and she had been living off base. Her husband was indeed under arrest for murder and a number of burglaries while Angel was arrested and jailed facing charges as an accessory to murder and receiving stolen goods involved in some burglaries conducted by her husband in Bristol. Her parents were good people and I readily agreed to go to Tennessee and do everything I could on behalf of their daughter. I had previously met the young woman in my office while tending to family matters for the parents.

Before I left for Bristol, I had called the lawyer who had been hired by Angel's parents to represent her. He told me that he was pressed for time and could not speak long, except that she was in trouble due to her involvement in the burglaries and retention of the stolen goods. When I asked about the accessory to murder charge, he told me he could not tell me anything about that, which I found to be strange since that was most serious charge. I told him that I was flying out the next day and looked forward to meeting with him. He replied that he would be in his office. Angels' parents were anxious about their daughter because the lawyer had not been returning their calls, and when they reached him, he had failed to explain what was really going on with regard to their daughter. Angel had been in jail for about three weeks and their only contact had been with her directly in jail when she was allowed to call them. According to her parents, she had not been contacted by her lawyer to whom they were paying his bill. Angel's parents instructed me to decide what should be done when I arrived in Tennessee, including firing her lawyer if I deemed it necessary and taking over the case. This was a most interesting task and I looked forward to learning the facts and circumstances of the case and meeting with Arnold Beachum, her lawyer. Everything turned out to be a surprise.

I arrived at Arnold Beachum's office in mid- afternoon. He was there and I was soon let into his office. He was tall, well dressed and formal in speaking with me. It was obvious to me that he knew I was there to question what he had been doing, if anything. His file had just a few documents in it from what I could see sitting across from him at his desk. He told me that in talking with the DA, Darrel Kingston, they had an open and shut case against Angel's husband since the local police had been suspicious about her husband for a series of home burglaries. The last one had involved a shooting in which a burglary had gone bad. The husband had been wounded and the homeowner was dead. As for Angel, I was told that she knew all about her husbands' burglaries since the police found some stolen goods in their search of the mobile home where she was living. When I asked about his conversations with our client, he told me that she was denying any knowledge about the burglaries and that she had apparently kicked her husband out of their home before the murder had taken place. Arnold Beachum had appeared on her behalf in court once but had not seen her since. He told me that "I was concentrating my time and efforts working things out with the DA, Darrel Kingston. Darrel is a good guy and things will be worked out in due course." I asked whether any negotiations about the terms of a plea bargain had taken place. His answer was. "Not Yet." I asked what was holding things up since his client and family were very concerned and upset with no news. "Well. You know. Things cannot be rushed under the circumstances." This meant to me that he was sitting on the case and not pushing forward with the DA who was in court daily real close to Arnold's office.

I did not believe half of what Arnold was telling me. I sensed that he was just telling me what he had been told by the DA. He was speaking to me in a formal and patronizing manner and made it obvious that he was busy with other matters that needed his attention. I then asked him to call the DA and arrange for me to see him so that I could report back to the parents as quickly as possible. I also requested to have it arranged so that I could visit her in the jail. Arnold told me that neither request would be a problem because the DA's office was close by and, actually, the jail containing my client was in the building next door. He said, "A visitation with Angel could be worked out very quickly. I did not know exactly what he meant, but soon found out.

I left Arnold knowing I had been bullshitted and also with the serious impression that he had not done any work at all on behalf of our client, and worse still, he had no feelings or concerns for our mutual client. His attitude was paternal and dismissive of her. She did not matter. I almost fired him on the spot since his parents had instructed me to do whatever I thought was necessary. However, I decided to wait until I had met with the DA and Angel before acting on my first impressions. The truth was, I was thinking about the proximity of the DA's office and the jail to his office just two blocks away and nothing having been done for several weeks. It was ridiculous that the lawyer had not done one thing while being so close to the DA's office and the jail. I said goodbye and left Arnold's office and walked the short distance to the courthouse, which, similar to small towns in Colorado contained the jail, courthouse and the DA's office near to each other. It was always pretty convenient to do legal business in criminal matters in small towns in the outlying counties in Colorado. It appeared to be the same in Bristol.

Darrel Kingston was in court when I visited the DA offices, so I walked next door to the courthouse and I soon found myself in the same courtroom where he was conducting business. I saw him standing before the Judge's bench and speaking to the Judge. The judge stood up and started to leave the bench through a door behind him. People were also leaving the courtroom as I entered and it was nearly empty. As I approached Darrel, I called out his name and he said." That's me." I approached the bench where he had been standing and introduced myself as the lawyer from Colorado who represented

Angel Porter. He greeted me in a very friendly way and after some small talk about flying in to Knoxville and driving to Bristol, we talked about criminal law in Colorado and how I enjoyed visiting the less populated areas similar to Bristol. Then, Darrel and I began speaking about my client and her present circumstances. Very quickly, he said to me that, "She has not been cooperating and this has been standing in the way of getting something done." I responded by asking, "Has her lawyer been cooperating to facilitate putting together a deal?" Darrel replied. "Oh, Arnold. He has a large civil practice and the Judge appoints members of the bar, one by one, to defend indigent clients. It was Arnold's turn. He showed up for the first hearing and I have not seen or heard from him since. I guess he is just too involved with this practice." There it was. Angel had an inexperienced and uninterested appointed counsel who did not have time for her and her predicament. Her parents had every reason to be concerned since I was learning that he was also inexperienced in the criminal law work. I then asked, "What do we need to do to get things rolling." Darrel replied, "We want her cooperation regarding the past burglaries so that we can sew them all up in a package and put her husband away for as long as possible. We have already obtained a bunch of stuff from the Mobile home, but we want times and dates so that we can tie him in with some of the unsolved burglaries. We are in the process of adding counts to the charges and we want to get them right." "Have you told that to Arnold?" I asked. "Yes, of course. But, as I said, he is busy with his cases making money" was Darrel's reply. This was the complete answer to the lack of information and contact with Angel's parents.

Next, I asked about the accessory to murder charge. I said. "If I fire Arnold, and take over the case and get whatever help I can from Angel, can we make a deal that will get her home to Colorado?" Darrel thought a minute and said, "Let's see if we can make it happen." Then, Darrel surprised me when He said, "You want to see her now."? "Yes, of course, that is why I came here from Colorado. I have been hired to do whatever is necessary, including becoming her lawyer and firing Arnold, if that is necessary. So, there is no better time than the present." This had all been taking place in front of the Judge's bench. Darrel picked up the phone on the bench and asked for the jail. As he did so, I looked around the courtroom and noticed for the first time that there were bars across all of the left side of the courtroom that stood from the floor to the ceiling. Inside that space were a number of chairs in sort of a row. The space was empty, but I figured that this was obviously set up to conduct business with the prisoners who had to come before the court on preliminary advisements and other court matters. I gathered that Angel would be brought out to speak to us at this time, and indeed, this is what happened. The deputy district attorney waited along with me until she was brought in to the barred space by a jailer. It was like nothing I had ever before experienced. Voila, there she was.

When Angel arrived and was brought to the bars dividing the jail from the courtroom, she was indeed followed by a jailer who stayed a few yards away and behind her as she came forward to the bars. It was a sad picture looking at her as she stood forlornly with her hands on two bars as she looked through them at me at me with tears in her eyes. She did not look well. I had met her once before in my office and she looked so much different from the young and fresh-looking girl I had met at that time. She was clearly depressed, tear-eyed and upset. Darrel had given us the courtesy of leaving the then empty courtroom saying he would check back into the courtroom in about twenty minutes. If I was ready to speak to him then, we could begin talking or, "If you are not yet ready, we can start talking later, whenever you are ready." He was certainly being cooperative, and I thanked him as he turned to leave us alone while the jail guard remained visible, but distant from where we were standing and talking. As the courtroom emptied and I was left to speak with my client standing opposite her at the bars, the uniformed jailer remained sitting behind Angel about eight or ten feet away. She and I automatically lowered our voices as we spoke.

When the DA left, he told me that the jailer would remain in the background and not to be concerned about anything being heard. He told me the voices did not carry well and," anyways, whatever you and she may say is confidential, as you know, and the jailers do not pay much attention." Of course, I was familiar with this and had had many interviews with clients with policemen or jailers nearby in courthouses or jails in different places in Colorado. I was left to conduct my interview with Angel with both of us standing. This created a problem as I juggled with my note pad to find a way to write and talk. I ended up placing it flat against the bars and holding it with my left hand as I took notes of the interview. That too, did not work. I put the note pad away and concentrated on what was being said by my client.

Angel stood close by at the bars as we looked at each other through them. She spoke in a whisper "I am so glad to see you. Can you please get me out of here? They do not treat us blacks here the same as they do in Colorado, Mr. Makaroff. It is terrible. My lawyer will not see or talk to me. I did not do anything. I know my husband shot a man, but I kicked him out of our home some time ago. I am going to get a divorce. I am glad the police took the things he stole out of my home. I did not have anything to do with that. He told me that he would hurt me bad if I told anyone what was there. He is a mean dude and I had to keep quiet. Please, please get me out of here!"

I guess she said it all and it was clear what I needed to do. I continued the interview and asked if she knew any other persons who may have participated in the burglaries. I figured that it would be helpful if she did since the DA would like to have additional names. She told me that" My husband did meet with some other guys from time to time." but she only knew a couple of names like, "Legs" or "Dog." Her husband was close mouthed about his comings and goings. She only knew that he had told her very seriously to "keep your mouth shut." He never told her where he had been to collect the "stuff "he left at their home and that he would periodically replace the goods with other goods that he would later take away. She came to understand that he would in the meantime be, "selling" or "cashing in" on some of the stolen goods because, from time to time, he had money and they would go out and celebrate. She did agree to cooperate with the DA and identify other possible suspects and the approximate dates or times when she saw some of the goods. All of this, of course, made Angel out to be an accessory as she was reciting her limited involvement to me. She told me that, "I was not brought up to live this way. I hated what he (her husband) was doing. As soon as you can get me out of jail, I want to leave Bristol and return to Colorado and divorce him."

I told her, "One thing at a time, Angel." Do you know anything about where he went to exchange the goods or receive the money?" She did not. We were not going to have much bargaining power. It was an altogether bad situation. She also volunteered that her husband had repeatedly told her that if she told the police anything about his stealing, "You will be sorry. You will pay for it and you will not like it." She was definitely scared of him and was visibly upset when she spoke about him. This was good to know because and it was something I had seen over and over again in such circumstances with wives and girlfriends of felons. Such information often helped in putting a deal together with considerate prosecuting attorneys. Her fear was visible and I realized that Darrel would easily see that she was telling the truth. It would sell itself to the DA.

Darrel came back into the courtroom and when I saw him, I met him halfway and briefed him on what I had learned from my client. I told Darrel that Angel would cooperate and asked for his help to get her released ASAP. He told me that he "thought something can be worked out." We then approached her standing at the bars. Darrel stood right next to me across from Angel on the other side of the bars. Without looking at her he spoke directly to me and told me that he had often conducted talks with lawyers in the same manner. He found that in this way the clients understood that he was not speaking directly to them, nor was he intending to be discourteous. Instead, he had found that under the circumstances of the bars separating us from the clients, that the prisoners generally understood that he was allowing them or her, in these circumstances, to learn and hear the full picture of what was taking place. It made sense and I had already determined that I could trust Darrel to act appropriately. I went ahead with talking to him in front of Angel after telling her to, "Listen carefully but do not say anything. I will do all the talking." Darrel said to us, "Our investigators will speak with your client if you agree and will be present. If all goes well, I will see what we can do about releasing her as quickly as possible." At that point, I stated for Angel to know that, "I will be with you for any interrogation which I hope will take place very soon." We then arranged on the spot for it to take place the following morning since I had stressed to Darrel that I needed to get back to Denver as soon as it was possible. Following the meeting and agreement, Darrel arranged for the judge to appear once again on the bench and we proceeded with a hearing so that I could formally enter my appearance as counsel on behalf of Angel that afternoon.

Soon after our negotiations had finished, Darrel left us and went next door into the judge's chambers and informed the judge that we were ready to appear in front of him. Since the judge's chambers were so conveniently next door to the courtroom opposite the barred prisoner area, no time was lost before we proceeded with a formal court appearance when the judge returned to the bench and called Angel's case to begin formal proceedings. The court approved my entry of appearance after hearing Darrel present me to the court as a practicing lawyer in good standing in Colorado. Darrel then proceeded to inform the Judge that effectively, I had the client's approval to take over the case from Mr. Beachum and about Angel's willingness to cooperate and that a meeting with his investigator was set for tomorrow. He asked that her case be reset for hearing on the following day in the hope that once the investigation had been completed we would be able reach a reasonable plea bargain and an end of the case. Finally, Darrel asked that the bond be continue pending the outcome of the investigation and inquiry. I informed the court that the defense agreed to all that was stated by Darrel and looked forward to a successful conclusion to the case with both sides in agreement.

Once this was accomplished on the record, the judge spoke with me about Colorado and his love of skiing and wished both sides well in working out the case. With that, the court was adjourned and everyone left but myself and Angel and her guard.

I visited the jail next door to spend time with Angel and fully explaining what would occur tomorrow and that what was needed was for her to inform the investigator and Darryl about everything she knew or remembered about the burglaries. I told her that I would be with her all the way. Naturally, she was concerned about what the final plea bargain agreement would be and when she might be allowed to leave the jail and Tennessee. I told her that I felt good about working out a deal that would release her and that she would soon be leaving Tennessee because that was going to be a part of the deal. "It will all happen, and soon." I told her. She was thanking me as we parted and she was taken back into the prison by the guard. Altogether, it had been an amazingly productive day as I turned and left the most unusual Tennessee courtroom to await the next day at 9 am in Darrel's offices where we had arranged to have the meeting with Angel. Darrel informed me that Angel would be brought directly to his office at that time.

It turned out that the jail did have a couple of attorney rooms available for use to speak at length with Angel. I did spend more time with Angel later that afternoon as we more fully prepared as best we could for the meeting with the investigator and DA by having her recollect as much as she could about the times, dates and observations she could remember about the various thefts, burglaries and evidence found in her home. She could not help in the murder case because they were already separated and her husband turned up at the home only a few times unexpectedly afterwards. She was not a murderer or axe killer. She was a frightened wife and an unwilling victim of her husband, but she did resolve to think about anything and everything she could remember about the "stuff" that her husband had deposited at their home, including times and dates as best she could. She was in full agreement. All she wanted was to get out of jail as quickly as possible. Same as she, I was hoping for it to happen without delay. I left her with the thought that "we will know it all tomorrow."

We met the next morning with the deputy DA and his investigator. Angel answered all of the questions to the best of her ability. She gave times and dates to the best of her recollection of the stolen goods being brought to the mobile home. She advised us that she and her husband had argued because she did not want the stolen goods to be left in their home. She wanted nothing to do with stolen property and felt degraded and betrayed by what her husband had been doing and bringing home. She reiterated several times that," This was not how I had been raised." Since I knew her parents and that she was telling the truth, I told that to Darrel as the interrogation was taking place. They were decent god-fearing people who were honest and hard working. I had known the family for many years. She went on to explain that her husband would not relent from his thieving and their arguments grew worse and had become physical. She broke down in front of us several times as the interrogation proceeded.

Angel informed the investigator that her husband was not living at home at the time of the killing for which he had been arrested. She relayed that she kept insisting that her husband take the goods out of the home. She wanted nothing to do with them, but her husband would not do as she wished. Moreover, he threatened her to "Keep her mouth shut and to do as I say." Her husband had explained that "getting rid of the stolen property takes time and I am working on it." They would argue over and over, and, finally, about three of weeks before the killing, they had broken up and he had not returned home. She did not know where he was at the time of the murder. They had spoken on the phone a few days before and he promised to pick up the last of the goods left at the home. He had not done so. She had been planning to obtain a divorce and return to her family in Denver.

As Angel's story unfolded, both sides came to understand that her crime was one of failing to report her husband's criminal conduct and the fact that she had permitted the stolen goods to remain in the home under duress. Same as in Colorado, the possession of stolen property amounted to either being at the level of misdemeanor or felonies depending on the value of the goods. Since she was charged with being an accessory and complicit with her husband in the burglaries, we heard directly from her that she was "physically threatened and under duress." It became clear that Angel did not know exactly what had been stored since she would not look inside the boxes and garbage bags in which they lay and only saw what had not been covered. She did not know from where or whom the goods had been stolen by her husband. He never told her where or when he would do a job.

Following the completed interrogation, in view of Angel's cooperation, Darrel announced that he was willing to peg the value of the goods in the misdemeanor range of less than five hundred dollars despite the fact that the total of all the stolen goods were in the felony range. Effectively, Darrel had been convinced that Angel was the person she had said she was and had been a victim of her husband's threats and violence against her will. In return for a misdemeanor plea to possession of stolen goods, he agreed that she would receive probation and the right to transfer the probation to Denver. We then worked out as part of the plea bargain that Angel would be allowed to be freed from jail as soon as the papers could be drawn up and we appeared in court before the Judge for entry of the plea and sentencing. There was nothing left for me to negotiate. It was everything I would have asked for. What happened in Tennessee was that my client had herself convinced the DA of who she was and that she deserved the treatment he offered to give her. We gratefully accepted the deal. Such things do happen and District Attorneys do have hearts and will act accordingly in most cases. I have actually had many such plea bargain agreements made during my career, but never one where I had to travel as far as I did.

The agreed upon entry of the plea agreement was made before the court the following morning. Angel and I had spent the morning with her being questioned by a good old boy detective who quickly and quietly took her through all of the facts and information that she was able to supply. I asked for an additional agreement to vacate the plea and charge completely after the probation in Colorado had been successfully completed. This was something that had been passed recently by our legislature in Colorado and also existed, it turned out, in Tennessee. It meant that once everything was done and her husband was found guilty and her probation was successfully completed, she could have her criminal record removed. Darrel agreed since he cared for Angel. She and I were both very pleased with the final provision of the agreement.

The final disposition was a plea to Failure to Report the crimes committed, a misdemeanor, with a two-year probation to be completed in Colorado. Angel would be free to pick up her belongings, report to the local Bristol probation office where arrangements would be made and signed off on a transfer of her probation to Colorado. We also agreed and promised that Angel would voluntarily return to Bristol if she were needed to testify in the case against her husband and if she failed to do so, this would be a violation of her probation. This was highly unlikely since they had such a strong case against her husband. In fact, he ultimately pleaded out and went to jail for a long, long time. Angel, on the other hand returned to Colorado, completed her probation, divorced her husband and resumed the way of life she was taught and raised by her parents. I learned a few years later that he had met and married a good man in Denver and they were happily married and expecting a child. Good news is always great to receive in my business.

At the end of the day of the interrogation and the court appearance that followed, for which we obtained the Judge's consent to the plea bargain and release of Angel from jail, I returned to the law offices of Arnold Beechum where I felt a final parting was necessary. He was actually expecting me since Darrel had called him. I did not say much since it was unnecessary, but did add to my farewell, "You owe it to your future clients and yourself as a lawyer to do a better job when you are appointed counsel in a case. What little you did and failed to do in this case is a disgrace. You could have easily done all of what I have accomplished on behalf of Angel and saved her and her parents a lot of money and, most important, avoided for a lovely woman extra time in jail. You failed miserably to live up to your oath as a lawyer. I guess I don't have to tell you what I think about you. Goodbye." He did not reply to my statement as I turned and left his office.

I spent that evening in lodgings in Bristol and returned to Denver on the third day. Angel was happy to be free at last and immediately began to pack all of her belongings into her car for her return to Denver as soon as she had completed the necessary forms for switching her probation from Bristol to Denver. On my part, I returned to Denver disturbed by the cavalier attitude of Arnold Beechum. His inaction had caused Angel to spend weeks in jail that could have been easily minimized if he had acted immediately as a lawyer should.

What happened to Angel represented by a lawyer who failed to do his duty repeats itself over and over in American courts. Many times, the client does not even know or understand the professional negligence that is taking place, but fellow lawyers and judges do know. Obtaining a lawyer to represent you properly in a case is a risky business. Advertising on TV or radio is not always a good solution. After all, it is the lawyer himself promoting himself. We are all very good at showing the best about ourselves. What matters is how the lawyer performs and how seriously he is committed to representing his clients. This is best known to the judges and fellow attorneys who watch or deal with their fellow attorney's in cases. For example, Arnold Beechum was well known to the prosecuting attorney and the local bar of fellow lawyers. Good lawyers stand out and are known to all of us, judges included. Bad lawyers are easily spotted and identified, but rarely to the public. However, few people get their referrals from court or counsel. This leaves all of us open to whatever friends, neighbors or anyone who has actually experienced how good or bad a lawyer performs in cases. This can be the best type of referral. It comes from people who have actually experienced a lawyer's work ethic, abilities and performance. Most of my business came from referrals from my clients, the second being from fellow lawyers and judges. If your case is serious, one must seriously pursue obtaining the right lawyer for your needs. It means fully exploring what the lawyer has done for the friends who are recommending him and whether he or she had had lived up to their commitments, this inevitably leads to one additional thought. Different lawyers have different specialties; what they do best. That is what you must learn in your search to obtain good counsel and avoid what happened to Angel Porter.

As I write this, I fully recognize that the present times have changed with the advent of the internet and instantaneous communication. I read and see newspapers, magazines, radio, TV and internet with advertisements about attractive lawyers; men and women shown to be masters of the different specialties that they practice in courts in Colorado and elsewhere. For the most part, I do not know them. As I read their wonderfully written and prepared biographies, a part of me shudders at the thought that they need to advertise what solid courtroom work establishes for the best trial lawyers; a well-earned reputation, which, in turn brings business to the lawyer's doors from satisfied clients. That is the best indicator of a lawyer's worth, not his or her self- proclaimed advertising. In the meantime, the grievances against lawyers grow and continue without stop. God help you in your search for the right lawyer.

CHAPTER 17

Jury Response to Racism

I am reminded of a case I tried in which my Russian client was charged with felony assault against another man. The incident happened, as it turned out, in front of many witnesses. When I took the case and obtained the discovery materials, they included two witness statements in support of the victim's statement that my client was the perpetrator of the direct assault against him with his fists. The client, Anatoly Labrinsky, told me a different story. He said that that there were at least two or three other witnesses who were with him at the time and place of the alleged assault that the police detective failed to interview. He went on to state that the other witnesses were with him in his car when he arrived at the vehicle repair store to locate some parts for his vehicle. When he exited his car close by to the store, Anatoly told me that he was attempting to determine from the man who approached him whether they had the parts he was seeking. Instead of answering, the man told Anatoly that he was parked in the wrong place and to move his car. Anatoly continued to explain his purpose in visiting the store and was asking if the parts he was looking for were available. The man insisted that he move his car immediately and the two men began to argue. As the words escalated between the them,' they squared off and the employee of the business attacked Anatoly and landed the first blow to which Anatoly immediately responded. The fight did not last long since Anatoly soon landed a punch across the other person's nose which ended up braking the man's nose. This stopped the fight just as one of Anatoly's friends had stepped in to attempt to separate the two men. Anatoly returned to his car with his friends as the other persons present gathered around the fallen man and helped him get up and leave to presumably seek medical assistance.

Anatoly explained to me that when the police arrested him soon after the fight, he had tried to tell the detective that he had witnesses who were there with him and had seen the fight from the beginning to the end. He told me that the detective asked him, "Are the witnesses Russian? Apparently, from Anatoly's accent, the detective had correctly guessed that Anatoly was Russian. "Anatoly replied, "Yes, we are." Then the detective said to him, "Ok. I know what they will say. I do not need to talk to them. They will support your side." Anatoly remembered then saying, "Yes, they will say that the other man started the fight, not me." Anatoly immediately understood that he would not get any help from the detective. He was aware of other Russian immigrants, like himself, having had similar credibility difficulties with these particular police department where the incident occurred. He could see that the detective was accepting what the victim's witnesses were saying about the fight, all of them apparently fellow workers or friends. The detective stopped listening to Anatoly and proceeded to arrest him and take him into custody. As he was being arrested, the detective told Anatoly that, "I know your Russian friends will tell whatever lies they may make up to help you. We get this all the time from Russians and we have learned not to pay attention." He proceeded to arrest Anatoly for an aggravated felony assault since it was clear that he anticipated that the injury to the victim, named, Don, would be sufficient to support a felony charge.

By the time the incident happened, we had many Russian immigrants in Colorado, including Denver, the suburbs and outlining cities. The particular city where this happened had been rapidly increasing in Russians and other immigrant groups since the late 1980s. The police were well acquainted with Russians as they joined with other ethnic groups moving into the suburbs. It turned out that the experience of the local police with Russians had developed into a bias that became the central problem in this case.

I went to the police station to obtain all the discovery materials, including the complaint and witness's statements before seeing my client in the jail located next door to the police headquarters. I would do this whenever possible since this always made the first interview with a client more productive. It allowed me to probe more accurately for information about what had taken place at the scene of the crime and the events leading up to the crime. Police documents always contained important information and, frequently, witness and victims' statements that gave counsel and client a real good idea about what the client was facing. Invariably, the client's recollections would be different from what was relayed in the police reports. This case was no different as Anatoly strongly denied what the alleged victim and his witnesses had said about the fight between himself and the victim. However, the police report contained only the statements of the two witnesses who sided with the man who was felled by my client's fists. My clients defense and any witness statements did not exist besides those of the alleged victim. Anatoly told me the police officer had refused to speak to them. This was highly unusual since it was my experience that the police almost always took down all the names, addresses and statements of witnesses to a crime and, certainly, in an assault case where the victim ended up with a bloody and broken nose.

This was a felony case and it was serious. I could see that Anatoly was also injured about his face and neck with contusions as a result of the short fight. However, nothing was broken and, according to him, he had won the fight with the victim who had started it. I immediately arranged for Anatoly to have photos taken of his face and hands so that we had a record of what he had endured. Moreover, I wanted to learn all I could about Anatoly's witnesses. As he gave me their names and phone numbers, I learned that they included a former Ukrainian heavyweight boxing champion, Ivan Valinenko, who had inserted himself into the middle of the two men immediately after the fight had been started by the other guy. Anatoly told me that his friend, the boxing champion, had been right next to him when the other guy had unexpectedly hit him hard with his right fist in the middle of the argument that had occurred as Anatoly and he were arguing before the fight started. He affirmed that there had been two witnesses standing behind the man with whom he had fought who had greeted him outside of the store. It turned out that they were not employees. They were the victim's friends who were there visiting.

Anatoly explained that he had driven to the particular motor vehicle store in order to obtain some parts for his vehicle. Upon stating that he was a customer, he was told loudly by Don that he had "parked in the wrong place." Then, once Don learned that he was Russian, Anatoly told me that Don told him to. "Get the hell out of here." Anatoly tried to explain that he was there to do business. Again, the response was that Don become, "angrier and came closer to me. At the same time, my friends had also gotten out my car, including my boxer friend, Ivan. They had come up alongside me as Don was shouting at me and in my space. Don had two friends who were also close by. It did not look good. The fight started with Don hitting me across my face as I tried to duck his blow. I recovered and was able to respond fast and hard. We exchanged a couple of hits and I could feel my last blow hit him flush on his nose. I could hear it break. He slumped to the ground and Ivan, who is big and strong, kept the other two men away from me. Don started it and I finished it."

I contacted both Ivan Valinenko, the boxing champion, and the two witnesses to arrange to meet with them at my office as soon as possible. All three men were upset with Anatoly being arrested and charged. They had all seen and heard everything and helped put together the money necessary to have Anatoly bailed out from jail soon after I had seen him at the jail. Their stories totally corroborated what Anatoly had told me about the incident. It was apparent that this was developing into a case with witnesses on both sides that would be testifying about opposite views of what transpired. It definitely looked like it would become a jury trial of the of opposing witnesses.

Igor Valinenko was a very interesting and soft-spoken man. He was about 5ft 10 inches tall and very big and strong as one might expect from a national heavyweight champion. He looked as if he weighed about two hundred fifty pounds. He was a formidable man. What I did not expect was how charming he was and able in Russian accented English to spell out in detail just how the fight had begun in front of him and how he had stepped in to separate Anatoly from Don. He was right there at the scene of the fight from start to finish. He saw the first blow by the alleged victim while he had been standing very close to Anatoly and saw Anatoly's response as the fight started. I asked Igor if he could show me just how fast it all happened by throwing a punch at me without hitting me. He readily agreed. He was used to such things from being in the ring and proceeded to demonstrate to me how fast the first blow was made. In doing so, Ivan did indeed stop just short of contact with my face as he punched at my face. This gave me the idea to have him demonstrate exactly the same thing with me in court in front of the jury. The fact that he was so fast with his punch made me believe that if this was done in front of a jury, they would see that it was entirely possible that no one but Igor actually saw the blow that started the fight. In fact, this was exactly what Igor was telling me as he was recollecting and demonstrating the fight that had taken place in front of him. He was going to be a great witness for the defense. I could visualize him doing the same demonstration of a punch with me in front of the jury. I loved it and believed from that time on that if we had to go to trial, we would win.

One of the other witnesses, Yuri, was also very good, but would need a translator in court because his English was not yet up to speed. I also learned that the third witness on behalf of Anatoly had just been visiting friends He had returned to LA where he lived. He also was not conversant in English and would need an interpreter. This is why I was so pleased that Ivan would be able to describe the immediate action to the jury in English with a Ukrainian accent. Having defended many Russians and Ukrainians with translators, I had learned how difficult this was to do. The translators were often poor in their English translations, which drove me crazy since I understood Russian and Ukrainian to a lesser degree and was able to follow all such testimony as it was being given in court. It always worried me in any of the other languages since I had a good idea how translators failed to appropriately translate Russian to juries and could only guess at how poorly the job was being done by the translators in the other languages.

The necessity for Russian translators had grown considerably in the 1980s when the then USSR had decided to allow a huge amount of their population to leave Russia and immigrate to other countries, with USA, England and Israel being the favored destinations. This forever made me skeptical about all translators in any language who were being increasingly used in our courts. Sadly, this was not well known to the Judges, lawyers, witnesses or the litigants themselves who had everything at stake in their cases. It was no different for me when I had to rely upon my translators in other languages. Naturally, I paid close attention to the Russian translators that appeared in my cases. If I found that they were not up to the job, I would make sure that we had a better translator the next time they were needed. I cannot stress how important it is for correct translations to occur in court for the benefit of your clients. Without one, the jury does not hear the tone or substance of what is being translated.

American juries have trouble with all the many languages of persons I have represented. We are not a linguistically talented country, except in the major cities and ports. When a translator is necessary, this often causes juries to fail to hear truly and correctly what the clients and witnesses are saying, through no fault of their own. Juries are denied the ability and senses to hear or understand the tone or feeling of what is really being said by the witnesses, their intonations or even the sense or meaning of their responses that are evident to all of us who speak the same language. If the lawyer himself does not know the language of the witness, he or she is often left without a true understanding of the failures in the translations to the juries that are happening in court in front of them. Sometimes, I was able to correct things with additional questions to cover the points that were missed or poorly translated from the Russian. I have even objected to the court about the Russian translations when I felt that the translations were incorrect or damaging in some way. This would put the Judge in an impossible situation of ruling on what he could not possibly decide. I learned to offer together with my objections that the translator and I speak to each other and work out the appropriate English word or words. The poor Judges had no way of deciding and they would allow me speak to the translator and get him or her to agree to say what the correct translation was to the court or jury. My English was always better than the translators involved and such discussions always worked out with the translators admitting their errors. Still, this would not necessarily solve the problem since the jurors would be distressed and uncertain about what they heard or were told. All of this always made it hard to try and win cases with a translator.

I have recommended to fellow lawyers, if the case was important enough, they should always have a person in court with them who understood both languages fully in order to be able to advise counsel of any mistake that had been made in the translations. In this way, an objection could be lodged for the record. A few followed my advice and thanked me when it paid off. It certainly was helpful for my clients when I was able to correct misstatements by Russian translators in my cases. However, it caused me to continue to wonder if I was receiving correct translations from interpreters in other languages that I was not familiar with.

It was time for me to meet and speak with the detective who had arrived at the scene and met with Don, his witnesses, and Anatoly. I had all the necessary information and actually hoped to be able to convince the detective that he had made a mistake. The Detective, named Jarvis, was experienced, direct and surprisingly frank in his replies to my questions. He told me that, "Yes, your client said that he had other witnesses. I was not going to be bothered by them since my experience with Russians has been that they will lie and say whatever was necessary. There was no reason for me to do additional work and attempt to obtain their statements." I immediately replied, "Detective Jarvis, it was your duty to hear and take the additional statements. You and I both know that. If you had, I can tell you that one of the witnesses was standing right there on the spot when the fight started. He saw who struck the first blow and the fight from beginning to the end. He was much closer than the other two witnesses you chose to interview. We will win the case in court. I am asking that you spare all of us and the city from having to go through the time and effort of a trial to prove that my client did not throw the first punch. Please meet with the witness and learn for yourself what happened. I understand that you may have been lied to by some Russians in the past, but that is not the case here. These witnesses are solid. Russians and Ukrainians are just as capable as we are to see and describe what they saw and heard." It was to no avail.

When I met the prosecutor, who was assigned to the case, she too was not convinced and accepted the detectives' witnesses and versions of the events. More importantly, she failed to ask about what our witnesses would say or to even meet with them. Having been a deputy city attorney when I was younger did not help me as the current deputy city attorney rejected my proffered evidence. As a former prosecutor, I found this to be appalling and unprofessional. However, I did not insist. I immediately realized that this would give the defense a great advantage if we were in fact going to go to trial in the case. She had no plans to interview my witnesses. This only helped my case when the chips would fall in the courtroom and the prosecutor would be hearing and seeing the evidence and witnesses for the first time. She was obviously willing to come to court unprepared. That was a real plus for our side.

Since Don had suffered a broken nose injury, the case indeed rose to the level of a felony. This was serious with unattractive penalties and the chance of Anatoly being sent to the penitentiary in the event of conviction. It was not a laughing matter and was a case that needed to be carefully and fully prepared for trial. I had no luck getting Don or his two witnesses to speak to me. When I called Don to speak with him, he informed me that he had contacted a lawyer to start a lawsuit against Anatoly. When I asked for the lawyer's name, he would not give it to me. He said his lawyer was going to wait until, "Anatoly pleaded Guilty or a jury decided that he was guilty." I answered, "This was a wise choice by your lawyer."

The trial began with detective Jarvis taking the stand to outline the date, location, jurisdiction and nature of the offense. He testified about the witnesses he had spoken to and what they had relayed to him. He also admitted that other witnesses had volunteered to tell him about the crime but that he declined to interview them. I asked, Why? "Because I already had sufficient evidence and witnesses to support the conclusion that Anatoly was the guilty party," was his answer. This was an obvious attempt by the City Attorney to cover the detective's negligence and bias in failing to speak to the other Russian witnesses who were on our side. I looked at the jury and felt that this was not something that was being well received. Now that we were in trial, I could see that the deputy City Attorney was beginning to truly face for the first time the dilemma created by her detective and herself in not learning what the other witnesses had to say. The jury was already showing concern.

When it came time to cross examine the detective, I took him back to the time he and I had met at the Police headquarters soon after he had arrested Anatoly. He admitted to rejecting the statements of the Russian witnesses. He also admitted that I had told him about the other witnesses and gave him a good idea about what they would say when I gave him copies of their signed statements. Those very statements and writings were soon to be placed into evidence as I was cross-examining the detective and were admitted by the Judge as Exhibits subject to later identification by the witnesses themselves. The detective testified in front of the jury that "I knew the Russians would get together and concoct a story anyway. I knew where this case was going." "You mean to a trial where all the witnesses would testify?" I asked him as the cross examination continued. "Yes." He responded. "Detective Jarvis, isn't it your job to meet with and check all witnesses, whether they knew the defendant or not so long as they saw what happened, whether they were Russians or not?" "Not in this case," he answered. "I had plenty of experience with Russian witnesses and knew what they would say." I was watching the jury during this exchange, and a woman in the front, in particular. She had been paying close attention during the trail and I could see that she was jarred by the Detective's answers. I could also see other jurors' who appeared to be similarly affected.

Things looked even better after the two witnesses that detective had testified about came across as extremely partisan against Anatoly. I found myself prodding each of them to tell more and more of the bad things they had seen since neither of them were allowed to see or hear what the detective had testified about before they were on the stand. This is the normal practice in court since witnesses are not allowed to hear what previous witnesses had said. The two of them ended up contradicting each other and the detective as they tried to add to the case against Anatoly. The jury was hearing and seeing this all unfold and I had not yet put on my witnesses and defense. I felt that the momentum of our case was already being established since juries do not miss among themselves the nuances and contradictions that evolve from the testimony of the prosecution witnesses or any other witnesses.

The most important part of the defense was the testimony of Ivan Valinenko, the former Heavyweight Champion of Ukraine. In preparation for his testimony, I had a meeting with him in my office to choreograph the presentation of his testimony. As a boxer, his training and fighting made him the perfect witness to explain and demonstrate to the jury the sequence of what took place. When he and I first met, I had been struck with the idea of showing exactly how fast the action had taken place at the time of the incident, so fast that it was possible that none of other witnesses had even seen it, including Don's friends who were behind him. Having boxed myself in college, I had a good idea about how fast things took place in the ring. I was knocked back on the ropes one time with a shot to my chin that I barely saw. Ivan had seen the first blow because he was closest to the action and right next to both men. Others may have missed it entirely and only seen Anatoly's response, making Don's witnesses very possibly 'truthful' but wrong. To accomplish this, I asked him to throw the punch at me same as he had done in the office, but now, in front of the jury where I stood in front Igor. With the consent of the Judge, Igor left the witness chair and joined me in front of the jury. We faced each other as if to fight same as Don and Anatoly did the actual fight as we had practiced in my office. I stood still as he punched at me and stopped his fist just short of my face. At that moment, I could see and hear the jurors react to the punch thrown at me by Ivan. Several of the jurors leaned back against their seats at the sight of seeing me almost hit on my face. It surprised everybody but the two of us.

Next, I had Ivan return to the witness chair and explain slowly and evenly that because he was so close, "I saw the punch that landed on Anatoly that any other person could easily miss. Anatoly had reacted by fighting back and successfully landed two punches that brought the other man down to the ground. I was not able to stop it before it ended. Then, I tried to help Don by picking him up. It was a fair fight and Anatoly won." Ivan was truly a star witness for the defense. He had impacted the jury. Soon after I also questioned Yuri with a translator, who also supported what Ivan had said from his standpoint a few feet away. Finally, Anatoly, took the stand and also made a good impression on the jury as he relayed the now familiar events that had taken place that day. The deputy DA cross examined as best she could each of our witnesses. However, I did notice that she had lost some of her vigor after Igor's testimony and demonstration to the jury. I rested our case and when I argued the salient points that the jury had been shown in the demonstration in my closing argument, I suggested that the city's other witnesses "simply missed the first punch but not the second by Anatoly," just as the jury members themselves may well have been shocked to see how fast a punch could happen so unexpectedly at me in front of them.

The jury was out two hours before returning the verdict. This worried me because I thought this was a case that would be decided quickly. When the Judge announced the verdict, which was indeed "Not Guilty," we were given the reason for the delay by the Judge. He told us that he had, "Received a letter statement from the jury signed by each of the twelve jurors." which he proceeded to read to us. The fact that the jury had taken the time to compose a letter to the court in which they explained the time that had been taken by the jury to reach its decision was very unusual.

The following morning, under the headline "JURY SLAMS COP AS RACIST," The Rocky Mountain News had an article covering the trial and the manner in which Detective Jarvis handled the investigation. In that article, it was stated that, "An Adams County Jury took the unusual step Thursday of censoring a police officer after he made racist remarks during his testimony about Russian immigrants. During his sworn testimony he stated that he had not asked for the statements from some witnesses because 'I knew the Russians would get together to concoct a story. I knew where this case was going anyway.' A statement signed by 12 jurors and an alternate said 'This is blatantly racist and unprofessional behavior on the part of the police officer. The Judge said that he was going to send the jury's letter to the police Department."

The lady juror whom I had initially noticed reacting to the Detective's testimony was quoted as saying, "I wanted the Defendant and his family to know that sort of behavior was not going to be tolerated, not accepted and not allowed." The article went on to quote me saying, "I have been practicing for 32 years, and I've never seen a jury make a statement like that. I have never seen anything like that." Detective Jarvis was quoted as saying that "I made a mistake and I apologize to anybody that I may have offended. I never intended to offend anybody. I should have worded it differently."

This case ran counter to the experience I have had dealing with allegations and prosecutions during my career. Almost always, the prosecution has good faith reasons to start and prosecute cases with evidence that is direct or with the accumulation of direct and circumstantial evidence that circles around your client to be the prime suspect. The very basic requirement of probable cause that must be found provides a good and solid foundation for cases to proceed in which the court and juries participate. By its very definition, probable cause is not sufficient to convict a person of any crime. The proof must rise to the higher level of proof beyond a reasonable doubt which is a strict and powerful barrier protecting all of us from wrongful accusations and or convictions of crimes. I can tell you that juries honor the historic standard of proof imbedded in our system of justice. It is a great system and it works well, most of the time. Only when one of the three parts of our system fails, does injustice occur.

In this case, the investigation, which is an integral part of any prosecution, did not live up to the standards required by justice. The prosecutor for state was equally guilty together with the detective for failing to pursue the evidence that existed in the case. The jury learned the truth about Anatoly and the facts behind the accusation as they listened and absorbed the evidence and the demonstration of how fast a punch can be. They not only rose up to do the job, they demanded further satisfaction. I had done my part by bringing forward the true facts and evidence which, in the end, the District Attorney rejected, but the jury did not.

I can tell you that almost all of the time, bringing forward the true facts works in dealing with District Attorneys and prosecutors in Colorado and elsewhere. It is true that sometimes our system will fail, but it is resilient and responds to good and hard work, investigation and the accumulation of evidence. And, if that fails, despite good faith effort on the part of the other two prongs of justice, trial and appeal, then only time and the hard work and efforts by interested parties can and do achieve a correction of a failure in our system. Achieving justice in our courts has stood the test of time and I believe will continue to do so. God bless our juries and the men and women who work and live within our system of justice.

CHAPTER 18

Appearance of Innocence

I had no idea when Tom Reed and his grandfather, Harlan Reed, walked into my office and sat down in the two chairs in front of my desk that this was a case that would try me to the limit of my physical and mental abilities. Harlan Reed looked the part of a Texan from the panhandle of Texas near to Amarillo. He placed his Stetson hat on my window sill, sat down next to his grandson and proceeded to tell me that he wanted me to defend his grandson, Tom, charged with sexual improprieties with two young girls under the age of eighteen while he was over eighteen years old. Harlan told me that I "know perfectly well that the case against Tom is made up because one of girls involved is my niece, Sara. Sara is well known to the entire family as a liar, cheat and mischief maker since she was a young girl. She had confounded and disheartened the family from the time she started walking and talking. My brother did not know what to do with her in Texas, and now that they have also moved to Colorado, things are just getting worse. Whatever she is saying, Tom did not do it. Mr. Makaroff, Sara is a psychopathic liar!" Wow. This was a most interesting introduction to a case, one I had never before experienced and it certainly grabbed my interest. Many clients claimed that the accusers were lying, but not to the degree of a serious mental illness. As it turned out, I was ultimately going to use this as the chief defense against the accusations in the case. I soon found myself caught in the web of the most intriguing, compelling, surprising and, ultimately sad and heart wrenching case of my career. However, all of that lay ahead as the case ended up taking over two years to wind down to the final scales of justice preordained by the truth of what had actually taken place.

Tom was a good looking, six-foot, dark haired young man who was then twenty years of age. He spoke thoughtfully and quietly. He was a high school graduate, working full time in an appliance store while attending junior college, part time, seeking a business type of education. He struck me as dependable and hardworking, making the most of his average intelligence. I immediately liked him and listened to his denial of the allegations in the criminal complaint and his repeated statements, "I did not do it. She (Sara) is making it up together with her close friend, Wendy. They have made up many accusations against me for all kinds of stuff. My family knows that she is a liar. Wendy always backs her up. It was never true and my family knows it. This is the worst thing Sara has said against me. I don't know what to do. I hated being arrested and jailed. She said I stole from her before, but this is terrible." I noticed in the criminal complaint that there were additional charges, called pattern charges, alleging lesser sex crimes on different dates with Sara and other persons at different times during a one and one-half year period.

The principal charges of sex with a minor under Sixteen and the pattern charges were alleged to have happened after Tom had turned eighteen years old which made the charges felonies. Pattern charges in cases generally include similar types of offenses that are added to the principal charges both in time or mode of behavior. Sara and her friend, Wendy, were both 15 and 16 years old at the time of the offenses. The main charges alleged both physical and oral sex while the girls were minors.

It struck me that this was going to be a very difficult case, not only due to the nature of the charges, but due to the varied dates and times of the alleged crimes to be investigated. I asked for and received the largest retainer of my career with the understanding that it would require additional smaller retainers as we progressed through the case. Harlan Reed agreed and we shook hands. I was now committed to a case and defense like no other I had ever experienced.

Tom did not have a criminal record, except for a few traffic tickets not involving alcohol. I learned from his employer that Tom was both trustworthy and dependable. I learned from his grandmother that he was the same at home, did not speak badly about people and had good and decent friends. He attended church with his grandparents since his parents had moved back to Texas and was very pleasant with people they knew or met at home, church or in public. He never seemed to be angry or upset. He had a calm demeanor about him and was open and friendly. He did not go out often and did not show up late at night. In short, he was a good kid and young man, contrary to Sara, who was forever in trouble and causing headaches and concerns for her parents and family.

It turned out that Sara was continually a truant in school and carefully watched by school authorities. She had been receiving professional help and counseling at school. Sara's parents had confided to Mary Reed, his grandmother, that they were at wits end about what to do with their daughter. Sara was failing in school, regularly in trouble and sometimes, out late at night. She lied all the time and was more than they could handle. It was not a pretty picture presented by the chief accusers, Sara together with her partner, Wendy, in the various alleged criminal sexual escapades. I was told that Wendy's mother did not reveal much about her daughter and was both close mouthed and private about what was happening with Wendy in her separate school.

I decided to focus first on Sara and see what could be developed about her reputation as a "psychopathic liar." At the same time, I put together a motion to the court requesting that Sara be seen by a court ordered psychiatrist to determine if her lying was truly the result of an uncontrolled psychiatric condition as was portrayed by the people around her, including family members and others. It turned out that in addition to the Reeds, other members of the family and close friends were easily persuaded to help me put together signed Affidavits of their similar concerns about Sara and how she distressed or outraged members of the family and close friends. In fact, it turned out that most friends and family members were deeply concerned about Sara's behavior.

There was a significant amount of evidence for such a request in the law of Colorado since an illness that causes chronic lying was certainly entitled to consideration by a jury that must decide on the facts, intent and the mental condition of an accuser. I filed the motion and the matter was set for hearing before the Judge with whom I had successfully worked together as counsel while defending, David Valerin, when he had been accused civilly of Conspiracy to Murder in front of the Russian restaurant many years before, referred to in Chapter 14, "Wrong Place at The Wrong Time."

We had a lengthy hearing before Judge Nikosabi that was vehemently opposed by the deputy District Attorney, Barry Langston. However, the many disturbing descriptions about Sara and she lies that were stated in the affidavits attached to the Motion prevailed and I received an order from the Judge that Sarah be examined by a psychiatrist about her psychopathic lying patterns, with a report to be rendered to the court. It was a good beginning to the case.

I began a detailed investigation of what family members could supply from their memories about Sara's behavior so that we would have a collection of incidents and behavior with which the psychiatrist could be informed about for his examination of Sara. We checked what we could at the school and subpoenaed whatever records they sought to be withheld. Other friends and neighbors were questioned, and in two instances, short term job fellow employees were willing to provide instances of sometimes bizarre behavior by this troubled youth. As the information accumulated and pointed with near certainty that Sara was a girl not to be trusted or relied upon, I started to occasionally speak with Barry, the DA, when I would see him in court or pass him in the corridors in order to give him a flavor of what I was learning. He was always friendly and receptive but would tell me that Sara was very believable and that their case against Tom was "Most disturbing due to the repetition and similarity of facts, dates and locations of their illicit sexual unions" He was not interested in a reduction of the charges and told me that this was a case that the District Attorney's office would be pursuing to the limit. This obviously did not give me any room for maneuvering or plea bargaining and limited the prospect of any solution as the case as it went forward. Both sides kept working but remained in contact.

It had become my habit to keep in touch with the opposing DAs in all of my cases since you never knew when something would spur them to consider a resolution. Sometimes, it was a schedule conflict with other cases, the statutes of limitations requiring that another case be tried or witness problems of one kind or another. Nothing in criminal law remained static. We were always dealing in the lives of distressed and broken people. Things would happen and priorities changed for either side. As this case developed, nothing was changing and trial appeared to be the only solution.

Then, two things happened which promised movement in the case. First, we received the psychiatric report which confirmed completely that Sara was indeed a girl afflicted with a mental condition that bordered on an uncontrollable condition of lying about big things or small. The Psychiatrist's interviews with Sara and testing showed that her illness had been a long-standing condition that was evident from past as well as present testing. It was not something that could be immediately cured and was likely to continue unabated without intensive therapeutic intervention. The psychiatrist did not attempt to deal with the facts or evidence in the case. Neither did his report find or suggest a way to know if or when Sara lied. She was indeed found by the psychiatrist to be a "Psychopathic liar" as it was commonly known and understood in the parlance of the psychiatric world and the rest of the population. It was left for the lawyers, judge and jury to figure out how to decipher the case and arrive at justice.

The second thing that came up was a direct result from the psychiatric report itself. About a week or so after the report was received and the trial date set for about three months later, Barry Langston called with a plea bargain offer. The offer was that Tom pleads guilty to two misdemeanor counts of sexual touching, one involving Sara and the other, Sara's friend, Wendy. The additional felony charges included in the three pattern charges would be dismissed as a part of the plea bargain. No agreement was suggested as to the sentencing by the Judge which meant that the Judge would be deciding on the punishment, including jail. This would give the court full latitude of a sentence for up to the two-year maximum terms in the county jail required by the misdemeanor offenses. I definitely liked the judge from my personal experience with him as a fellow civil defense counsel but had no idea how he would react to Sara if such pleas were entered in the case. It was definitely an offer that had to be seriously considered since it did not include pleas to any of the additional pattern felony charges which created separate problems for the defense. The pattern charges were to be dismissed. Obviously, the District Attorney's office believed that the psychiatric opinion exposed their case to far more uncertainty then they had previously believed. That was a good sign. I called Tom and his grandfather and we set up a meeting at my office to discuss the pros and cons of the offer.

Our meeting took us back over the same territory we had previously discussed. Tom reiterated that Sara and her girlfriend were lying about all the incidents in which he was charged. He said once again, "I did not do these things. They are not telling the truth. I do not want to enter pleas or to go to jail." I asked him and his grandfather, "What if I was able to reach an agreement as to the pleas to the misdemeanors and no jail? You would have to serve the probation requirements of not more than two years. Would that work?" They sat there and looked at each other. I asked again. The answer from both of them was, "No." It was clear that they were both of a same mind. No deals. I reported this back to the DA and returned to continuing to speak with family members, friends and prospective witnesses who knew Sara to determine who I would be calling to testify for the defense. I had numerous people to pick from and continued the process of learning about Sara from many different eyes and ears. Everyone was able to describe instances of outright fabrications and a few of the younger ones also confirmed that she would steal from stores, smoke pot and skip school.

School teachers and counselors were less forthcoming, citing the board of education rules of confidentiality and what they termed to be "privileged communications." There was no such legal privilege, but their unwillingness to cooperate was a problem I had experienced in many other cases. I ended up without using any teacher, counselor or other person connected with the high school or prior grade school. Another thing I learned in the investigation was that few witnesses on behalf of Tom knew anything about Sara's friend, Wendy. She remained an enigma and all the while, as the younger minor, her mother would not allow anyone to interview her daughter. I was limited to whatever was stated by her in her statement located in the police report in support of the allegations.

I spent several sessions with the psychiatrist in preparation for his testimony. He was a pleasant and cooperative person happily complying with the use of his time for which he was paid. We spent a considerable amount of time going through the various test results he had obtained as part of his analysis and his direct findings from his meetings with Sara. She was not his first "Psychopathic liar" and she fit well into the normal symptomatology of the illness. I asked about her ability to turn it on or off and learned that this was not clear or certain. It appeared that this was something she lived with consciously and unconsciously. And, of course, everyone was different. He was able to spot some lies and called her on them. She handled this without rancor and dismissively, such as "Why bother." However, he was confident that he missed others. It was like having a bad cold. It would come and go and could not be predicted or effectively controlled. "What about making up stories and sticking to them?" I asked. His response was, "Sometimes "yes" and sometimes "no. There does not appear to be a pattern." I asked." Do you believe that she lied in this case about what happened?" His answer was, "I cannot say with any certainty. This is what she does. One can only speculate if the incidents that are claimed actually happened." Finally, I asked whether he could state his opinion about her illness to be one beyond a reasonable doubt." His answer was "Yes. She is a psychopathic liar in my professional opinion." There, in short, was the major part of our defense.

The other question became, how would this carry over to her friend, Wendy? Also, I was wondering, what is the story with her? Apparently, she was there with Sara in all of the sexual encounters. Her mother would not let me speak to her daughter and the DA would not set up a meeting over the mother's objection. In fact, Wendy's mother told me not to call again because she would, "hang up." When the deputy called Wendy to the stand in the trial, it would be my first and only chance to see her or speak with her and assess her, all in front of the jury. I had the distinct impression that her mother was against her daughter testifying at all. This was the DA's problem which he confirmed when we spoke about it during several court appearances before the trial. I was probably not going to know what Wendy was going to say beyond her very short statements to the police which were in the discovery materials before she was called to the stand. In those statements, she confirmed that Tom had committed the sex acts on Sara and her at the times designated in the criminal complaint. It was not the first time that I would be cross examining an alleged victim in trial for the first time. In the preliminary hearing, Sara had done all of the testifying establishing probable cause with her descriptions of the alleged sex acts in considerable detail with regard to both girls. Wendy remained an unknown right up to the trial. This was a serious and distressing concern that had no resolution in sight.

Trials do not provide many surprises for the lawyers who are trying the cases. Almost all of the evidence in the form of documents or things are known, examined and agreed upon beforehand. It is rare for something unknown to be presented at the last minute. If something is a serious legal issue, it can be dealt with in a hearing before the Judge and outside the presence of the jury. The testimony of witnesses is another matter. Although both sides generally know what to expect from prosecution witnesses, since each has spoken or tried to speak to each known witness, if at all possible. However, this is where the advantage tilts in favor of the prosecution since most of the people scheduled to be witnesses in criminal cases avoid cooperating with a defense lawyer preparing for a trial, often with the stated or unstated approval of the prosecutors. As one can imagine, this problem is compounded in a sex charges case. Often, the prospective witnesses have been advised that there is no requirement for them to speak to defense counsel, which is true. Others simply do not want to be bothered or profess disdain or objection to voluntarily sharing information with the defense lawyer. It takes time, good investigators and persistence to speak with and learn what witnesses saw, heard or know. Witnesses are not required to cooperate. If they are subpoenaed, they must come to court and testify. However, you are stuck with what they may say. It makes it far more difficult for the defense to personally learn all of the facts or evidence that may be available from witnesses beyond what is provided under the Rules of Criminal Procedure involving prior statements or evidence. This does not include discovery of real evidence such as weapons, written statements or confessions which are provided to the defense as a matter of course. In this case, I was facing a lot of uncertainty because almost all of the possible witnesses simply would not cooperate beyond their statements to the police. Those that did still left unknown a major problem that could only be resolved in trial; how would their testimony come off before the jury? Good, bad or indifferent? Such questions were always unanswered and uncertain as the cases progress to trial.

The amount of preparation or lack thereof was not the final decider. More important was how the witnesses would present themselves in court and before the jury. Expected good witnesses can turn sour, poor or uncertain, Others became gold. It was always a tossup and trial lawyers are accustomed to what amounts to the roll of the dice. This was exactly what happened in this case as I worked my way through witness after witness for the prosecution.

Once the trial began, the District Attorney presented his case by first focusing on what was learned by the detectives assigned to the case. The police witness and assigned detective stuck close to their reports and graphically described what was said to them by Sara and Wendy about their and Tom's behavior. This allowed the contested facts to be first presented by the prosecution with credibility that is generally attached to the testimony of the police to be followed later in the case by the actual prosecution witnesses and the victims themselves in what was hoped to be both disturbing and convincing. This calls for different types of cross examinations by counsel. The police officers come to court with juries wanting to believe them since they represent law and order. As a result, the idea is to handle them carefully and have them admit that no actual physical evidence or other type of evidence existed to support what Sara and her cohort had told them other than their specific claims. In fact, both officers admitted that at the time they spoke with Sara that they did not know that she was a" Psychopathic liar." Moreover, they had no way to check or confirm if either Sara or her close friend, Wendy, were both lying to them since there was no physical evidence of the alleged crimes available from one or two years before. The predicate to questioning Sara's credibility was placed before the jury without much difficulty since both the officer and detective admitted that this was outside of their providence and ability to confirm.

The next witnesses were a school homeroom teacher and counselor who testified about particular problems they encountered with Sara's disturbing behavior which they remembered to have occurred after the dates of the alleged sexual encounters were reported to them. Cross examination established that neither witness had heard directly from Sara any complaints about what was now being alleged to have happened at or about the times it was alleged to have taken place. In fact, both witnesses only learned about the alleged claims against my client after the criminal case had been filed and Sara had filled them in on the incidents that she claimed had occurred. To cover this problem, the deputy DA called a couple of classmates who testified that they remembered that Sara acted depressed and differently around the time that a couple of the alleged incidents were claimed to have occurred. However, as before, with the school homeroom teacher and the counselor, neither one was able to connected unusual behavior by Sara's to the dates or times when they allegedly had happened. Once again, the evidence was limited to what Sara had said to them after the actual criminal charges were brought two and one-half years later.

Time was spent by the prosecution with witnesses who were family members who testified to Tom's interactions with Sara and other friends. In fact, on some occasions, Tom was asked to drive Sara to appointments or even to school. This had been a longstanding practice in the family, once Sara and her parents had moved to Denver from Texas. They were family and treated as such. On the morning of the fourth day of trial, the prosecution called Sara to the stand.

She presented herself as young and innocent as Barry Langston carefully took her through the tangled web of her upbringing and behavior. She admitted to school problems and truancy, taking drugs which, she did not like, causing problems with occasional lying and minor thefts from friends for which she was very remorseful. She was working hard on changing and bettering her behavior that was now openly being talked about in court. She also testified that she had taken to heart and was trying to change her behavior that the jury learned about from her homeroom teacher, school counselor and psychologist. Growing up and understanding about herself was a difficult process for her, but she felt good about what she has been accomplishing. In response to a question about her being a "Psychopathic liar," she admitted that she did a lot of lying, but was." getting better," and, "I recognize that this is a problem that I must deal with. But, I would never lie about the things that Tom did to me or Wendy. I always loved him and looked up to him like an older brother."

Next, Barry began to question Sara about the details of the times, places and specifics of the actual sex acts that she engaged in with Tom himself and together with Wendy, including the acts with one or two other persons that were contained in the Pattern charges. She proceeded to graphically tell the jury about spending time with Tom, alone and with Wendy on the occasions listed in the criminal complaint. She explained specifically what had been done to her alone or together with Wendy and that it was all done by Tom on those occasions. The courtroom was silent and you could hear a pin drop. What we adults were hearing was deplorable. But was it true? When Sara's testimony was finished, I rose to stand at the lectern and began the cross examination.

After establishing and obtaining Sara's admissions once again that she had been a lifelong liar, I asked Sara whether she had read the psychiatric report ordered by the court. "Yes, I read the report." She replied. "Do you believe it was accurate? "I do not know," she answered. This was the answer I expected and I went to my next planned question, "If you do not know and understand what a psychopathic liar is, how is the district attorney, the Judge, the jury, myself, my client or anyone able to tell while you are testifying when you are telling the truth or when you are lying?" Sara thought for a minute and responded, "I do not know. What I have said is the truth and these are the things that Tom did to me and Wendy. It all happened and this is what I have to live with." Following this answer, which I realized had been planned by Sara and the DA, I took Sara through a series of questions about her school, teachers, parents, cousin's family and friends and obtained her admission that she had lied repeatedly to each of them. With those admissions, I was also able to obtain her agreement that she lied daily and effortlessly. In fact, she admitted that much of the time she did not consciously think or plan the lies. When I asked if she knew whether she was lying during my questions, she responded, "No, I do not believe that I am lying. I looked at the jury wondering if they were thinking the same as me, that this answer, like so many others was canned testimony and a lie.

We went through her store thefts, absence from school, drug use and other sexual escapades beyond what was charged against Tom. Concerning the other sexual episodes, she said," Everything I did was with Tom. I trusted him. This, of course, contradicted her previous testimony. I was feeling that all of us in the courtroom were had become used to hearing her lie. I turned the fact that she had kept quiet about Tom for almost two and a half years. "Why now," I asked. "Why bring the charges now? Her answer was, "It was bothering me and I needed to bring it all out in the open," I then asked,

"How are we to know now if you are lying or not? She looked back at me and said, "I don't know. I guess that is why we are here." I then asked her why Wendy was with her during most of the encounters. She thought a minute and said that, "We do everything together." I then asked, did either of you question what you were doing? Her reply was that, "We were accustomed to it. It was what we did." I looked at the jury members as I returned to my seat. I saw puzzlement. Was it possibly uncertainty? They were all serious and contemplative. It was now all out there for the jury to decide.

Opposing counsel elected not to call Wendy to the stand. This was a serious decision by counsel since she was directly involved in most of the main charges. I wondered if Wendy's mother was still blocking her testimony, or was Barry waiting until the conclusion of our defense and his rebuttal? Time would tell.

Our defense began with the testimony of the psychiatrist himself which took the entire Friday morning and into the early afternoon for direct and cross examination. He was very good and thorough as he explained his examinations and conclusions. He stated that Sara was indeed a psychopathic liar and unable to contain or change herself without long term psychiatric help and support. He did not believe that she had the internal mechanism to change, without therapy. He was unable to say what was or was not truthful, made up or fanciful, including her earlier testimony before the jury. He shrugged and put up his hands. "I can't say, it is beyond my ability as a Doctor to enter her mind based upon my study and conclusions." After that, Barry conducted his cross examination in which, I believe we both recognized, only supported the Doctor's conclusions.

I then called Tom's grandfather, Harlan Reed, to the stand. I knew that his honesty and total grasp of family situation, including the failure of Sara's parents to deal with their daughter's obvious problems and wrongdoings would resonate with the jury. And so, it did. Once Harlan Reed's testimony and cross examination was done, I opted not to put two other family members on the stand that had been ready and willing to corroborate Sara's behavior. I decided that since grandfather had done so well in his testimony and presence before the jury that I would not risk any testimony that may occur from less effective witnesses. It was one of the many decisions that we have to make in calling witnesses or not during a trial.

I had decided that the jury needed to hear and see Tom in order to judge his credibility against Sara and Wendy, if she testified. I had spent a lot of time going over Tom's testimony with him and believed that he would do well in front of the jury and the cross examination by the DA. I was right. Tom did do well. He remained placid, courteous and answered all questions on direct and cross examination without evasion. I asked Tom if he had done any of the acts charged by Sara. He answered forthrightly, "No, I did not. It did not happen!" looking straight at the jury. Barry was unable to break through his calm demeanor. Tom did not fight the DA as he was questioned. He just kept saying, "No, it did not happen. I do not know why she keeps making things up or Wendy for that matter." After, Barry ended his cross examination, I told the judge that we rested our case. This happened just before lunchtime. At that point, Barry informed us that he would call Wendy to the stand as his rebuttal witness. Obviously, he had overcome her mother's opposition to allowing her daughter to testify. Maybe, he convinced the mother that he needed the girl's testimony to win the case. I did not know for sure, but without Wendy's testimony, the prosecution case was sitting on an edge. As I left the courtroom to go to the cafeteria, I knew that it would be one of the worst lunches I had ever experienced. I sat there without much of an appetite as I tried to figure out how I would question this alleged young partner to the psychopathic lying Sara.

As expected, Wendy corroborated just about everything that had been testified about by Sara including her participation in sexual activity. I had little to go on to attack her other than her close friendship with Sara. She was a pleasant looking teenager which made things still worse. I approached her from the standpoint of the findings that Sara was a psychopathic liar. Her response was that Sara was actually very dependable and that she rarely caught her in a lie. As she gave this answer, I looked at the jury members and saw several looks at each other as they were taking in the testimony. Often, when faced with a difficult witness who was appearing credible or giving unexpected answers, I would change my script in the middle of cross examination. This is what I did knowing that Wendy had not been present to hear Sara's testimony in the trial. Instead of trying to impeach her strong belief in her friend, Sara, I decided to ask her a series of questions about Tom. Was he a sex and drug addicted young man? Was he in her presence prone to odd behavior? And if so, what? Did he steal in her presence? Did he drink heavily? One by one, Wendy responded that Tom had done and been each of those things and said that she and Sara had been telling him to stop all such behavior. It turned out as I hoped. Wendy thought such questions had been asked and been answered affirmatively before by Sara when, in fact, Sara had affirmed in her testimony that Tom was a straight arrow. Wendy must of thought that she was adding more fuel to fires that had not been lit. There had been no such testimony and the DA were unable to rehabilitate her on re-direct. Damage had been done as to Wendy's credibility since such evidence had not been presented by the Sara or the other prosecution witnesses. This was helpful to our side. I looked at the jury and thought that I saw hesitancy and thoughtfulness on the part of several jurors. After Wendy was dismissed, I thought for a moment to call one of Tom's parents to affirm that their son was a young man who was far straighter then what Wendy and Sara had made him out to be. Instead, I decided to let it go and allow the case go to the jury with what was on the table. I felt that I had done all the damage that could be done to the prosecution case. Such are the decisions we must make during trial as the occasions arise. There was no way to know if it was a right or wrong decision.

What followed that afternoon was to meet with the Judge in chambers to work out the final wording of the contested jury instructions to the jury and to argue before the judge about the wording of certain jury instructions. As is often the case, each side had presented differently worded instructions for the Judge to decide upon. This normally took a while and this case had a number of difficult legal issues to tackle. The Judge, therefor, excused the jury until Monday when we would reconvene to have counsel make their final arguments and the judge would read the final jury instructions he had decided upon to the jurors before dismissing them to the jury room to begin deliberations. The trial had lasted an entire week and two days before the jury was adjourned to deliberate. There was no way to know how soon they would decide. It was a complete toss-up and there was nothing to do but to wait over the weekend for them to hear our final arguments and begin their deliberations.

We waited for two and one-half days while the jury deliberated over twenty hours. This jury asked the court several questions on legal points that required counsel to be called to chambers to help decide on the language of the Judge's responses. This meant that counsel would be called from wherever they may be to help the court and, together with the judge, work out the best answer to be provided to the jury questions. This happened, I recollect, three times. The first two times, counsel was called by the judge and we conferred by phone on the appropriate answer for the judge to give to the jury. At the end of the second time, the Judge decided that counsel should come and stay in the courthouse since it appeared from the questions that they were closing in on a final verdict. In this case, the jury questions were loaded with legal issues and it took time to work out the best answers in consultation with the Judge as the jury waited. All of this added to the time the jury was out. Finally, in the third day of deliberation and ninth day of the trial, they reached a verdict.

A couple of the questions raised by the jury were very troubling since the jury was reporting that they were having a hard time making a final decision and, maybe, they were hung. On the afternoon of the third day of deliberation, we received word that the jury had decided some counts but was totally hung and undecided on the others. The court had instructed them to reconsider their positions, and if they could not break the ties or reach final decisions, to inform the court and he would have them appear in the courtroom with the verdicts they were able to achieve. This happened on the ninth day of the trial.

A couple of hours later, in the afternoon of the third day of deliberations of the second week of the trial, we assembled in the courtroom. The jury foreman informed the court that they had reached a verdict on some counts, but not others. The Judged asked for the verdicts to be given to him. After he read them, he asked his bailiff to read the verdicts. It was "Not Guilty" as to each of the four basic felony counts. However, they were still hung on the three pattern felony counts. The court asked each of the jurors if these were their final verdicts and non-verdicts. Upon receiving affirmative replies from each of the jurors, he thanked them for their service and excused the jury.

Barry Langston informed the court once the jury had left the courtroom that the District Attorney's office would pursue the pattern counts left undecided by the jury. We were excused by the court but were ordered to appear in two weeks to set a time and date for the retrial of the case on the remaining pattern charges. The verdict was half of a loaf. We won, but not everything. Any celebration was muted. The case remained in limbo with another jury to be selected to decide Tom's fate. In truth, nobody was happy; not the jurors, judge, DA, defense and certainly not Tom, his family or even Sara.

I can tell you that it was a tough mental process to go back and reassemble the facts and evidence for a re-trial of the case on the pattern counts that were left. In this case, it was going to be doubly difficult since we had taken the case to its conclusion with evidence and rebuttal as to the pattern counts. What does either side do to change or improve the way the remainder of the case would be re-tried? Each witness would have been in court once before and under oath and with a complete record of what had been asked and answered. This was not an alluring prospect for either side. On my part, I had expended a great amount of time and energy in the case on top of the emotional wear and tear. Having been a trial lawyer at that time for over thirty-five years, I strongly felt the wear and tear and began questioning whether I could command my best performance once again. I spent time considering the issue and decided to meet with Tom and his grandfather to discuss obtaining another lawyer for the retrial of what remained of the case. I was doubting my ability to retry the case with my best efforts. I was beginning to think that someone else, with fresh thinking and approach, may be better for my client. This was something I had never faced before and I was surprising myself with my thoughts and doubts.

We did not meet until a few days later since I had much work to do to re-enter and take hold of my business and law practice. You always pay for time away. When I met with Tom and his grandfather, they were adamantly against my leaving the case or hiring some other lawyer to get another view on how to proceed. However, they did agree to meet with another lawyer who would be able to put a fresh mind and face on the facts and issues of the case. I recommended a lady lawyer I knew who had tried many sex cases in her capacity as a Denver public defender and had developed a very good reputation among the judges and counsel who had seen her in court, worked with her or against her. She had entered into private practice and continued to take and defend sex-type cases.

Both Tom and his grandfather did not want to accept my decision, but they did agree to meet with Carol Conner. A meeting was arranged. They met, and she was hired. They reported that not only did they like her but were impressed with her experience and know how. This made me feel good and relieved with my decision to withdraw from the case. It had been the first time I had ever done so. However, I believed that I had done the right thing. I had left all my strength and energy for the case in the courtroom. It was better for someone else to take over with new and fresh ideas.

About a month and a half later, I received a phone call from Carol Conner. She had just finished reading the transcript of the trial and had obtained a continuance of the trial date since it had taken so long to obtain the transcript. After the usual pleasantries, she told me what was on her mind. "Mike, I have just finished reading the transcript of the trial. You did a great job! How did you do it?" She went on to add that she was really concerned about the fact that the DA could now focus on the three separate Pattern incidents allowing for three bites at the apple with witnesses already prepped due to the initial trial. We both recognized that

Wendy would become an even greater issue for the jury to consider since their focus would be limited to the pattern charges and her participation along with Sara. Barry Langston had focused real hard on convincing the jury about Sara in the first trial with Wendy as a last-minute bonus since her status was always in doubt. This did help my defense. Now the emphasis would not be divided with Wendy as a co- principle victim along with Sara. This gave then a second victim and two bites at the apple. Wendy had never been labeled to be a "Psychopathic liar". She had admitted to being present at all the times when the alleged other sexual felonies had occurred. We agreed that the dynamics of the remaining case would take a different turn. When we finished the back and forth discussion of the case and I had supplied her with my thoughts about the remaining undecided charges, our conversation ended. I put down the phone relieved that I would not have to plan or prepare the defense. However, Carol had informed me that, once again, the Arapahoe DA's office had offered her the same plea bargain to two misdemeanor sexual assaults with two years in the county jail that Tom, his grandfather and I had previously turned down before going to trial. She was negotiating to lower the pleas to a single count with the same two years in jail and probation. This made me realize that the DA's office was no more interested in retrying the case than she, Tom or his grandfather were. The time and the agony of the case had taken its toll on all the participants and a plea bargain was more attractive than ever before.

Tom did in fact agree to take the plea bargain and entered a plea of guilty to the same two misdemeanor counts we had previously turned down. He went to jail for a two-year term in the county jail. According to Carol, his prime motivation was to get it all over with so that he could go on with his life. I was surprised, but it was not the first time I had experienced a defendant deciding to take a plea and endure the punishment to have a final solution despite claiming innocence to the charges. I thanked Carol for calling me with the update, shook my head and returned my attention to the cases and trials that lay ahead for me and my clients.

I received a phone call from Tom about a year later. He was out of jail and working at the same place he had been working at when we went to trial. He had completed his jail term in the normal amount of time, months less than one year of the two-year term for good behavior. The problem was that he was having a hard time with probation and had failed to meet the requirements that included attending classes and counseling for his sex offense convictions.

Tom was scheduled to appear in court in a few weeks for a trial on the issue of his failure to comply with the probation requirements. If convicted, this could cause the court to jail him for another term of up to two years, the same as he had previously served. He and his grandfather wanted me to handle the case and defend Tom regarding the probation violations. After some talk back and forth, I reluctantly agreed and went about preparing for what would amount to a mini-trial in which the probation officer would be the sole witness before the Judge since no jury was allowed under Colorado law for probation violations.

I met with the probation officer and found her to be informative and factually well prepared to make out the case that Tom was willfully and repeatedly violating many of the probation requirements. She had his signatures on the appropriate documents informing him of the penalties for violating the rules and her notes containing the reports of meetings with Tom about his failure to attend the meetings and counseling sessions involved. It was truly an open and shut case against Tom. It was apparent that he would lose in the trial before the Judge. This was not a pleasing prospect.

When I appeared in court for the trial which was set for the afternoon docket together with several other matters, I noted that we were reassigned to a well-known hardnosed Judge who was likely to make Tom serve the full two years of time required. Tom was in the courtroom sitting several rows in front of his grandparents. I went over to them first and visited with them. They were very concerned that Tom would be sent back to jail and were hoping that I could somehow save Tom from more time. It was hard to tell them that the deck was stacked against their grandson. I left them and went to sit next to Tom and prepare with him as best as possible for his testimony. At that point, Tom said that he needed to tell me something and asked that I go with him to the corridor outside the courtroom. I said "Fine. I'll check with the DA and make sure how much time we have since the Judge is not yet on the bench." I did so and learned that we were fourth on the docket and there would be several pleas being entered before our case was called. This gave us ample time to talk. I waved for Tom to meet me outside the courtroom. I did not realize that I was in for one of biggest surprises of my legal life when Tom joined me in the corridor.

Tom began by saying, "I did it." I said, "Yes, I know you did it. We need to explain to the court what was going on in your head to cause you to fail to comply with the probation requirements." "No, Mike, that is not what I meant. I did to Sara and Wendy what she and Wendy testified about. I feel terrible that I lied to my grandparents and to you. It has all taken too long and too much money to bring this to an end. I did some research and learned from "Helen" (the probation officer) that if I do the time for violating the terms of probation, I will not have to do probation when I get out. I know I can do the time. I am tired of lying and I want to get this over with once and for all."

There it was. The long hours of study and preparation, fighting and battling in court and arguing to the jury knowing in my mind that Tom was innocent was flushed down the drain in a few short minutes. The jury had been half convinced and acquitted him on half of the counts. I stood their shell shocked and sad. Perhaps, I sensed it when I chose not to fight the case a second time. Maybe, that was what was behind my unwillingness to return to the fray. I'll never know, but it was my job to return with Tom to the courtroom and tell the grandparents what I had just learned, which was one of the most difficult things I ever had to do in my role as defense counsel. I went back into the courtroom and asked the grandparents to join me outside the courtroom while Tom remained seated in the courtroom. When they came out and joined me, I proceeded to tell them what I had been told by Tom. It was a terrible heart rendering thing to do. They stood there stoically taking in the terrible truth. There were no questions or replies. They looked at each other and returned with me to the courtroom as they were groping and swallowing the admissions made by Tom to me. I did the same walking behind them. I was soon standing next to Tom and entering a plea of guilty to the probation violations. He was sentenced once again to the County jail where he was familiar with the life and routines. This is what my client wanted and is what we did. When we finished the plea and sentencing, Tom was placed in custody and sat with other defendants in the jury box to await being taken to jail to begin serving his two-year sentence as his grandparents and I watched until he and the other Defendants were taken out of the courtroom to the county jail next door.

I accompanied Tom's grandparents as they left the courtroom to go home after the plea had been entered. This is one my saddest memories of my law practice. For the grandparents, this was an agonizingly slow and painful walk to the parking lot during which they were ruminating about the sad admissions made by their grandson and his sentencing to serve, for a second time, two years in the county jail. This was what it was going to take to free him from continuing to lie about the criminal acts he had committed so many years before. It was heart breaking as we walked together, no doubt each of us thinking about the cost in money and emotional upheaval that had been expended because Tom had lied to us all for so long.

Knowing whether a client is innocent or guilty of the crimes charged is not essential or a prerequisite to representing a person under our legal system. Our system of justice in America is based on proof beyond a reasonable doubt which provides all defendants the license to argue for acquittal when the proof is insufficient or simply not convincing to a jury. We have already explored in this book the many ways facts, evidence and culpability are decided upon by juries. It is not a perfect system. However, it is nearly perfect, except when racism plays a role. Outside of racism, when the system does not work, it is mostly the result of negligence, malpractice or the failure of one of the integral parts of the system that can be identified and corrected. What cannot be controlled is what goes on in a lawyer's mind as he tends to his clients in the varied and different ways they go through the maze of our justice system. The attorney-client relationship fluctuates from being fluid, professional or at odds between client and counsel. Yet often, you become a fan of your client and even a teacher and adviser beyond the cases themselves. The personal part is hard to keep out of the equation and gives us all hope and good wishes for our clients mixed with the realities and dangers that we experience with them at the same time. Sometimes, you feel the need to separate yourself from the bricks and arrows that are thrown at you and your clients. At other times, the client's trauma gets through the personal defenses and you are stuck with concern for them and their situations. That is what happened to me with Tom and his grandparents as his case moved to its ultimately sad and unexpected conclusion. It hurt. It hurt bad!

I had to pick myself up, brush myself off and concentrate on the other clients and cases in my office. It was business as usual, but the smoke from Tom's case took a long time to clear. I had been so confident and committed to Tom's innocence that I found myself upset with the truth that he himself had declared. It made me wonder, how many other times had I been fooled. Was this a problem of my own making, taking on the burden of innocence that so many of my fellow lawyers simply took off the table? Innocent or guilty, it did not matter to them. I had never achieved such a mindset in my head. Was it time to do so? Was this an unnecessary burden I had inflicted upon myself? Frankly, I never resolved this internal debate. I know that when I believed in my client's innocence, I was able to work harder and more passionately for my client. My strong belief would help me with the prosecutors and the juries. In fact, I had developed a reputation with the DAs for being a true believer in my cases. This was a good thing, wasn't it? What did happen to me after the Reed case was that I became harder to convince by the clients' stories and protestations of innocence. Maybe this was better and at the same time in the best interests of my clients. Unknowingly, this may well have been the best approach all along.

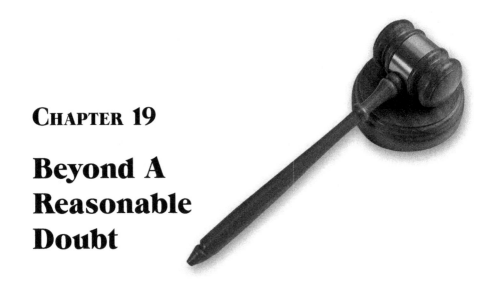

CHAPTER 19

Beyond A Reasonable Doubt

When Howard Reston entered my office, introduced himself and sat down, I immediately recognized that he was not an ordinary client. As it turned out, this was true in more ways than I first realized. Howard was well over sixty years old, grizzled looking with gray hair and the look of a person who was both confident and defiant. Without any prompting, Howard told me that he wanted me to defend him in a "bullshit case." He gave me what turned out to be a Weld County Criminal Complaint in which he was charged with felony assault with a gun against a husband and wife in Greeley, Colorado, located about fifty miles north of Denver. He explained that the alleged victims were his tenants living in a trailer home he had rented to them. On the date and time of the charges, he had visited them to pick up their rent, which was late," As usual," requiring him to regularly visit them to collect the rent. Without giving me a chance to ask any questions, Howard went on to describe the husband and wife to be "losers, obnoxious and a continuing pain in his neck." He informed me that "when he arrived at the trailer home and knocked, the two of them responded and stood side by side in the doorway while he told them what they already knew. "I have come here once again to pick up the rent. You are overdue!" As the wife stayed in the doorway with Howard, the husband went back into the trailer. Howard waited with the wife until the husband returned. About two minutes later, the husband returned and, similarly to previous visits, gave him some money which Howard proceeded to count. It was not enough and as Howard was about to say that to the husband, John Bremer, Bremer started yelling at Howard, called him a "stupid jerk" and yelled "Get the hell off our property!" At the same time, John Bremer said "I will pay the balance off in two weeks. "Now, get the hell out of here." At this point, Howard, money in hand, told me that he turned around and walked away from the trailer, got into his car and drove away without saying another word.

At this point, I began to ask Howard some questions to develop some background information about him. He answered curtly." I used to live in Greeley, but now I conduct my business and live in Denver." However, before I could learn anything else, Howard started another monologue and told me that "the charges are balder dash. I did not have a pistol on me when I went to the door. I left my pistol and shotgun in the car. What they said is simply not true. It never happened!" As Howard was speaking, his face became flushed, his voice hardened, his lips clenched, and his eyes darkened. I saw a look that I did not want a jury to see. He needed to settle down. I asked him to stop talking and to compose himself and told him that," I cannot represent a person who is unable to control his emotions. It would be like a time bomb. I need you to pull yourself together and speak to me rationally. I realize that it is hard to be charged with a felony, but anger and being emotional will not get us anywhere. Can you do that?" Howard looked at me and was quiet for a few moments. Then, he replied slowly thinking the words as he spoke. "Yes, I can do that, but those sons bitches are going to pay for this!" This was not a comforting reply and I took a few moments to decide whether to take the case. Now was the time to say, "Thank you for asking for my representation, but I am going to decline. It does not appear that you can control yourself. I can't help you." However, I did not say that. Instead, I told Howard," Ok, let's get started and work out how your case can be won." I was in and began to live through one of the most incredible cases I had ever experienced.

It was clear from the beginning that this was going to be a different kind of case, far different from anything that I had ever handled before. Howard Reston was unlike any client I had ever represented. During that first conference, I could see that he was opinionated, cantankerous and hard headed. None of these traits worked well in court and if they were out of control and were being exhibited together, it could be disastrous. He calmed down a little bit and told me that his family had lived in the Greeley area for a long time and the rental in question was one of several that he owned, including farm land of many acers that had been passed down to him by his family. He and his wife had moved to Denver when he decided to move his law practice from Greeley to Denver. Howard was a lawyer! I was surprised that he had any business at all from the way he conducted himself in my office. As it turned out, he handled mostly property matters and was indeed struggling with his practice in Denver since most of his clients were still in Greeley. Not surprisingly, he was having trouble developing new clients and business in Denver. Slowly, in between outbursts about the lies and falsehoods in the charges, I learned the basic facts about his encounter with the Bremmers. He explained that he had no weapon on him when they spoke. They were left in his car. "I did not threaten them. My pistol and rifle were in the car and I left with a partial payment of the rent telling them that I would return in two weeks."

When I entered my appearance in the case, I learned from the Sheriff's Department and the prosecuting attorney in Greeley that Howard was not only well known in the area but was often on people's nerves due to his lack of normal courtesies and just plain obnoxiousness. My own experience and similar observations of Howard corresponded with what I was being told. He was a work in progress at best and his own worst enemy. I was not receiving any good signals and there was much work ahead to be done. People were happy that Howard had left for Denver and only saw him when he would return for business or court. He was clearly a character whose manners and outspoken behavior left lasting impressions, all bad! He had no criminal record other than traffic tickets and apparently fought long, hard and vociferously for his clients in his cases. He was simply a hard man to deal with. This was not surprising as I became more acquainted with how he acted while he was seated in my office and giving me his thoughts and facts in the midst of declarations against the Bremmer's and many other people and things in general.

The charges against Howard presented a very real and serious problem since a felony conviction meant the loss of his license to practice law in addition to the normal criminal penalties and possible jail. Howard told me that he decided to hire me because of the parachuting murder case he had heard about and another client whom he could not name that I had represented in Greeley.

The prosecuting attorney was a good guy. His name was Robert Ugara. He was a Japanese American and I had seen him before in court and liked the way he handled himself. Soon after I entered my appearance, we ended up in a conference with the Judge about how the case would proceed. The Judge turned out to be a Harvard Law school graduate who was laid back and conducted himself and his docket extremely well. His name was Harold

Houston. He was the Chief Judge of the District who was well liked and respected by his fellow judges and attorneys. I was pleased with the judge because I had learned early on that good counsel and good judges meant a case that would be conducted well and tried well. In fact, I had found good lawyers and good judges to be, often, easy to get along with, sharing information and professional courtesies. This always made things better for the court, counsel and, ultimately, served the best interests of the clients. This was all helpful if I could convince Howard to act in better control of himself and not give in to his need to spray his unchecked opinions out randomly about everything. This became the major question mark as the case proceeded. Would I be able to keep Howard in check? I was now in the case and there was no turning back.

Not long after I had entered my appearance in the case and before the preliminary hearing, I learned from Robert Ugara, the assigned deputy DA, that they had another witness to the alleged event. It was the six-year-old daughter of the Bremmer's,' who they said was present at the doorway at the time of the incident. Robert was considering adding the little girl as a witness to the incident since she, too, had been frightened by Howard's demand with the gun pointed at her parents. The final decision had not yet been made. This was more trouble for Howard. Robert informed me that his office was holding off on the girl to see if we can work the case out. However, there did not appear to be any such chance of that occurring, so I understood from the beginning that the girl, named, Jamie, would soon be a part of the case.

The pressure of the case mounted heavily as I contemplated cross-examining a six-year-old girl in the defense of my client. I had done this before in a few cases, with six, seven and eight-year children. Each time, it was in divorce and custody cases, never in a felony case. It was difficult each time, and I knew it would be the same in this case.

The first question to be decided by a court in a separate hearing in chambers was whether the child had a sufficient understanding of the proceedings and the importance of telling the truth. Was the child competent to be allowed to testify? Then, if the judge decided that the child was fit to testify, counsel was faced with the prospect of cross examining the girl in the courtroom before the jury in the criminal case or before the judge in the divorce case as if he or she were an adult. This was not a pleasant experience for any judge or counsel. However, it had to be done and I began to gear myself up for what was going to be a very painful process. I had a client who was dreadful in his relationships with others and now, the jury would be hearing from a cute little girl whom I would have to cross examine. The odds of success had changed dramatically. It was all downhill and I could feel it in the pit of my stomach.

There were really no options available for resolving the case. Since Howard was an attorney, even a plea to a lesser misdemeanor offence would pose serious problems for him before the Supreme Court Grievance Committee and a suspension from practice would be the result. We both recognized that a plea bargain was out of the question. A plea bargain to a lesser grade of felony relating to the unlawful use of a weapon that would decrease the possible sentence to two years. However, neither side was willing to explore reaching a plea agreement. Unfortunately, this was a case that had to go to trial and both sides knew it. There were no serious negotiations after the initial offer had been quickly turned down. Howard repeatedly told me that he did not do it and, "Never would have done such a thing." There was no room for negotiation. Even as he was saying that to me, I found myself thinking, "Will anyone believe him?" He was adamant and kept telling me that, "We will win." With Howard, I noted that he included me in "we" as he would repeat that to me. "Don't worry. We will win this case. They are lying, and we will show that to the jury." I felt little comfort in Howard's words. Still, he truly believed what he was saying. On my part, I was not reassured.

I was never able to reach Howard's level of certainty in his case and believed that I had a deeper appreciation for the dangers he faced in court, most important of which was himself as a witness. He was unable to see beyond his frustration and denials that a serious case existed against him. Howard admitted that he had only tried a couple of cases to juries, one a traffic case and the other a civil contract trial. This was not significant experience from which to understand how a jury would respond to the litigants or the case facts. After all, a husband and wife, no matter how vulnerable they each may be, were going to be supported by a child also testifying about what took place on the fateful day in question. The wife had testified at the preliminary hearing and that was enough for the Judge to decide on probable cause. She was weak and tearful but said more than enough for the case to be bound over for trial. I was unable to get much out of her in cross examination. She was quite able to testify to all the necessary elements of the crime charged and responded patiently and politely to my questions and the feeling out process of my cross. Her testimony indeed covered all the elements of the alleged assault; how Howard approached her and her husband and child at their home and doorstep, the fact that he held a gun pointed at her and her husband, his threatening remarks that included, "I will kill you," and what was said and where the little girl was standing as the events took place. In any cross examination of such testimony, you look for openings and possible misstatements, without necessarily revealing where you may go. That must be left for the trial and the jury. There was little to hold on to from her testimony which added to my growing pessimism.

Cross examination of the two sheriff deputies and Ellen Bremer at the preliminary hearing was limited to learning as much as possible about the facts that will be presented later to the jury. I used the preliminary hearing cross examinations for that purpose and to get a feel for each of the witness and, Ellen. In fact, once the case was bound over for trial, I found myself more fearful than I had ever been about the result of a trial since the Lopez murder trial. It kept racing through my head that all the elements of the crime were there and being filled even more with Howard's temperament. It will boil down to the credibility of the parents, plus Jamie versus Howard. They were the only persons present. It will be three against one. I found myself thinking, "Howard is not going to change. He will be his own worst enemy in the trial. How can we possibly pull this case out and win? It will take a miracle."

I prepared myself as best I could for the trial, spending many hours and many sessions with Howard preparing him for his testimony, direct and cross examination. He did understand that it all depended on his testimony and how the jury would be reacting to him as they were making their final decision. However, he poos pooed this and kept repeating that the husband and wife were, "liars and the jury would will see through their efforts to not pay the rent and use their child to beat me in court." This was the attitude he maintained throughout the ordeal of this case. I would reply, "Maybe, but the odds are piled up against you and you know it! It will all depend on how well you behave in the courtroom." This was going to be new ground for Howard and he knew it but would not let on while maintaining his outward confidence.

To his credit, none of this changed his confidence or his irascible nature as the trial date approached. If anything, he grew more querulous and cantankerous. It was difficult to sit and talk to Howard without hearing his epitaphs and poor opinions about everything and everybody involved in the case and beyond. When we would finish a conference, I would be exhausted because it was always hard to keep him on the subject at hand. He would express his opinions about this or that person, the DA, cops, renters and people in Greeley and, now. Denver. It never stopped. What was going to happen when he was in court and required to answer the questions by the deputy DA? He was not listening to my advice and I did not see any change in his manner or behavior. If anything, it seemed to get worse as the trial date approached. All my senses told me that it was going to be bad, even very bad. I was not experiencing a normal growing confidence as we approached the trial date. In fact, it was just the opposite. The trial of this case was quickly becoming very scary to me and I was full of foreboding and deep concern. This was not going to be a walk in the park.

There was one hope left before the case went to trial. I had raised the issue of the competence of the child to testify in a Motion to the court. However, Judge Houston decided that the Motion would be heard during the trial whenever the child was called to testify instead of sometime before the trial. This was very disappointing since neither side would learn what the child's testimony would be or if she was going to be permitted to testify by the Judge until we were already in trial and with a jury seated and hearing all the evidence. The court decision to delay the hearing about the child was well within the prerogatives of a trial judge, but it placed us in a box unable to discern what the child's testimony would look or feel like until the last moment. The little girl, Jamie, was likely to be the most important witness in the case and, as defense counsel, I would have no clue as to how she would appear to the jury as we tried the case.

I knew that the Judge would inevitably allow the child to be questioned by counsel for both sides in chambers and he would also personally question the child as to her understanding of the court process and the importance of telling the truth in front of counsel and the jury. However, the problem was that this would be done only when the Deputy DA called the child to the stand at some point during the trial. The more I thought about it, I believed that Robert Ugara was going to wait until the end of his witnesses before calling Jamie to the stand. I figured out that the Judge knew and understood this as well and figured that Ugara would decide to put Jamie on the stand only if he determined it to be necessary. On my side, it became a game of waiting until the end of the case for the last foot to drop, this was not a pleasing prospect as the case unfolded.

Judge Houston did tell us by way of explanation that "I want to give the parties every chance to resolve this case before I expose the child to the trauma of examinations by the court and counsel for as long as possible. For that reason, I have decided to do it during the trial only if it becomes necessary." In domestic cases, sometimes the judges would speak to the children themselves, but in a criminal matter, everything would be on the record, and so it was to be. This meant that during the selection of the jury, both sides raised the issue of a minor child testifying and what the individual jurors thought about this. On my part, I questioned whether the jurors from their experience could trust what a little girl might say. Most of the prospective jurors would not commit themselves beyond saying that they would listen and decide based on what they saw and heard. There was wisdom in their answers and by that time, I had become resigned to the inevitable. It was the Judge's call and we were proceeding in accord to his wishes.

Once the trial began, Robert Ugara started with the two sheriff deputies who responded to the scene. They presented the basic facts and the allegations of the Bremers against Howard as they reported what they each said had allegedly transpired. Both deputies affirmed that neither parent had said anything about Jamie being present during their initial meeting with the deputies. This had happened in a second meeting. This was appropriately asked by Robert Ugara since prosecutors often will bring out discrepancies in their cases to build confidence in the juries with their cases. They had to live with the facts, same as the defense. The next witness was a district attorney investigator who had been called in by Robert Ugara to take the statements of the parents when they appeared at the DA's offices to tell him about Jamie being present at the incident. This had occurred just before the preliminary hearing and the investigator gave the jury a summary of what the parents had stated about Jamie and the reasons why they had initially withheld the information. He stated that it was. "Not unusual for victims to come in and add to their testimony or other witnesses after they had had a chance to think it over and relive the crimes, particularly if it involved a child or youngster." This was a point well taken, but under cross examination, the investigator admitted that there could be other possible motives, including that the parents were worried that their testimony alone may not prevail.

The next witnesses called to the stand were the parents and accusers. In cross examining each of them, I verified that their rent payments had been spotty and irregular. They each agreed that Howard had reason to be upset with them and, in fact, they lied to him regularly about when they would pay or make up the rent money that was due. Susan Bremer was more willing to agree than her husband. The husband fought me and continued to refer to what Howard had done by pointing the pistol and threatening to" kill" them. The Judge had to keep reminding him that he was required to answer my questions and not extemporarily give his thoughts and opinions to the jury. This is a frequent problem in criminal cases where victims keep referring the alleged criminal acts rather than answering the questions being asked. I had asked each of them why they had initially withheld the fact that "Jamie was present?" Both gave the same answer, "We wanted to protect Jamie." However, when Susan Bremer answered, she said that, "After we learned that Howard was denying the incident had happened as we had stated that he had pulled the gun, we felt that we had better let the DA know all of the facts." When I asked her husband the same question, his reply was that, "the DA had suggested that the child be added as a witness." I followed up with the question, "Your wife said in her testimony that the two of you purposefully decided not to tell the investigators about Jamie being present and there was indeed nothing mentioned about Jamie in the police report. If that is true, how could Mr. Ugara have known that Jamie was present?" The father looked at his wife and then looked at Robert Ugara. I saw jury members leaning forward waiting for his reply. He then answered, "I don't know. At some point we told the DA. He told us that they would have to reveal that Jamie was a witness. We did not like that but felt that there was no choice." This was discrepancy, but how much would it count? I continued and asked, "Did you forget the same as you forgot to tell the two police officers who responded that you and your wife were not alone when Howard came to the door." He immediately replied "No, we reported what happened. He had a pistol aimed directly at us!" I asked immediately, "But not at your daughter? He said "Yes, at her also." To which, I asked. "So, you lied to the police then and this jury now?" He answered "I am not lying now. "It was all a terrible thing and we wanted to get it over with." I returned to the defense table from where I had been standing while cross-examining Howard. I had drawn some blood, but there was no way to tell how it had affected the jury. I could see that they were thoughtful. The trial proceeded with the remaining witnesses without much fan fair.

Counsel and the Judge knew that Jamie was to be the last witness. We were near the end of the trial. It was the morning of the 3rd day and Robert Ugara called Jamie to the witness stand. We all watched as her mother led Jamie into the well of the courtroom. They stopped, and the Judge announced to the jury that they were to retire to the jury room while he was going to conduct a hearing with the parties and Jamie. There is no doubt that this was very intimidating for Jamie and surprising to the jury members. After they left for the jury room, we proceeded into the judges' chambers together with Susan Bremer holding Jaimie's hand as the stenographer and her father followed. When we were all arranged and seated in Chambers, the Judge proceeded to question the child very lightly and professionally. He asked if she knew why she was there. She replied "Yes, my parents have told me that I must answer questions!" The Judge asked, "Did your parents say that you must tell the truth?" "Yes, they did tell me to tell the truth." The Judge went on, "How do you know the truth? She answered. "It is what I see. What I know." The judge then asked "Do you know that people lie sometimes? "Oh, yes. My father says people lie on the TV all of the time." To which the Judge asked," Do you know that you must not lie in court? That it would be wrong to do? "Yes, I know it would be wrong to lie." The girl replied. "Thank you, Jamie." the judge finished. He turned to counsel and told us to proceed, "with care and caution with our questions." I went first.

It did not go well. Jamie was cute and friendly as she explained that she had been with her parents when they went to the door and Howard was there. "I knew Howard from his visits before." She said that he had immediately taken, "A pistol out of his pocket and started yelling at my parents and telling them to pay or else! I was so frightened. I held tightly to mother's hand and I began to cry. Howard kept yelling and Dad went inside and got some money that he gave to the Howard. I could not stop crying. Then Howard went away. It was awful." There it was, words from a child that were devastating. As I questioned her, she stayed with the story she had told. Hearing all this as it was likely to be told in front of the jury was very unpleasant. After my questions, Robert Ugara followed with just a few questions same as the Judge when he had questioned Jamie before me. Jamie answered pretty much the same as she had previously said to the judge. She was holding to her story. It was a forgone conclusion that the Judge would determine that Jamie was competent to testify and we all returned to the courtroom.

I was mindful of a witness we intended to call who a neighbor was living in a trailer nearby on the day in question who had seen Howard leaving the mobile home on that date without a gun in his hand after hearing loud arguing. I had this lady under subpoena to testify for the defense in the case in the event the DA failed to call her to the stand. To his credit, the DA did call the lady to testify and I was able to cross exam her and make sure that we gained every inference possible from her testimony.

Jamie's testimony in front of the jury, not surprisingly also came across well. The child told them, "Howard spoke loudly and scared me. I saw the gun in his hand and I crouched next to my mother. She put her arm around me. I heard Howard say that he wanted money from my parents or he would shoot us!" As I sat at defendant's table with Howard next to me, I could only see that the case was being lost. My mind kept churning and trying to come up with a different way to question Jamie. Then, while Robert Agara was finishing his questions to the child in front of the jury, I came up with an idea that might work when it was my turns to cross- examine Jamie. If it worked, there might be chance. If it failed, I realized that we had next to zero chance of winning a not guilty verdict. Soon, it was time for me to stand up and cross examine Jamie. I could feel in my body and my own trepidation.

Nothing in law school, fellow attorneys or Continuing Legal Education Seminars prepares a lawyer for a cross examination of a witness that is killing his case, let alone, a six-year-old child. My idea was our only chance, and there was nothing to do but to see if it would work. Since, I had already questioned Jamie in the judge's chambers, I began by asking Jamie if she was at ease with me to answer some more questions. She said, "Yes, I am." I then asked her if she remembered what she had said in front of the judge just about ten minutes before. She replied," Yes, I remember, I heard Howard say that he wanted money from my parents or he would shoot us." I then asked, "Did you see him do this before with a gun?" She replied without hesitation. "Yes, I saw him do it before." "Did he do that two, three or four times?" I asked. "Oh yes, I am not sure. Maybe two or three times," she replied, and I then asked, "Were you scared each time?" "Yes, it was scary each time." Did you tell your parents each time it happened? "Oh, yes. I told them each time it happened." She replied as she looked at the jury and they, in turn, were looking intently at her. I was watching the jury to see if they were catching on to the huge discrepancy by the child remembering not one, but several events. I thought I saw that they were troubled as they were taking this in. I turned back to Jamie and thanked her and said. "No more questions your honor."

It had worked better than I had dreamed. Robert Ugara tried as best he could to rehabilitate the child's testimony. However, he was in the position of having to not shake up Jamie while getting her to admit that she had not mentioned "two or three times" before in her testimony before the Judge about Howard having a gun pointed at her and her parents. It was an impossible task with the child remaining firm in her recollection of the events. Robert stopped after what turned out to be futile attempts to get through to Jamie. The result was that we ended up on a high at the end of the prosecution case. Unfortunately, we still had our own defense ahead and it all boiled down to Howard facing the jury on the witness stand.

After the prosecution rested its case, we had a lunch break. I drove

Howard to a restaurant near the outskirts of Greeley where I had often met with other Greeley clients, including Howard, before or during trials. We sat down for a final prep session before his testimony. He and I had become accustomed to speaking directly and frankly. I did not pull any punches. I told him, "Howard, the jury already has a bad picture about who you are and how you act. If this continues with your own behavior in front of them, you lose. Maybe, we should consider you not taking the stand. I could argue that it was clear from the child's testimony that the parents had coached her to say you held a gun and threatened them. This can be a huge blow to their credibility. It might work." Howard would have none of that. "I did not do it and I will testify," Was his response. He was the client and I was the lawyer. He certainly knew his right to testify and to not accept my thought that maybe he should remain silent. Even as I raised the idea, he was shooting it down. It was probably best, for better or worse that he testifies. I accepted his decision and was relieved. I did believe that we had to put it all out there for the jury to decide. However, it would be with fear and trembling. I proceeded to tell Howard. "When you take the stand, you can control and change how they may think about you. You will fill in the blanks. The more unpleasant and bad impressions you give them, the more likely they are to rule against you and convict you. You will not be able to overcome still another bad impression. Remember, we have wounded the parent's version by exposing that their daughter was coached to support their charges. It is up to you. I am asking you to tell your story without striking out against the cops, deputy DA or the child. Keep those things within yourself. What matters is that it did not happen the way they have stated. You did not have a gun and did not threaten them. Will you do that?

"Howard pushed and shoved, went this way and that, but in the end, he promised me that he would behave himself in front of the jury. I thought that I had convinced him that he simply had to state the truth that he did not have a gun in his hand or threaten the parents. I told him once again, "That is all you need to say, plain and simple." He would be cross examined at length and needed to keep repeating that he did not do it. I repeated to Howard that, "My experience is that when clients' speak the truth in court, juries hear, feel, sense it and respond to it, no matter who you are or how it comes out." I was asking Howard to believe that and let his words come out without being scrambled by his anger and desire to strike back. He agreed with me and said that he would stay calm when we returned to court. I was hopeful that he would follow my advice and stay away from being his cantankerous self.

I took Howard through his direct testimony without any serious problem or breakdown. I turned him over to Robert Agara for cross- examination and sat down to listen. Robert asked his first question and Howard answered by saying, "I do not understand your question" Robert repeated the question. Same answer. After Robert had asked the question for the third time, Howard answered, "I do not understand your Jap accent, and you need to speak English to me!" I put my hand to my face and looked up in shock. This was the beginning of a cross examination that was full of efforts by the DA to get answers to his questions while Howard was being discourteous at best, evasive and downright hateful of the Japanese American lawyer at worst. Howard never did admit to anything. On the contrary, he stood solidly that he had never acted the way in which the Bremers' and Jamie had portrayed. However, his answers were always accompanied with putdowns and anger at the questions. I objected whenever I could but was later told by jury members that at one point when I had stood up to object once again, I had just stood there, and then sat down with them understanding that there was nothing I could do. It was the most painful cross examination of a client I had ever endured up to then or since.

In my argument to the jury I asked them to try to understand how "deeply a person is hurt when his honesty and integrity is attacked. One must experience it to comprehend it, particularly if that person is a lawyer and has taken an oath to be honest and truthful. As a defense lawyer, I have seen it many times and am able to relate to it. I am hopeful that you as jurors are be able see this and to relate to this as well. We are not here today to judge whether Howard handled these accusations well. We are here to decide if it ever happened. If it did not happen, then, there is no crime to be judged by you or the court." After that, I concentrated on Jamie and her testimony. I argued that "what has been exposed is that her parents were people willing to convince and prod their child to present their lies to a judge and jury. You must reject Jamie's' testimony under the instructions you have received from the judge allowing you to do so and then use that insight to reject the charges that were made malignantly by the parents against Howard. If you cannot accept the child's testimony, then the house of cards and lies must fall. This is because it would mean that you have a reasonable doubt. It is a knowing, present and serious doubt due to the use made by the Bremers of their child. I am asking that you return a verdict of 'Not Guilty.'"

The jury took twenty hours over the rest of that day and the next wo days to reach its verdict. After waiting the first day in Greeley, the court allowed me to return to Denver and go back to work in my practice during the second day. Already, over one week had transpired and no one knew how long the jury may take. I was grateful to the Judge for his understanding as I started to pick up the pieces of my practice with the jury and outcome always in my thoughts. I received a phone call from the judge's clerk that the Jury had reached a decision on the third day. I immediately went to my car and began the hour and one-half drive to court. The charges had been amended before we went to trial with a misdemeanor charge that I do not remember exactly. It had to do with the weapon. However, as I drove towards Greeley and the verdict, I remember thinking and hoping that, maybe, the jury would find Howard guilty of the misdemeanor and not the felony as a compromise verdict. I was worried about the verdict and how long the jury had taken. I knew that the question of the child's testimony was probably the biggest factor in their decision with Howard's antics and behavior a close second.

Soon after I arrived and entered the courtroom, the Judge adjourned the case he was hearing, and our jury was called to the jury box from the jury room. Howard was sitting beside me as we waited together at the defense table for the foreman to hand the verdict to the court by way of the bailiff. He remained confident but was quiet. The Judge, upon receiving the verdict from the bailiff, read it to himself. He then handed the verdict form to his bailiff who proceeded to read the verdict out loud to counsel, the defendant and a few people sitting in the courtroom. The verdict was "Not guilty" as to the felony assault and "Not guilty" of the misdemeanor. Somehow, we had won the case! Howard was correct. It was the result he kept telling me would happen. Still, I felt not just relieved, but as if we had miraculously escaped despite Howard's dismal performance on the stand. The jury had refused to convict while I had become doubtful and resigned to defeat. It was as if we had come back from the dead. Part of me felt it to be unreal, like a dream. Yet, we did win! Howard was very happy and, at the same time angry at the parents and Robert Agara for bringing the charges. He kept repeating. "I told you so. I told you they would not convict me." I do not remember him thanking me. I found myself watching over him to keep him from personally expressing his thoughts against Robert Agara or the child's parents who had come into the courtroom to sit in the front seats and hear the verdicts when they were read by the Judge's bailiff. As Howard and I were leaving the courtroom, the parents remained huddled together, obviously upset. It was quiet and a bit surreal as we left them alone the courtroom.

When I spoke to the jury members who stayed after being dismissed by the court with his thanks for their service, I remember more stayed than usual even though the trial and verdict had taken more than one week. After long trials, jurors are often anxious to get home. The lady foreman whom I had liked from day one of jury selection stressed to me that they had listened carefully to my admonition that the child's testimony had to be rejected. She informed me that the jury had taken over nine hours over two days to decide whether to accept or reject Jamie's testimony. Once that was decided, the remaining time was spent arguing back and forth about which side they believed, the Bremers or Howard. They finally decided that since they could not decide between the Bremers and Howard that this was the reasonable doubt that was explained in the court's jury instructions that they had read over and over in the jury room during their deliberations. At that point it became the unanimous decision of the jury to acquit.

There it was. The jury was describing to me how they studied, reviewed, argued and finally attained the verdict in our American system of justice. Effectively, they realized that they could not accept the parents' testimony beyond a reasonable doubt despite how awful Howard had behaved in court. Several of the jurors' expressed their understanding and sympathy about how difficult it was for me to have a client like Howard. Nevertheless, they were all saying that Howard's behavior in court did not prove that he was guilty. This was music to my ears and impressed me once again with the wisdom and comprehension exhibited by jurors almost as if they were trying the case themselves. Both before and after this verdict, I had come to understand that jurors, between themselves, and during the interactions occurring in the jury room, often collectively feel, understand among themselves what the lawyers are feeling and going through as the cases unfold. This is not something that can be hidden, even if you try. Just as we trial lawyers can read them, they can read us. It is a two-way street. It is as if they had entered our minds and hearts. The more cases I tried and the more experienced I became, the more I could feel and see that jurors were often seeing and experiencing exactly what I was experiencing in court, good and bad. We were silent partners in the unfolding of the evidence and drama of a trial.

The jurors are an integral part of any trial. From time to time, I would connect with one of the jurors through our eyes, his or her facial response or the shrug of their shoulders and mannerisms. Such signals would often be later verified by the verdicts themselves. Jurors were not an open book, but the glimpses we trial lawyers receive are real and were to be paid attention to. I thanked them several times for their verdict and left the courthouse feeling more relieved than I could ever remember. I had a hard time accepting that we had won. It was truly so improbable. It was as if it were a made-up story. I had spent the entire case worrying about the result. Howard took it in as if he knew it was going to happen all along. He acted and spoke as if he expected the verdict. He was speaking to a few jurors while I was doing the same. I do not know what he said or what they had asked him. I never inquired.

In the aftermath of this case, the District Attorney's office opposed the return of the pistol and rifle to Howard that they had in their possession. They claimed that they had received several complaints about Howard during their investigation raising concern about his handling and showing of weapons. The court was told that their office believed that in the public interest that they should retain the weapons. This was at the very beginning of the time when all DAs' offices in Colorado began to fight the return of all weapons seized by police and Sheriffs, no matter what the outcome of the cases were. We ended up with having a hearing on that issue and the court accepted a compromise agreement that I was able to achieve with the DA's office whereby I was to pick up the weapons and keep them in my home for one year before Howard could receive them.

Howard never picked up the weapons from me before he died a few years later. His widow did not want the weapons and I ended up disposing of both without ever using them. Howard was grateful for my work and efforts but had a hard time separating his anger and distress from having to go through the whole process of a trial by jury. It was not easy for him. I will never forget him. He was the most disturbing and amazing character I had ever represented.

A lawyer must learn to separate his feelings about what his clients' have done or not done from their idiosyncrasies and character deficits. Most clients are far different from what Howard exhibited during his case. They come in a wide variety from misfits to connivers, despondent to angry and seeking retribution, discouraged and defeatist or seemingly without hope. The best of them become stoic and some, are very resourceful and helpful help in their own defense. Such clients make good witnesses and we win the cases, particularly if they have a sense of humor. Clients' act out in a multitude of ways, including attacks upon the accusers, prosecutors and their own counsel. Each type of client requires counsel to be alert, flexible and mindful of their peculiarities and reflexive to their separate identities. This takes a lot of street psychology and often being supportive with smiles and humor. Humor works since it does cause people to reflect on their position and even smile in return.

I learned to pass on to my clients my faith in the jury decisions. This was a strong faith developed after so many years in the trenches. In some cases, clients accepted my faith and told me it helped them get through the ordeal of trial. Another benefit was that the crucible of trial often brings the lawyer and client closer together in dealing with the problems in the client's case. You end up experiencing the pressures, doubts and fears of your clients together with them. This creates a bond that brings you closer to your client that suddenly ends when the result is obtained. You celebrate or commiserate and you each go your separate ways. However, because you have been to edge with your client, you part with the common memory and bond of having been tested together and survived. It is a good feeling for both of you. Often, the winning and losing clients return with more business.

It is also true that some persons caught in the web of criminal justice are not only sympathetic, but strong and capable of dealing with the insults brought about by the accusations in the criminal process, sometimes because they have been through it before. A good example is the man I represented in Chapter 13, "The Wrong Place at the Wrong Time," David Valerin, who was simply standing nearby smoking a cigarette next to the homicide, and then wrongly pursued civilly for money. Injustice does not recognize any barriers and lives freely among us. The truth is that if you make yourself available to handle criminal defense cases and their offshoots, you are bound to be caught up in situations that test your temperament, equilibrium, personal relations, sensitivity and stomach for the details of a given crime or disturbing criminal behavior. You will run a full gamut of thoughts and emotions as you guide your client through the twists and turns of their cases and trials. It is not easy, but if it fits, you are in for an amazing ride and ready for more. There is no other way to describe it. You enter a world in the courtroom not bound by the ordinary rules of life and society. It is a place of high drama where winning and losing is always at stake. It draws you in and you want to become better and better. People or things are not always what they appear. You see and experience the good and the bad in people. It is not for the faint of heart and is a harrowing and uncertain process. It is called, justice.

The End

Printed in the United States
By Bookmasters